NEOLIBERAL CITIES

NYU SERIES IN SOCIAL AND CULTURAL ANALYSIS
General Editor: Phillip Brian Harper

Nice Work If You Can Get It: Life and Labor in Precarious Times
Andrew Ross

City Folk: English Country Dance and the Politics of the Folk in Modern America
Daniel J. Walkowitz

Toilet: Public Restrooms and the Politics of Sharing
Edited by Harvey Molotch and Laura Norén

Unhitched: Love, Marriage, and Family Values from West Hollywood to Western China
Judith Stacey

The Sun Never Sets: South Asian Migrants in an Age of U.S. Power
Edited by Vivek Bald, Miabi Chatterji, Sujani Reddy, and Manu Vimalassery

Chronic Youth: Disability, Sexuality, and U.S. Media Cultures of Rehabilitation
Julie Passanante Elman

Abstractionist Aesthetics: Artistic Form and Social Critique in African American Culture
Phillip Brian Harper

Fashion and Beauty in the Time of Asia
Edited by S. Heijin Lee, Christina Moon, and Thuy Linh Nguyen Tu

Neoliberal Cities: The Remaking of Postwar Urban America
Edited by Andrew J. Diamond and Thomas J. Sugrue

Neoliberal Cities

The Remaking of Postwar Urban America

Edited by

Andrew J. Diamond *and* Thomas J. Sugrue

NEW YORK UNIVERSITY PRESS

New York

NEW YORK UNIVERSITY PRESS
New York
www.nyupress.org

References to Internet websites (URLs) were accurate at the time of writing. Neither the authors nor New York University Press are responsible for URLs that may have expired or changed since the manuscript was prepared.

Library of Congress Cataloging-in-Publication Data
Names: Diamond, Andrew J., editor. | Sugrue, Thomas J., 1962–   editor.
Title: Neoliberal cities : the remaking of postwar urban America /
edited by Andrew J. Diamond and Thomas J. Sugrue.
Description: New York : New York University Press, [2020] | Series: NYU series for social
and cultural analysis | Includes bibliographical references and index.
Identifiers: LCCN 2019043630 | ISBN 9781479828821 (cloth) | ISBN 9781479832378
(paperback) | ISBN 9781479827046 (ebook) | ISBN 9781479871391 (ebook)
Subjects: LCSH: Cities and towns—United States—Social conditions—20th century. |
Cities and towns—United States—Economic conditions—20th century. | Neoliberalism—
United States—History—20th century. | City and town life—United States—History—
20th century. | United States—Race relations—History—20th century. | United States—
Economic policy—History—20th century.
Classification: LCC HT123 .N37 2020 | DDC 307.76097309/04—dc23
LC record available at https://lccn.loc.gov/2019043630

New York University Press books are printed on acid-free paper, and their binding materials are chosen for strength and durability. We strive to use environmentally responsible suppliers and materials to the greatest extent possible in publishing our books.

Manufactured in the United States of America

10 9 8 7 6 5 4 3 2 1

Also available as an ebook

CONTENTS

Introduction

Historicizing the Neoliberal Metropolis

ANDREW J. DIAMOND AND THOMAS J. SUGRUE

How do we explain the profound transformation of metropolitan America in the latter half of the twentieth century and the beginning of the twenty-first? What are the origins of now-commonplace urban policies such as tax increment financing, charter schools, enterprise zones, special services districts, public-private partnerships, and the outsourcing of city services to the private sector? Why have public employee unions struggled for survival in heavily Democratic cities? What explains the disappearance of public or social housing at the same time that cities provide massive tax abatements for corporate headquarters and luxury housing? How can we make sense of the politics and policies of gentrification? Why have governments gone from regulating businesses to incentivizing them, often at a substantial loss to municipal revenue? Why do city officials often identify as "CEOs"? Why have cities become magnets for extraordinary wealth at the same time that a majority of their residents face austerity budgets that lead to rundown parks, poorly paid teachers, and shabby, overcrowded neighborhood schools? How have local politicians and community leaders as well as grassroots organizations—community groups, unions, civil rights and black power activists—challenged but also reinforced urban plans and policies that have created and maintained inequalities by race and class?

Over the last few decades two currents of scholarship—one centered in social theory and geography, the second in history and urban sociology—have offered powerful explanations for the fate of American cities. The first focuses on the emergence of neoliberalism, emphasizing macro-level transformations in finance, modes of production, and governance, all with global origins and reach. The second is resolutely local in its orientation, focusing on specific cities or metropolitan areas, with attention to electoral politics, social movements, and racial and ethnic conflicts. As historians, we find most work on neoliberalism to be insufficiently historical, lacking the specificity and attention to context and chronology that characterizes historical scholarship. But as scholars who have read widely across the social sciences, we are critical of historians who have, at best, ignored the vast body of work on neoliberalism and at worst dismissed it outright. In the pages that follow, we argue that it is high time to bring the conceptual framework of neoliberalism into urban historiography and, in addition, bring rigorous, place-based historical research to enrich and challenge social scientific scholarship on neoliberalization.

The very mention of the term neoliberalism arouses feelings of annoyance and skepticism among many historians, often for good reason.[1] Few terms in contemporary scholarly discourse have been deployed more imprecisely or polemically. Today neoliberalism is a polyvalent concept that bears only superficial resemblance to its appearance in the writings of the German Ordoliberals and intellectuals associated with the Mount Pèlerin Society in the mid-twentieth century who hoped to breathe new life into nineteenth-century notions of classical liberalism in the fight against regulation and social welfare.[2]

Since the 1990s, scholars, mostly on the left, have deployed neoliberal as a blanket term to denounce contemporary capitalism and inequality. Neoliberalism is sometimes a name for the deregulatory and anti-welfare policies of Margaret Thatcher in Britain and Ronald Reagan in the United States and their successors. It is sometimes a loose description of an orientation toward the market and a faith in market-based solutions to social problems. It is most often a synonym, usually pejorative, for right-wing or conservative economic programs. In the work of many scholars, neoliberalism is also a totalizing term that blurs geographical distinctions. It has been deployed variously to describe public policies promoting free market forces and limiting the reach of the state in countries as divergent as the United States and Zambia, and as the basis for the strengthening of an oppressive state apparatus in nations as diverse as Chile and China.[3]

Many influential theoretical works on neoliberalism share one underlying premise: Change happened from the top down. Economic elites and their political allies, with the support of right-wing think tanks and research centers, engineered a neoliberal "turn" or "takeover" in the 1970s and 1980s that effectively restructured governments to preserve the interests of capital by deregulating financial markets, weakening labor power, cutting taxes while imposing austerity and anti-welfare policies, and privatizing education, housing, and social services. Neoliberals valorized the market and delegitimated the public sector as inefficient, corrupt, and sclerotic, even as they used the power of the state to spur financialization and restructure tax policies in service of the financial sector. In the most familiar version of this story, the triumph of a neoliberal agenda entailed or was achieved through the ability of capital to capture the state, political parties, and other institutions of civil society to forward its agenda.[4]

This top-down story of neoliberal triumph, laden with the theoretical trappings of Marxist political economy, has been most associated with the work of David Harvey, an urban geographer who, despite being one of the most widely cited scholars in the social sciences today, has had, until quite recently, surprisingly little influence among urban and political historians. His book, *A Brief History of Neoliberalism*, has become the default account of the neoliberal ascendency. But few historians of postwar metropolitan politics and economics have embraced Harvey's story of neoliberal takeover and hegemony—in large part because of his schematic framework for understanding modern political and economic history. Harvey's analysis relies on a powerful but oversimplified distinction between two ideal types of political economy and governance. One—the social democratic—prevailed from the Great Depression through the early 1970s. Social democratic regimes promoted pro-labor policies, strong economic regulations, state-funded economic development, and a robust system of social welfare. The second—neoliberal—took form in the years following the global economic shocks in 1973. Neoliberal regimes were increasingly oligarchic, with a commitment to untrammeled capital, economic austerity, and financialization.[5]

To many modern American historians—including many of the contributors to this volume—Harvey's framework appears both ahistorical and reductionist. His premise that a social democratic order prevailed in the period from the Depression to the early 1970s has been undermined by the revisionist work of scholars of the New Deal and post-

New Deal American politics. Scholars of race and gender have focused on the limited scope of the American social welfare state during the supposed heyday of liberalism, particularly its underpinnings in a system that created a two-tiered set of social policies that subordinated or excluded African Americans, Latinx, and women to the advantage of white men. Labor historians have emphasized the fragility of worker protections and unionization, particularly during the Cold War years, as corporations consolidated power and bankrolled a campaign to market the ideology of "free enterprise." Urban historians have pointed to the deep illiberalism of urban whites, particularly around questions of racial equality in housing, workplaces, and schools. Political historians have documented the growing influence of pro-business conservatives, the religious right, anti-communists, and the resilience of a discourse of small government in the post–World War II years. If social democracy was weak at best in the United States, then the post-1973 period seems less discontinuous than Harvey and his school might suggest. The emphasis often placed on chronology by historians is not trivial in the context of understanding neoliberalization: It is impossible to understand the depth and persistence of market-based policies and political skepticism toward the welfare state that theorists of neoliberalism see emerging de novo in the 1970s and 1980s, without realizing that social democracy was always weaker than its most fervent supporters and passionate critics believed.[6]

One of the strengths of urban historiography—and perhaps its most generative challenge to social scientific scholarship on neoliberalism—is its attention to local and regional contexts and to history from below. Because most work on neoliberalization begins its analysis at the national or international levels, through the global workings of financialization, the maneuverings of institutions like the International Monetary Fund, the World Trade Organization, and the World Bank, and the rise of the Anglo-American political right in the 1980s, neoliberalism appears as an insuperable force swooping in from beyond rather than a process that was shaped and sometimes constrained by local political actors, community organizations, and social movements. Neoliberalism, as historian Julia Ott has argued, "is not a historical actor itself. We should not treat 'neoliberalism' as if it possessed a pre-determined historical trajectory or an essential nature." We thus need to consider its specificity. Neoliberalism was as much local as transnational. As the chapters in this volume show, urban activists and policymakers and citizens shaped neoliberalism, sometimes reinforcing it, sometimes limiting it, sometimes adapting it to their own agendas, such as school reform, economic "empowerment," or community economic development. Neoliberalization was deeply contested and always incomplete.[7]

Historians have good reason to be skeptical of many of the fundamental claims of scholars who write about neoliberalism, but theorists of governance and political economy ask questions that pose substantive challenges to historians. We find particularly useful the work of political scientist Wendy Brown, who posits neoliberalism's evolution from political theory to political ideology and then to a dominant rationality within a political culture that, in Brown's words, "figures citizens exhaustively as rational economic actors in every sphere of life."[8] Grappling with Brown's insights holds the promise of pushing the history of neoliberalization beyond its current state as a framework for describing the circumstances and dynamics of late capitalism toward critical questions of causality—namely, those related to the triumph of market rationalities and the "'economization' of political life."[9] If neoliberalism, as Marion Fourcade and Kieran Healy have argued, has developed as a project that celebrates "the moral benefits of market society" and identifies "markets as a necessary condition for freedom," it is vital that we better understand the forces and circumstances on the ground that legitimated this project and made it popularly appealing. Historians are particularly well-situated to explain what made neoliberalism hegemonic in the Gramscian sense. With attention to the particulars of place and politics, of identity, interest, and ideology on the ground, historians can explain what brought about the "construction of consent" necessary for neoliberal policies to have staying power. This volume proposes an intervention along these lines.[10]

Two recent historiographical currents—the revitalized subfield of American political history and the vital subdiscipline of urban and metropolitan history—can help us understand neoliberalism on the ground, as it emerged in the context of everyday life, gained consent, and shaped public policies. Particularly in the burgeoning field of the "new political history," scholars have been finely attuned to the relationship of political ideology and political institutions. But American political historians have to a great extent remained trapped in the binary of American partisan politics, usually conflating neoliberalism and the New Right. In accounts of the rise of the New Right, a range of political languages and ideas—consumer rights, homeowners' and property rights, meritocracy, entrepreneurialism, individualism, freedom—are crowded under the umbrella of modern conservatism, which, seen from another perspective, could be read as symptomatic of the penetration of neoliberal values into US political culture.[11]

While neoliberalism germinated among conservative activists and intellectuals and found its staunchest support on the political right, it gained broad assent across the political spectrum. American Democrats, like their counterparts in Britain's New Labour Party and in many European socialist parties, came to embrace market-oriented policies, austerity, privatization, and to varying degrees enacted policies that undermined trade unions, weakened the social welfare state, and rationalized pro-business initiatives as necessary.[12]

Few places were more significantly affected by neoliberalism than urban centers. Municipal governments became the sites of experiments in privatization, austerity, housing, deregulatory and pro-market policies, as a number of recent studies on "the neoliberal city" or "neoliberal urbanism" by urban geographers and critical planning scholars have demonstrated.[13] Innovations in urban governance proliferated because they enjoyed support across the political spectrum, part of a process of historically contingent political development. As many of the chapters in this book demonstrate, neoliberal urbanism in the United States is scarcely the distinctive product of right-wing thought or of Republican policy initiatives. It took deep hold in many Democratic Party–dominated municipalities. Indeed, beginning in the post–World War II years and intensifying in the 1970s and beyond, many liberals themselves began to challenge New Deal programs, calling for lean government, budget cuts and the reduction of municipal workforces, and the redistribution of tax revenues in the form of abatements for developers and businesses. What had been key missions of municipal governments— the provision of quality education, affordable housing, public transit, and public works and employment—withered.

The historiography of the conservative ascendency has been ill equipped to explain how figures like Richard M. Daley, mayor of Chicago in the 1990s and 2000s, whose aggressive neoliberal agenda would be elevated to the national stage during the Obama era, fits into the history of modern American conservatism. It has been hard-pressed to explain how Democratic politicians, including Bill Clinton, Arne Duncan, and Barack Obama, embraced ideas about budgetary restraint, welfare cuts, public-private partnerships, or charter schools with all of the zeal of their original proponents on the political right. It cannot help us understand why mayors in big cities as diverse as Atlanta, Boston, Cleveland, Detroit, New Orleans, Los Angeles, Philadelphia, and Pittsburgh, turned to corporate philanthropies to underwrite such urban amenities as parks and transit lines, and to fund experiments in "school reform." Neoliberalism became a "dominant rationality" precisely because it could not be confined to a single partisan identity.[14]

Urban history, in particular, offers a powerful tool to understand neoliberalism in practice. Since the 1990s, the urban history of the modern United States has witnessed an extraordinary revival, launching what Matthew Lassiter calls "the spatial turn" in American history, with attention to the ways that macroeconomic policies and partisan politics reconfigured housing, education, employment, and place in the post–World War II United States.[15] Historians who have examined racial divisions and racialized boundaries in metropolitan America offer insight into one of the central dimensions of neoliberalism, namely the reshaping of the very notion of the public.[16]

Many prominent theorists of neoliberalism ignore or downplay the importance of race. Urban geographers David J. Roberts and Minelle Mahtani have criticized their field for analytically separating questions of race and neoliberal political economy, arguing that the two need to be considered as "co-constitutive." Neoliberalism, they argue, is more than a "socioeconomic process that has racial implications." Instead, "neoliberalism modifies the way race is experienced or understood in society."[17] In the United States, it has been impossible to separate structural arguments about markets and privatization from moral, political, and cultural frameworks that create, reinforce, and perpetuate racial ideologies and inequalities.

American urban history offers an important corrective to the frequent silences on race in many theoretical accounts of neoliberalism. Neoliberalism shaped the opportunities, the politics, and the everyday lives of

Americans across racial and ethnic divisions but had a disproportionate effect on urban people of color because of the entanglement of race with economics. Race was also central to how Americans constructed citizenship and understood the "moral benefits" of markets. One cannot understand such neoliberal phenomena as the privatization of social housing without understanding the racialized history of American housing markets and their role in constituting different categories of citizenship. One cannot make sense of the intensification of anti-welfare and pro-carceral politics—and the belief in the salutary effects of the "discipline of the market"—outside of other disciplinary projects such as the racial stigmatization of welfare and criminal justice. One cannot discuss the challenges to publicly funded urban spaces without considering the racialized perceptions of who used and who was entitled to public spaces.[18]

It is a short step from the spatial turn to a nuanced history of neoliberalism in practice. If cities have been the central sites of neoliberal innovation, the insights of urban historians who have written detailed place-based case studies can help us examine the operation of neoliberalism on the ground. The scholars in this book, drawing from their original work on a diverse group of American cities, examine neoliberalization in different policy arenas, including housing (Pattillo), commercial development (Adams), municipal finance (Phillips-Fein), public-private partnerships (French-Marcelin), carcerality (Murch), gentrification (Tissot), and the non-profit sector (McQuarrie).

In this volume, we argue that the process of neoliberalization is critical to understanding politics, policy, and power in the modern American city. The actors in this history, as the contributors to this volume demonstrate, include legislators, planners, developers and business leaders, political representatives, state and civic institutions, community organizations, and ordinary citizens. While the authors of these contributions have somewhat differing visions of the contours and character of neoliberalization because our histories of the topic are still emerging, they agree on the basic idea that its advance in the postwar era has witnessed the proliferation and normalization of principles, policies, and modes of governance favoring free market solutions to a range of social, political, and economic problems facing metropolitan society, with the state playing a key role in creating the institutional frameworks for this shift.

Taken together, these chapters argue for a fresh methodological approach to the trajectory of neoliberalism. First, they offer up a new history of neoliberalization over the *longue durée* of the postwar decades to replace the prevailing story of a neoliberal takeover beginning in the mid-1970s. Second, they suggest the need to view this long march of neoliberalization from both the top-down and bottom-up in order to trace its dynamics and operations. Finally, the chapters in this volume point toward a rethinking of connections between race and neoliberalism and go a step further to consider how shifting understandings of race and its role in urban policymaking also colored neoliberalism. In the United States, it has been impossible to separate structural arguments about markets and privatization from moral, political, and cultural frameworks that create, reinforce, and perpetuate racial ideologies and inequalities.

Urban geographers Jamie Peck and Adam Tickell have powerfully argued for "a careful mapping of the neoliberal offensive—both in its heartlands and in its zones of extension—together with a discussion of how 'local' institutional forms of neoliberalism relate to its more general (ideological) character."[19] This is a set of questions that has generated important research in their field. But to understand the process of neoliberalization requires more attention to chronological variation and the ways that local, metropolitan, regional, national, and transnational scales interact. Spanning the entire United States, from the New Deal to the early twenty-first century, and including original scholarship on cities as diverse as Boston, Cleveland, Los Angeles, New Orleans, and New York, the contributors to this volume hope to enrich theoretical discussions of neoliberalism with a focus on context and, at the same time, generate productive questions that can guide future research on neoliberalism across disciplines, bringing a deeper historical perspective to bear on questions of contemporary importance. The chapters that follow are a starting point.

NOTES

1 The leading intellectual historian of the 1970s and 1980s, Daniel T. Rodgers, for example, has argued against the use of the term; it only appears twice in his important account *Age of Fracture* (Cambridge, MA: Harvard University Press, 2011). See Scott Spillman, "Splinters," *n+1* (June 8, 2011), https://nplusonemag.com/online-only/book-review/splinters/. Rodgers has more recently offered a

strong critique of neoliberalism as a category of analysis in "The Uses and Abuses of "Neoliberalism," *Dissent* (Winter 2018), 78–87. For responses to Rodgers's essay, see "Debating the Uses and Abuses of 'Neoliberalism': A Forum," with comments by Julia Ott, Nathan Connolly, Mike Konczal, and Timothy Shenk, and a reply by Daniel Rodgers, *Dissent* online (January 2018), www.dissentmagazine.org/article/uses-and-abuses-neoliberalism-debate.

2 See, among others, Angus Burgin, *The Great Persuasion: Reinventing Free Markets Since the Depression* (Cambridge, MA: Harvard University Press, 2012); Daniel Stedman Jones, *Masters of the Universe: Hayek, Friedman, and the Birth of Neoliberal Politics* (Princeton, NJ: Princeton University Press, 2012); Nancy MacLean, *Democracy in Chains: The Deep History of the Radical Right's Stealth Plan for America* (New York: Viking, 2017).

3 For critical overviews of the term and the field, see Stephanie Mudge, "The State of the Art: What Is Neoliberalism?" *Socio-Economic Review* 6 (2008), 703–31; James Ferguson, "The Uses of Neoliberalism," *Antipode* 41:1 (2009), 166–84; Terry Flew, "Six Theories of Neoliberalism," *Thesis Eleven* 122:1 (2014), 49–71. Gary Gerstle has recently argued that it is problematic to use neoliberalism as a synonym for right-wing or conservative politics. See Gerstle, "The Rise and Fall(?) of America's Neoliberal Order," *Transactions of the Royal Historical Society* 28 (2018), 241–64.

4 David Harvey, *A Brief History of Neoliberalism* (Oxford: Oxford University Press, 2001); see also Gérard Duménil and Dominique Levy, *The Crisis of Neoliberalism* (Cambridge, MA: Harvard University Press, 2011).

5 Harvey, *Brief History of Neoliberalism*.

6 The revisionist work on the New Deal and the limits of liberalism is extensive. Influential books include Ira Katznelson, *When Affirmative Action Was White* (New York: W.W. Norton, 2011); Kim Philips-Fein, *Invisible Hands: The Making of the Conservative Movement from the New Deal to Reagan* (New York: W.W. Norton, 2009); Thomas J. Sugrue, *The Origins of the Urban Crisis: Race and Inequality in Postwar Detroit* (Princeton, NJ: Princeton University Press, 1996); Robert O. Self, *American Babylon: Race and the Struggle for Postwar Oakland* (Princeton, NJ: Princeton University Press, 2003); Alice Kessler-Harris, *In Pursuit of Equity: Women, Men, and the Quest for Economic Citizenship in 20th-Century America* (New York: Oxford University Press, 2001); Margot Canaday, *The Straight State: Sexuality and Citizenship in Twentieth-Century America* (Princeton, NJ: Princeton University Press, 2009); and Linda Gordon, *Pitied but Not Entitled: Single Women and the History of Welfare* (New York: Free Press, 1994). For a historical viewpoint more compatible with Harvey's, see Jefferson Cowie, *The Great Exception: The New Deal and the Limits of American Politics* (Princeton, NJ: Princeton University Press, 2016). See also Jefferson Cowie and Nick Salvatore, "The Long Exception: Rethinking the Place of the New Deal in American History," *International Labor and Working-Class History* 74 (2008), 3–32, with commentary by Kevin Boyle, Michael Kazin, Jennifer

Klein, Nancy MacLean, and David Montgomery, and a response by Cowie and Salvatore, 33–69.

7 Julia Ott, "Words Can't Do the Work for Us," *Dissent*, January 28, 2018, https:// www.dissentmagazine.org/blog/neoliberalism-forum-julia-ott. On the importance of the local, see Thomas J. Sugrue, "All Politics Is Local: The Persistence of Localism in Twentieth-Century America," in *The Democratic Experiment*, ed. Meg Jacobs, William J. Novak, and Julian Zelizer (Princeton, NJ: Princeton University Press, 2003).

8 Wendy Brown, "American Nightmare: Neoliberalism, Neoconservatism, and De-Democratization," *Political Theory* 34 (December 2006), 694.

9 For a discussion of this terminological shift from "late capitalism" to "neoliberalism," see Sherry B. Ortner, "On Neoliberalism," *Anthropology of This Century* 1 (May 2011), http://aotcpress.com/articles/neoliberalism/. Wendy Brown refers to the "widespread economization of heretofore noneconomic domains, activities, and subjects" as "the distinctive signature of neoliberal rationality"; on the notion of "economization," see Wendy Brown, *Undoing the Demos: Neoliberalism's Stealth Revolution* (Cambridge, MA: Zone Books, 2015).

10 Marion Fourcade and Kieran Healy, "Moral Views of Market Society," *Annual Review of Sociology* 33 (August 2007), 287; for an important comparative study that demonstrates how neoliberal policies gained the support of electorates, see Monica Prasad, *The Politics of Free Markets: The Rise of Neoliberal Economic Policies in Britain, France, Germany, and the United States* (Chicago: University of Chicago Press, 2006).

11 See, for example, Lisa McGirr, *Suburban Warriors: The Origins of the New American Right* (Princeton, NJ: Princeton University Press, 2001); Matthew D. Lassiter, *The Silent Majority: Suburban Politics in the Sunbelt South* (Princeton, NJ: Princeton University Press, 2007); Kevin Kruse, *White Flight: Atlanta and the Making of Modern American Conservatism* (Princeton, NJ: Princeton University Press, 2007); Bruce Schulman and Julian E. Zelizer, eds., *Rightward Bound: Making America Conservative in the 1970s* (Cambridge, MA: Harvard University Press, 2011). Neoliberalism does not appear in major overviews of political history in twentieth-century America such as Julian E. Zelizer, *Governing America: The Revival of Political History* (Princeton, NJ: Princeton University Press, 2012).

12 There is much need for work on Democrats and socialists who embraced neoliberalism. The term "neoliberal," rather vague in its outlines, was applied by some centrist Democrats to themselves in the 1980s but has gone with only brief mention by historians. See Corey Robin, "The First Neoliberals," *Jacobin*, April 28, 2016, https:// www.jacobinmag.com/2016/04/chait-neoliberal-new-inquiry-democratssocialism/. Important starting points are Lily Geismer, "Agents of Change: Microenterprise, Welfare Reform, the Clintons, and Liberal Forms of Neoliberalism," *Journal of American History*, forthcoming, and especially Stephanie L. Mudge, *Leftism Reinvented: Western Parties from Socialism to Neoliberalism* (Cambridge, MA: Harvard University Press, 2018).

13 Jason Hackworth, *The Neoliberal City: Governance, Ideology and Development in American Urbanism* (Ithaca, NY: Cornell University Press, 2007); Neil Brenner and Nikolas Theodore, eds., *Spaces of Neoliberalism: Urban Restructuring in North America and Western Europe* (Malden, MA: Blackwell, 2002); Jamie Peck, Nik Theodore, and Neil Brenner, "Neoliberal Urbanism: Models, Moments, Mutations," *SAIS Review* 29 (Winter–Spring 2009), 49–66.

14 On Daley, see Andrew J. Diamond, *Chicago on the Make: Power and Inequality in a Modern City* (Oakland: University of California Press, 2017); on Obama, see Julian E. Zelizer, ed., *The Presidency of Barack Obama: A First Historical Assessment* (Princeton, NJ: Princeton University Press, 2018); Reed Hundt, *A Crisis Wasted: Barack Obama's Defining Decisions* (New York: Rosetta Books, 2019).

15 Lassiter, *The Silent Majority*, 7. For examples, see Lily Geismer, *Don't Blame Us: Suburban Liberals and the Transformation of the Democratic Party* (Princeton, NJ: Princeton University Press, 2015); Mike Davis, *City of Quartz: Excavating the Future in Los Angeles* (New York: Verso, 1990); Kenneth D. Durr, *Behind the Backlash: White Working-Class Politics in Baltimore, 1940–1980* (Chapel Hill: University of North Carolina Press, 2003); Self, *American Babylon*; Sugrue, *Origins of the Urban Crisis*; Kruse, *White Flight*; Diamond, *Chicago on the Make*.

16 Kevin M. Kruse, "The Politics of Race and Public Space: Desegregation, Privatization, and the Tax Revolt in Atlanta," *Journal of Urban History* 31:5 (2005), 610-33.

17 David J. Roberts and Minelle Mahtani, "Neoliberalizing Race, Racing Neoliberalism: Placing Race in Neoliberal Discourse," *Antipode* 42:2 (2010), 248, 250.

18 Marisa Chappell, *The War on Welfare: Family, Poverty, and Politics in Modern America* (Philadelphia: University of Pennsylvania Press, 2010); Julilly Kohler-Hausmann, *Getting Tough: Welfare and Imprisonment in 1970s America* (Princeton, NJ: Princeton University Press, 2017); Joe Soss, Richard C. Fording, and Sanford Schram, *Disciplining the Poor: Neoliberal Paternalism and the Persistent Power of Race* (Chicago: University of Chicago Press, 2011).

19 Jamie Peck and Adam Tickell, "Neoliberalizing Space," *Antipode* 34:3 (2002), 381.

1

Race, Poverty, and Neighborhood Planning in Chicago from the New Deal to Neoliberalism

MARY PATTILLO

Newton C. Farr was the president of the National Association of Realtors in 1940, and he lived in the Kenwood neighborhood on the South Side of Chicago.[1] The neighborhood is now slightly famous because it is the Chicago home of President Barack Obama. Back in the 1930s and 1940s, however, Newton Farr worked hard to ensure someone like Obama could never move into South Kenwood. For many years, Farr served as president of the Oakland-Kenwood Property Owners Association and he aggressively fought racial integration of the two neighborhoods. He once called the methods of the Ku Klux Klan in the South of the United States "extreme" but "justified" and "certainly effective."[2] Chicago's black newspaper, the *Chicago Defender*, deemed Newton Farr "more than any single person, responsible for keeping the city's expanding Negro population packed 'in their place'" and characterized the organization that Farr ran as "the wealthiest and most active anti-Negro organization above the Mason-Dixon line."[3]

The 1930s through the 1950s—an era that includes the New Deal expansion of social welfare programs and post–World War II economic prosperity—predates the dawn of neoliberalism, which scholars usually pin to the 1970s. Indeed, these years of Keynesian welfare logics are often portrayed as running counter to both the unfettered capitalism that led to the Great Depression and the neoliberalism of the post-industrial era.[4] Yet, as I show in this chapter, the seeds of neoliberalism can be found growing at the very local level during this period. In other words, the rise of neoliberalism and the neoliberal city does not constitute so much of a break with mid-century big state interventions, but rather an intensification of practices that have long been central to a capitalist political economy. This point should be obvious, of course. Neoliberalism builds on liberalism, which is at the core of the US and European political economies, which privileges the autonomy of the market and private profits in the economic sphere, and which promotes individual freedoms over the collective good in the political sphere.

Yet, in the field of housing in the United States, the federal insurance of home mortgages through the New Deal of the 1930s and 1940s was a huge public-private partnership, using public monies to support the investments of private banks in private households. As Andrew Diamond writes: "How can we discuss the adherence of Americans to neoliberal forms of reasoning in the 1980s without describing the ways in which federal housing policy cultivated an 'ownership society' in the exurbs and suburbs of the postwar metropolis by making homeownership affordable to a whole new class of people?"[5] The story in this chapter is not about those suburbs and exurbs, but instead about the neighborhoods and people that were excluded. The case of the immediate pre– and post–World War II period shows the austerity of the state in matters of redistribution and racial equality, but not in matters of lubricating private investment and accumulation, both of which are hallmarks of the neoliberal city.

The explicit racism of Newton Farr also illustrates how much the discourse about race and neighborhoods has changed in this neoliberal era, and how it also has roots in these pre-neoliberal processes. Unlike in Farr's era, neighborhood planning today never overtly champions a "for whites only" ideology. Quite the opposite, as political scientist Lester Spence argues, under neoliberalism, diversity and anti-racism become feel-good public principles, but with the work to be borne by the former targets of racist exclusion. Spence writes, "the key distinction is that under neoliberalism the most effective means of combating racism are developing entrepreneurial capacities in populations, institutions, and spaces deemed as 'non-white.'"[6] Black and Latinx urban residents are charged with solving their own problems and saving their own neighborhoods. The neoliberal city socializes black leadership into the rational and technical planning of the city and away from collective politics and organizing. This shift of responsibility from the state/collectivity to the individual began in the pre-neoliberal period with the promotion of private housing consumption and individual mortgages and credit, or what sociologist Monica Prasad calls "mortgage Keynesianism."[7]

Many black urban stakeholders have today bought into these forms of governance—anchored by neighborhood organizations and alliances with powerful institutions and city administrations—which in earlier periods had been utilized to exclude them.

I chart the prehistory of neoliberalism and its contemporary legacy by using the case of one neighborhood in Chicago, North Kenwood–Oakland (NKO). NKO is located roughly five miles south of the city's downtown and just north of the University of Chicago, one of the important birthplaces of neoliberal economics.[8] The University of Chicago plays a key role in the mid-twentieth-century urban renewal policies that would transform cities across the country, starting with its own immediate surroundings. Beginning in the 1940s, NKO experienced a complete racial transition, going from nearly all-white to nearly all-black by the mid-1960s, a story that was common to neighborhoods across the urban north. While the first wave of black newcomers to NKO were middle-class like the white families who were leaving, the neighborhood grew poorer over time, such that by the 1980s it was one of the poorest neighborhoods in the city of Chicago. The lower socioeconomic status of blacks as compared to whites has always been a salient part of the fear of neighborhood change, and thus it is always important to see race and class as connected, but not the same thing. The late 1980s and early 1990s ushered in renewed attention to NKO by city planners, private developers, the University of Chicago, and black residents of various political persuasions and economic positions. The planning activity during this period is more evidently characteristic of the neoliberal city. The purpose of this chapter is to highlight various threads that connect the 1930s, 1940s, and 1950s to the 1980s and 1990s.

This chapter begins in the 1930s, when the federal government pledged to make major investments in housing and neighborhoods in cities, but soon undermined those investments with even greater support for white suburbanization. This first era is not neoliberalism as we know it today, but rather its predecessor. Political theorist Wendy Brown writes:

> In contrast with the notorious *laissez faire* and human propensity to "truck and barter" of classical economic liberalism, neo-liberalism does not conceive either the market itself or rational economic behavior as

purely natural. Both are constructed—organized by law and political institutions, and requiring political intervention and orchestration. Far from flourishing when left alone, the economy must be directed, buttressed, and protected by law and policy.[9]

The federal government supplied that law and policy by jump-starting housing construction and all of the ancillary materials and trades involved in that endeavor; transferring risk from private banks to the public coffers;[10] and engineering a massive subsidization of individual wealth through homeownership. For cities—and urban black neighborhoods in particular—the largesse was decidedly more restrained, more in line with the contracted welfare state of contemporary neoliberalism.

I then transition from the earlier years to the defining decades of neoliberalism, the 1980s and 1990s. During that period, the NKO case illustrates the growth of the do-it-yourself ideologies of the neoliberal city among middle- and upper-income black urbanites in the post–Civil Rights era. This local activism manifests in exclusionary practices that had been directed at all black people by the likes of Newton Farr in the 1930s and 1940s, now more narrowly targeted toward poor black people. Looking across this long time period uncovers the cultivation of neoliberal sensibilities of exclusion and individual worthiness long before Reagan "sought to link [access to] housing to individual work ethic" and "wean the existing tenant base from the federal government by improving [their] work ethic and entrepreneurialism."[11]

A New Deal for Urban Neighborhoods

Newton Farr faced a painful reality. Lending institutions, both public and private, deemed his neighborhood a high risk for investment and therefore generally avoided it. For Farr and many other white real estate and civic leaders, one of the ways to demonstrate their neighborhood's worthiness of investment was to successfully hold potential black neighbors at bay. The white response to dubious lending guidelines and the exodus of public and private mortgage monies was clearly racist. At the local level, residents formed neighborhood improvement associations and erected restrictive covenants, which barred white homeowners from selling or renting their homes to African Americans. At the municipal level, anti-black attitudes drove much of the history of urban renewal and public housing. This racism at the individual, neighborhood and city levels was partially triggered by federal housing policies that favored newer developments at the city's fringes and in the suburbs, and disfavored the city's core.

A two-tiered system of federal housing policy was initiated during the Depression, persists to the present, and is characterized by, as historian Gail Radford notes, "well-legitimized, relatively generous state support for the middle and upper segments of the population and poorly regarded, poorly funded programs for the least affluent." Peter Dreier and his colleagues report that federal tax breaks (e.g., mortgage interest deductions, property tax deductions, etc.) for homeownership totaled $1.7 trillion from 1978 and 2000, compared to $640 billion spent by the Department of Housing and Urban Development on all low-income housing subsidies.[12] In addition to differentially treating and funding classes of beneficiaries, such tiered policies have had distinct ramifications for places. Plentiful and popular subsidies to middle-income families built the suburbs while the penury directed at the poor further impoverished the cities in which they lived. While this divergent legislative infrastructure is frequently juxtaposed in the literature[13]—and often implicated in the simultaneous rise of suburbs and decline of cities—it is not often analyzed for its impact at the neighborhood level, where the two strands worked at turbulent cross-purposes. Working-, middle-, and upper-class white Americans had the Home Owners Loan Corporation of 1933 and the Housing Act of 1934, which created the Federal Housing Administration (FHA), among other programs. The former supported homeowners hard hit by the Depression and the latter (along with the Veterans Administration in 1944) jump-started the homebuilding industry and put homeownership within the reach of millions of new families through smaller down payments and thirty-year repayment terms. The FHA also *denied* that privilege to many others.[14] Through its blatantly racist and classist appraisal practices, the FHA insured loans primarily in newer white suburban areas. Nationally, African Americans received less than 2% of federally insured loans between 1945 and 1959. In his book *Crabgrass Frontier*, historian Kenneth Jackson tells a vivid story of how, in place after place, the FHA "helped to turn the building industry against the minority and inner-city housing market."[15]

While the FHA-insured mortgages were underwriting suburban homebuilding, federal transportation policy was paving the way to get there. Federal highway legislation is what Peter Dreier calls a "stealth urban policy," or one that on its face seems unrelated to the care and sustenance of cities but has great impact under the radar. Scholars have shown repeatedly that highways—those used to exit the city and those that cut through cities on their way to the next one—had profound effects on city neighborhoods. The Federal Highway Act of 1944 and, even more, the Interstate Highway Act of 1956 funded the building of new roads at a cost of $2.9 billion by 1960, while neglecting the care and modernization of public transportation. Within cities, the land proposed for highways almost always had people already on it, and their dis/relocation caused further distress. Ultimately, all of that free money was far from free, costing cities their residents (and their tax dollars) as urbanites who could afford it and whom the government would support took those highways right out to the suburbs.[16]

For city residents—and city populations were becoming more black as World War II inspired a second Great Migration from the South—public housing, slum clearance, and urban renewal were the answers. The Housing Division of the Public Works Administration first authorized public housing in 1933, building roughly 25,000 apartments for poor and working-class Americans across the country over the next four years. It was followed by the Housing Act of 1937, which was "the first time the federal government accepted permanent responsibility for the construction of decent, low-cost homes."[17] The Chicago Housing Authority (CHA) was chartered in 1937, the same year as the enabling federal legislation. The federal government funded public housing construction, but only through local housing authorities, to which it also delegated site selection, tenancy, and management, and all of the contentious politics involved in such decisions. The Housing Act of 1949 authorized the construction of 810,000 public housing units over six years, but to illustrate the half-hearted commitment to housing the poor, less than half of those homes were actually funded in the succeeding eleven years.[18] Moreover, public housing was subject to exacting cost limits, which pushed local housing authorities to build denser and taller developments with fewer amenities. The most absurd of these cost-cutting measures was the skip-stop elevator buildings like St. Louis's Pruitt-Igoe, which saved money by cutting out the mechanicals and materials needed for elevators to stop at every floor. In the case of Chicago, historian Devereux Bowly argues that the cost constraints imposed by the federal government were most consequential because of local authorities' unwillingness to build in out-lying white areas where land was cheaper. Their interest in maintaining the racial status quo trumped the social goal of housing the poor in buildings that would last.[19]

The 1949 Housing Act covered more than just public housing. Title I of the Act established federal support for slum clearance, including land acquisition, demolition, and relocation. Slums were cleared not to be rebuilt for the displaced residents, but to be *replaced* by middle-class housing in a desperate attempt to shore up downtown consumer markets and the city's tax coffers. Later, the Housing Act of 1954 changed urban "redevelopment" to urban "renewal," now focusing on areas that were threatened by blight but were not yet slums, and expanding the kinds of construction the federal government would support beyond residential.[20] Since the states were often ahead of the federal government on urban initiatives, Illinois had already enacted the Urban Commu-nity Conservation Act of 1953, which granted public dollars to imperiled communities. Chicago's Hyde Park neighborhood, with the strong lobby of the University of Chicago, was the first project to take advantage of the 1953 state legislation and the 1954 Federal Housing Act's "conserva-tion" allowances. Together these acts granted powers of eminent domain for the "removal of dilapidated buildings and other obstructions"; zon-ing powers for the "discontinuance of property uses that downgrade the neighborhood"; aggressive code enforcement with the ability to place liens on private property; and state and federal loans for rehabilitation and new construction. "Nowhere," wrote Arnold Hirsch about the role of the University of Chicago in promulgating urban renewal, "was the role of private initiative, power, and interest in the postwar reconstruc-tion of Chicago more evident."[21]

Just as there is compelling evidence that FHA and VA mortgage insur-ance primarily benefited banks and served individual white families—presaging the preferred groups under neoliberalism—the record is also clear that public housing and urban renewal were targeted at the poor and racial minorities. African Americans were so uprooted by urban renewal—they occupied roughly 70% of homes demolished—that the aphorism "Negro removal" became a commonplace in that era. In Chicago between 1948 and 1963, black families made up 79% of those displaced from urban renewal sites, 74% of the families cleared to make way for public housing, and 33% of the families whose homes were demolished in order to build expressways.[22] When white people were victims of urban renewal, they were almost always lower- and working-class whites.[23] Public housing has been disproportionately concentrated in central cities and in minority neighborhoods in those cities. In Hartford, for example, 90% of the family public housing was located in minority neighborhoods by the late 1970s, as was 79% of the public housing in Atlanta, 88% in Richmond, and 67% in Denver.[24] While some working-class families got new apartments, the mortgage guarantees, land write-downs, and clearance assistance of the 1940s and 1950s were an even bigger boon to private investors, institutions, and developers who could transform whole parts of the city with aid from the federal government. Historian Gail Radford notes that "even though representatives of real estate groups argued that state-provided shelter was tantamount to communism or socialism, they never questioned federal support for the activities of their own members."[25]

Funding disparities were directly related to the power of the constituencies who lobbied on behalf of distinctive priorities and interests. "Public housers," the self-applied nickname for early public housing advocates, envisioned a generous program that fully addressed the considerable housing needs of low-income Americans. Yet they lacked the resources and the influence to convince lawmakers of the rightness of their position. On the other side, organized business interests, such as the National Association of Real Estate Boards and the National Retail Lumber Dealers Association, held considerable sway with elected officials in Washington and bent the range of building programs during the era to their advantage.[26] Hence, even in this supposedly pre-neoliberal moment, when "prosperous states focused their attention on improving the welfare of their citizens,"[27] the stratification of housing policy to favor big business and to grow a consumer-based white middle class, while scorning the poor with stingy welfare all through ostensibly nonracial policies, prefigures post-1970s neoliberal market domination and welfare retrenchment.

These mid-century government subsidies of suburbs and, to a lesser extent, cities are clearly different from the post-1970s deep cuts in public funds to cities. The shift in low-income housing ideology and policy is perhaps the most telling. The negotiations in Washington that resulted in the Housing Act of 1949 "took a bold, inclusive approach to the housing issue," as historian Alexander von Hoffman notes.[28] Even Senator Robert Taft, who had been a staunch critic of President Roosevelt's spending, "had frequently visited the urban slums of Cincinnati, his hometown, and was convinced that only a government program could provide good homes for low-income families."[29] Today's policies suggest the precise opposite: The government is the least capable of providing homes for poor families; instead, the private market is best able to do so. Hence, the largest low-income housing production vehicle today is the Low-Income Housing Tax Credit program, which attracts private firms to invest in privately developed low-income housing by reducing their federal tax burden. The two approaches couldn't be more different.

At the same time, however, there are important continuities between the mid-century and contemporary approaches to low-income housing policy in how they defer to the private sector and provide minimal funding for low-income housing. The Housing Act of 1949, for example, was more generous toward slum clearance and urban renewal—offering funds that could be used for the acquisition and clearance of land for private redevelopment—than toward public housing for low-income residents. And of course this was all within the context of the boons to private builders, banks, and insurance companies that were building the suburbs. For public housing, on the other hand, urban planning scholar Charles Orlebeke concludes that the act "was not much of a victory. 'Authorization' means little unless it is followed by appropriations—actual commitment of money. . . . Thus, 10 years after the 6-year, 810,000-unit total had been set, less than a quarter of the units were in place."[30] While contemporary neoliberalism has introduced new technologies that perhaps extend and perfect the goals of enriching private interests while contracting provision for the needy, the history in the urban housing arena shows that the United States' short years of welfare capitalism were never as generous as often assumed, and often privileged the interests and demands of the private sector.

On the Ground in North Kenwood–Oakland

The litany of housing policies enacted during the New Deal and around World War II (many of which were mirrored in Illinois state legislation) were acutely felt in North Kenwood and Oakland. The Ida B. Wells Homes was the first public housing built in Chicago for African Americans. The site was chosen in 1934 by the Public Works Administration, but the federal outsiders were not ready for the controversy that their decision would stir up in Chicago. The northwest corner of Oakland, where part of the 43-acre, 1,600-unit Wells Homes (then called the South Park Garden Homes) would be located, was 90% black in 1930. It was the only part of Oakland that had a sizeable black population because it was a small sliver of land that jutted west of Cottage Grove Avenue, the dike of black advancement. In the Oakland census tract farthest from Cottage Grove, along the lakefront, the black population was less than 1%. North Kenwood, to the south of Oakland and also east of Cottage Grove, was still all-white. Nonetheless, the Cottage Grove barrier was weakening, and white Oakland and Kenwood residents were concerned.

Hence, the residents of these white neighborhoods were none too happy with the PWA's choice for the siting of the Wells Homes. They argued that clearance for the project's construction would push unwanted black families deeper into their neighborhoods.[31] "We say that if the government desires to erect a housing project for colored families it should be over to the west of South Park way, where the colored population has its schools, churches and other social and civic advantages and not placed at the gateway to the Kenwood and Hyde Park areas," remarked Chicago Real Estate Board spokesman and Kenwood Club member Louis T. Orr. An op-ed from an Oakland resident J. L. Doyle cried foul: "We are the sacrificial lambs [or rather goats] on the altar of the Roosevelt-Ickes-Dresser & Co. philanthropic scheme to turn the Chicago lake front into federally subsidized slums." "Feelings became so strained," wrote historian Devereux Bowly, Jr., "that some people feared a repetition of the massive Chicago race riots of 1919."[32] White protests, and even a lawsuit, delayed the construction of the Wells Homes for years. Black residents hungry for new housing countered with protests of their own, demanding that the PWA and the Chicago Housing Authority complete the housing development in order to address the crisis-level housing needs in the black community. The Ida B. Wells Homes development was cheered by the black community when it was finally completed in 1941. The need for housing was profound; there were ten applications for every one apartment built in the project.

It is striking how planners seemed so unsuspecting about how the great suburban drive would ravage their cities. Chicago's Master Plan of Residential Land Use of 1943 began with the following hopeful forecast:

> It is believed that now is the most appropriate time to plan the future residential pattern of Chicago and this report has been prepared on that premise. The interruption to normal building caused by the war furnishes a pause that affords the opportunity to analyze and evaluate our city, and to make plans for a new and better Chicago in which Chicagoans and potential Chicagoans will want to live. When peace comes, not only will our people want better communities; they will also want the opportunity to make a living in Chicago, not by haphazard "make-work" programs, but by employment in constructive channels. The vast reservoir of available manpower and technical experience must be used in the building of a better city. What could be a more constructive utilization of this manpower than in the building of new attractive communities in which families may live in comfort and enjoyment.[33]

These city architects were correct that the labor power freed up by the end of World War II would be put to good use in building much-needed housing at home, but they were sorely mistaken as to where most of that power would be unleashed. As impressive as the central city redevelopment projects were, they paled in comparison to the Levittowns and superhighways being built outside of cities. The "new attractive communities" that the master planners of Chicago looked forward to were not built in places like Oakland and Kenwood, but on virgin swaths of prairie outside the city limits. So, when the new black tenants of the Wells Homes arrived in Oakland, white residents exercised their exit option. Between 1940 and 1950, Oakland's white population declined by 6,821 residents, more than 60% of the population.

White residents also left because there was no profit in staying. The notorious federal "security maps" of the 1930s and 1940s evaluated mortgage-lending risk in Chicago (and other cities) and revealed discrepant plans for investment and dis-investment. The maps established some neighborhoods as high-risk (rating of "D") and thus not eligible for federally insured mortgages, and other neighborhoods as good bets ("A" neighborhoods) for insuring mortgages.[34] Sometimes they marked off neighborhoods with red boundaries—as in "redlining"—to indicate areas that were to be avoided when making loans. At this time, North Kenwood and Oakland were still predominately white but sat just at the edge of the Black Belt. This proximity created a situation of "inharmonious racial groups" that the FHA warned its appraisers about. Consequently, North Kenwood and Oakland were both given "C" ratings by the FHA, a notation that allowed the insurance of ten-year mortgages only, as opposed to the thirty-year mortgages available in "A" areas. The Chicago Housing Authority summarized the message of this map bluntly: "[A]ll Negro census tracts fall within the area where loans have not been made by the major loaning agencies, and loans will not be made."[35] If the displeasing possibility of having a black neighbor pushed white North Kenwood–Oakland residents out of the neighborhood, then the discriminatory FHA-lending geography pulled them to the edges of the city and beyond with the assurance of low-cost housing with long-term financing.

Post–World War II Urban Renewal and Public Housing in North Kenwood–Oakland

Across the United States, and definitely in Chicago, urban renewal was the big game in town with its mandate for eradicating slums and rescuing threatened communities through the widespread use of eminent domain, institutional expansion, middle-class fortification, and black containment. In the 1950s and 1960s, North Kenwood–Oakland was sandwiched between two of Chicago's largest urban renewal projects. Situated to the north and west was Chicago Land Clearance Commission Project #1 in the Douglas neighborhood, later known as Lake Meadows, and soon followed by other clearance and reconstruction projects that involved local hospitals and the Illinois Institute of Technology. To the south of NKO was the Hyde Park–Kenwood Southeast Urban Renewal Project, which was the model for state and federal urban conservation policy that emphasized the preservation of threatened communities.

Urban renewal may have officially passed over NKO, but its effects were profound.

David Wallace, a PhD student in planning at Harvard in 1953, analyzed the data on families that were moved from the Lake Meadows site. He found that twenty-seven families displaced from the Lake Meadows urban renewal site bought homes in Oakland and at least fifteen families bought homes in North Kenwood (out of 235 displaced families who bought homes). Looking at the entire sample of displaced families, not just the homebuyers, Wallace noted further that "single-person families, as might be expected, clustered around the original site and moved in large numbers to Oakland and north Kenwood, where rooming houses predominate." A quarter of the families moved into public housing, with the nearby and new Victor Olander Homes in Oakland a likely destination. Wallace concluded that the Lake Meadows project directly contributed to the rapid racial transition of white neighborhoods like Oakland and North Kenwood that bordered urban renewal sites in the core of black Chicago.[36]

To the south, Hyde Park–South Kenwood residents and officials, Newton Farr most notable among them, criticized the Lake Meadows project because it threatened Hyde Park–South Kenwood's tenuous racial balance by pushing black people farther south and east.[37] But Hyde Park–South Kenwood soon had an answer in its own urban renewal plan, which hardened the 47th Street dividing line between North and South Kenwood and leveled the neighborhoods nearest to Cottage Grove Avenue, where black people had begun to predominate.[38] The federal government, which for twenty years had rejected loan insurance for urban neighborhoods, now stepped in to financially support urban renewal efforts within cities, but only when they were managed by large private institutions or investors. The Housing Act of 1954 instituted a mortgage insurance program for existing buildings or the construction of new buildings in urban renewal areas, known commonly as Section 220.[39] Whereas individual homeowners and landlords could not get money to maintain their buildings, large institutions garnered federal funds for their master plans. As the federal dollars flowed in, and the city funneled the money to institutions, developers, and investors, it was truly every neighborhood for itself. Given the adverse diagnosis and bleak prognosis for NKO, Hyde Park turned inward and closed its doors.

Organizations within NKO attempted to fight back. The interracial Kenwood–Ellis Community Center (KECC) located at 46th and Ellis in North Kenwood issued a series of survey reports, the last of which in 1959 laid out a broad development plan for the neighborhood. The plan ended with a kind of grassroots manifesto, which accused urban renewal of "urban removal"—not quite as strong as "Negro removal" but still critical—that had been "visited on the people in the affected neighborhoods and communities from above." The indictment became even more charged as the statement continued:

> Indeed, only a few people have benefitted [from urban renewal] while at the same time family and community life has become increasingly demoralized for the greater part of the population in these areas . . . A successful community organization in North Kenwood-Oakland could result in an important contribution to the city's orientation in urban renewal. It could prove the very urgent problem of renewal planning for people outside the ever-rigid framework of large institutional and economic interests. For eventually, if urban renewal is to become meaningful here, it will have to go beyond the process of squeezing the weaker economic groups from slum to slum, and, rather, attack their problems directly where they are. An awareness of what the renewal process can really be means that this area, and others as well, will not stand idly by while the less fortunate of this city's people are treated as second-class citizens in the name of urban renewal.[40]

This is a critique launched during the supposed pre-neoliberal golden years of state intervention and egalitarian economic growth. Though scholars often contrast the New Deal and the Great Society with the neoliberal era,[41] the tropes of undemocratic planning, the dominance of private interests, and the disinterest in systemic approaches to improving the lives of the poor were apparent well before the 1970s.

Caught between the University of Chicago in Hyde Park and the formidable alliance of the New York Life Insurance Company, Marshall Field and Co., and the Chicago Title and Trust Company that was developing Lake Meadows, North Kenwood-Oakland—with no immediate powerful institution or investor—got the castoffs of both ventures. At least some of the families being "removed" from renewal areas would be re-housed in the new public housing projects built in Oakland—the Victor Olander Homes in 1953 and 1956 (300 apartments), Clarence Darrow Homes in 1961 (479 apartments), Lake Michigan Homes (457 apartments), and Washington Park Homes (300 apartments on two sites) in 1962 and 1963, and the last large public housing project built by the CHA, the Madden Park Homes in 1970 (450 apartments). Many of these projects were part of Chicago's bold plan in 1956 to build thirty-five new developments with 13,000 apartments in five years on the South Side. As Devereux Bowly writes, "This was the great era of construction of public housing in Chicago, and the source of the current popular image of public housing as being long rows of sterile tall buildings."[42] Staking its claim in history, the fifteen-story Olander Homes building was the tallest of Chicago's public housing projects when it was constructed in 1953. It ushered in more than a decade of feverish high-rise construction, including the sixteen-story Lake Michigan Homes that topped it next door.

William Kean, executive director of the CHA, reportedly did not favor high-rise buildings, but "would prefer row housing but it is too costly. To stay within the cost limits set by the public housing authority the CHA must build high-rise structures." Yet, contradicting himself, Kean also boasted that the CHA only needed to use half of the federal funds available to it to build public housing. The agency, he said proudly, had an $8 million surplus.[43] Hence, while cost contributed to the decision to build high-rises, it was not determinative. Rather, it gave cover for other goals that could be realized with federal support, such as containing and constraining black population movement. Chicago's Mayor Richard J. Daley presided over the most segregationist era of public housing construction in the city. His biographers wrote:

> It was a year into his mayoralty, on May 9, 1956, that Daley obtained City Council approval for the first two public housing projects that were truly his own. Plans for the Robert Taylor Homes and the Clarence Darrow Homes left no doubt that the Daley era of public housing would be marked by densely packed high-rise towers that vigorously reinforced the city's racial boundaries . . . Daley's decision to build his first projects as high-rise towers in the ghetto underscored another advantage of public housing: it gave him power to control the demographics of the city. In

the post–Elizabeth Wood era, there were no limitations on using public housing to maintain the city's racial separation.[44]

Hemming in black Chicago was only possible when used together with the other tools in the urban policy arsenal: the strategic placement of highways and the discriminatory lending practices that incentivized white families to move far away from the black community. The salutary intentions for cities contained in the series of federal housing acts were almost completely offset by the crippling effect of more generously financed suburban flight. Quite different from the "vicious cycle" of pathology often used to describe the behaviors of poor African Americans, their neighborhoods and families, the web of federal policies with their stingy appropriations and their local discriminatory purveyors viciously and cyclically condemned black central city neighborhoods like North Kenwood–Oakland. The lesson is not that public housing or urban renewal failed, but that they were doomed by incessant ideological wrangling over their importance, at the same time that funds were flowing to banks and builders who were moving white people to the suburbs. The tightfisted welfare state of the neoliberal era was already in evidence for the black urban poor in the mid-twentieth century, as was the concentration and privatization of wealth through the big business of suburban expansion and small lots of individual suburban homes.

Conservation and the Submersion of Racial Exclusion

From its introduction as a planning category in the 1943 Master Residential Plan of Chicago to its codification in Illinois state law under the Urban Community Conservation Act of 1953, the notion of "Conservation" floated just below the waves of plans and policies that touched North Kenwood–Oakland. The term re-appears in the documents of community groups and city agencies that on most matters were or would have been avowed adversaries. The Oakland–Kenwood Property Owners Association—which peddled racial restrictive covenants in the 1930s and 1940s—quickly latched on to the Conservation idea and hired the former director of the Chicago Plan Commission to produce a specific plan for Kenwood–Oakland that would use the Conservation weapons against the growing black population.[45] Ten years later, the Kenwood–Ellis Community Center, with its chartering mission of racial harmony, also sought to "stimulate citizen participation in community conservation."[46] Another ten years passed, and the Kenwood Oakland Community Organization (KOCO), whose motto was "Black People Serious About One Another," asserted that "Kenwood–Oakland should be declared a Conservation Area."[47] Around the same time, the city's 1967 Comprehensive Plan of Chicago similarly stated that "a conservation program would build upon and strengthen the improvements already made both to the north and the south" of North Kenwood–Oakland.[48] Another ten years later, in 1978, KOCO issued yet another plan with conservation aims. Simultaneously, but separately, groups of block clubs began talking with the University of Chicago about how to improve the area. This wave of community research and planning through the 1980s culminated in another call for a Conservation Area, which was heeded at last in 1990, nearly fifty years after the Master Plan originally contemplated such a designation.

The Conservation Area concept is a particularly rich policy to investigate because of the seemingly innocent phrase used in the 1943 Master Plan: "what is good." "Planning is as much concerned with what is good and should be maintained as it is with that which is in need of reconstruction."[49] Establishing "what is good" transforms policies into politics. This is why so many disparate organizations in North Kenwood–Oakland could enthusiastically support and propagate a Conservation strategy. The Oakland Kenwood Property Owners Association valued the whiteness of the neighborhood. They saw it as *good* and worth maintaining, thus their strident defense of restrictive covenants.[50] KOCO self-righteously heralded the goodness of the *black* community that gained control of North Kenwood–Oakland in the 1960s. "All those people in the suburbs just realized what they left behind," opined the Reverend Herbert Eaton, one of KOCOs founders. "Now they want to get our black bodies off the lakefront."[51]

Following the logic of assets and liabilities, the Illinois Urban Community Conservation Act of 1953 emphasized that what is good should be "protected" in order to "prevent" decline. "[I]n order to promote and protect the health, safety, morals and welfare of the public," the legislation reads, "it is necessary to provide for the protection of such conservation areas and prevent their deterioration into slum and blighted areas."⁵² What and whom should be protected or prevented is another axis upon which to analyze the divergent utilizations—or the specific politics—of the Conservation idea. In the Conservation Area planning processes from the 1950s to the 1990s, the main characters change, but the threads of neoliberalism from previous decades persist, especially the role of private institutions and the marginalization of poor residents. What is different in this era, however, is the submersion of explicit discussions of the racist history of neighborhood development. Instead, rebuilding these now all-black neighborhoods does not entail confronting and undoing the uneven investments of the mid-twentieth century, but instead relies on the technical and entrepreneurial capacities of local black leadership.

The University of Chicago played a pivotal role in the implementation of the 1953 Conservation Area legislation. It transformed the Conservation approach from a tool used primarily against black people to a tool to be used against the poor, with the understanding that the latter category would indirectly and disproportionately affect black residents. In the 1930s, the University of Chicago was a key player in organizing property owners' associations in Hyde Park and the neighborhoods that surrounded it, including the Oakland Kenwood Property Owners Association.⁵³ The University financed the establishment of racial restrictive covenants to keep black people from moving into nearby neighborhoods. By the 1950s, however, the University had changed its rhetoric.

The progression of the University of Chicago away from race per se to class as the basis of exclusion was facilitated by a 1953 report it commissioned by the Metropolitan Housing and Planning Council (MHPC) to study the possibilities of Conservation as a legal and practical development tool. The qualifier "per se" is evocative of the inability to separate race from class, as illustrated in the tangled language of the MHPC document. The MHPC report declares without reservation that targeting one race for removal is untenable. "Conservation based on any policy of racial exclusion," stated the MHPC, "is not only morally reprehensible, but practically impossible." Instead, Conservation Areas can be examples of "interracial communities maintained at a middle- or upper-middle-class level." Here the substitution of class for race is straightforward, but later the authors equivocate. "In a sense the criteria to be evolved are economic rather than racial. Because of the structure of the non-white community, such criteria will in a sense promote exclusion. This exclusion, however, will be at a different level in different conservation areas, and will not be based on race."[54] "Per se" might be appropriately added at the end of this last sentence. Literally meaning "by (or of) itself," the MHPC guide to Conservation conveyed clearly that exclusion would not be based on race *by itself*, but on race and class simultaneously and in tandem. As Hirsch points out, class was used "not as a *substitute* for race but as a *back-up* for it."[55]

In light of the University's historically sordid relationship with the neighboring black communities, its deployment of Conservation provided an example of the incomplete submersion of racial antipathies in favor of socioeconomic creaming.[56] Because the University's answer to the Master Plan's implicit question "What is good?" was ultimately "middle-income residents," Hyde Park's Conservation efforts tolerated middle-income black residents but stubbornly resisted public housing that might house poor African Americans. The University's evolution on the aims of Conservation constitutes an important segue to the assumption of the Conservation mantel by African American North Kenwood–Oakland residents in the 1980s and 1990s. Moreover, its central role in both eras highlights the long-standing role of private institutions—and universities in particular—in the development of the neoliberal city, well before they had been theorized to be such key players.[57]

Conservation Against the Poor

By 1990, NKO was nearly 100% African American and had a poverty rate in excess of 50%. In other words, it was a predominately black low-income neighborhood. It also had small but growing black middle and upper classes who were attracted to the stately greystone homes and brick apartment buildings, and who wanted to move back to an area that had been the center of so much black cultural production in the 1950s and 1960s. These newcomers took advantage of the Conservation legislation with rhetoric that echoed the University of Chicago's emphasis on class, not race. Indeed, it would be odd for a black community to promote planning that excluded black people. Instead, NKO's Conservation in the 1990s would rest on promoting class integration, which in this context meant encouraging the entry of upper-income black families into what was then a very poor neighborhood. Their approach to neighborhood planning fits with what political scientist Lester Spence has called the neoliberalization of black politics. Spence writes: "We live in a period in which many of the central problems we face, problems that have political roots and political solutions, have been taken out of the realm of the political because blacks increasingly present these problems as technical problems that should be treated with very specific practices rather than as political problems that call for political organization and mobilization."[58] For the newcomers to NKO, improving NKO and establishing the Conservation Area was an exercise in technical efficiency, rigor, and deal-making.

There were several major players (individuals and institutions) in the establishment of the NKO Conservation Area, making for quite a complicated story. This complexity further underscores the technical acumen and social capital necessary to realize what was ostensibly a "community" process. The roster of key stakeholders in creating a conservation area and plan illustrates the neoliberal ethos that privileges private interests over public deliberations.

Shirley Newsome moved to Oakland with her husband in 1979. Newsome had for a time lived in Hyde Park, and that's when she became familiar with North Kenwood–Oakland, particularly through warnings to avoid it. With her memories of the supposed dangers north of 47th Street, Newsome moved to Oakland with some trepidation. She nonetheless became an intrepid community organizer, demanding and commanding the attention of her neighbors, private investors, and elected officials. One of her first action items upon arrival was to meet with the local city council representative. Typifying her fiery determination, Newsome recalled:

> I found out that the alderman was Timothy Evans, where his office was, his number. I made an appointment to go and meet with him to talk about the state of this community. And I must say he probably wishes he had never ever met me in life. But he was gracious. He was, I guess, really surprised. He didn't know what to think of me, but then he understood that I was about getting this place straightened up. And I meant what I was saying to him.[59]

From her initial meeting with the Alderman in 1980, Shirley Newsome and her husband worked with their neighbors to re-energize the block clubs, the same level of community organizing that had been used by the Oakland–Kenwood Property Owners Association to get white residents to sign racial restrictive covenants. They worked diligently until home-owners from the entire area from 43rd Street to Oakwood Boulevard, from Cottage Grove to Lake Michigan, were organized into one large block club.

Searching for strategies to "straighten up" the neighborhood, New-some enlisted all the help she could get. Making a move that might have been unthinkable for someone steeped in the local history, she contacted the University of Chicago. Given its role in excluding black people from Hyde Park and the surrounding neighborhoods, distrust of the Univer-sity ran deep for more than a few community residents. At the Univer-sity of Chicago, Newsome contacted Jonathan Kleinbard, who was Vice President for Community Affairs. Kleinbard had arrived at the Uni-versity in 1965 when urban renewal tensions between Hyde Park and nearby black communities were combustibly high. Because of this, he was cautious about getting the University embroiled in another battle over community ownership, but he nonetheless connected Newsome to an array of people who might be able to provide direction.

White real estate developer Ferd Kramer declared his interest in developing a plan for NKO in 1987. When the Chicago Housing Au-thority emptied the public housing high-rises it had built in the 1950s and 1960s to supposedly renovate them, Kramer proposed their demo-lition instead. He imagined public housing reconstructed as low-rise, low-density buildings scattered across the larger NKO community. Kramer convinced the state's Illinois Housing Development Authority (IHDA) to be the official sponsor of a planning process for the neigh-borhood. This instigated more meetings. Some were held downtown with downtown types, but many were conducted in the Newsomes' living room. The looming, rotting high-rises across the street from their home reminded the group of the work that needed to be done, while the small number of public housing residents who participated in the process meant that they were unlikely to have much of a say in the final plan.

Robert Lucas of the Kenwood Oakland Community Organization became a very vocal sponsor of the resulting plan, often claiming it as the KOCO/Kramer Plan. Along with Kramer, the state of Illinois, Lucas, and the Newsomes was a long list of interlocutors including Jonathan Kleinbard from the University of Chicago; representatives from Michael Reese and Mercy Hospitals to the north of the neighborhood; block club members; Chicago civic and industry leaders; bank representatives; and private developers. The group's visions—for which Kramer saw himself as the "catalyst"—were put to paper by a design team from the nationally renowned architectural firm Skidmore, Owings, and Merrill. Kramer paid the architects out of his own pocket.[60] The final product was an elaborate urban design initiative for the neighborhood including new parkways, community squares, and a commercial "town center." The plan was soon called a "conservation plan," with a small "c" and small "p" since it was not the same as the Conservation Plan authorized in the Illinois Conservation Act, which needed the City Council's approval to become law. But it was the precursor.

The Kramer Plan was not without its staunch critics, however. Given the plan's call to demolish the high-rise public housing, the displaced residents of the buildings were the most passionately critical. The former residents had with no small effort brokered an agreement with the Chicago Housing Authority that promised the renovation and repopulation of the high-rises, and they were not keen on any plan that would endanger those assurances. A handful of the residents stayed in the high-rises even after the Chicago Housing Authority ceased maintenance and management of the buildings. It was their way of resisting invisibility. Carlos Roberts, a leader of the Lakefront Community Organization, conveyed the residents' resolve: "Just because we're poor and living in public housing doesn't mean we'll allow ourselves to be taken advantage of. We'll do whatever is necessary to ensure that we remain where we're at." As the steward of public housing, CHA Chairman Vincent Lane also did not support the Kramer plan. Years later, sounding as much like an untrusting resident as a former appointed bureaucrat, Lane believed that the Kramer Plan was simply a thinly disguised strategy to "demolish all the Lakefront and replace it with market rate housing. It would have just been the northern expansion of the University of Chicago." The federal Department of Housing and Urban Development was lukewarm about the proposal and also concerned with the dispossession of poor families from the site. Mayor Harold Washington voiced his opposition to early versions of the Kramer plan, but then suffered an untimely death just after his re-election to a second term. His successor, Eugene Sawyer, was leaning against it, commenting reticently, "I'll think about it, and I'll pray."[61]

Within North Kenwood–Oakland there was a contingent of residents who worked to prevent the development of NKO by what were framed as outside institutions and interests. James Fitzhugh, a resident of the neighborhood, was active in, but always skeptical of, the various planning processes. "They'd look down on us then," he felt, particularly about the University of Chicago and its representatives. "It was a poor area, but it was poor because of what they had done in the 1950s, when they had their urban renewal plan. [But] the circle is turning now that [Hyde Park] has developed out. They need to expand and so they started trying to entice people to come into this area."[62] Fitzhugh's comments represent a toned-down version of those put forth by a group of residents who distributed newsletters, made testimonies, filed affidavits, and circulated petitions all outlining the conspiracy that they believed the Kramer Plan represented. A letter to the Commissioner of the Department of Planning illustrated this group's opposition: "[T]he Kramer Plan will not be mixed with our plan, because we don't need Mr. Kramer. This community will be revitalized and stabilized without Mr. Kramer, IHDA, or any of the people whom [sic] have proven in the past to harm us, we have rights, and the civil war is over."[63]

In other words, North Kenwood–Oakland was a hotbed of development attention. Local residents and organizations, city agencies and leadership on up to the mayors, state and federal departments, business leaders, and the federal courts were all taking sides on plans for the neighborhood. Everybody worked the political ropes. "I had a meeting with [Mayor] Gene Sawyer who was acting mayor, and I told him what we wanted. And as a matter of fact, I had a meeting at his house," recalled Robert Lucas about his role in getting the city to establish a Neighborhood Planning Committee, a necessary precursor to a Conservation Area designation.[64] He also remembered accompanying Ferd Kramer to meet with Sawyer's successor, Mayor Richard M. Daley, who needed to be convinced of the neighborhood's worth, the force of the planning process under way, and the fit of a Conservation designation. Jonathan Kleinbard was also calling in old favors: "I went to see [Mayor Richard M. Daley] a couple of times and I said, you know, you really ought to spend some time in North Kenwood–Oakland because these people want change. I don't know if you'll have the will at all to do it but that is something that you ought to look at."[65]

Working quietly and purposefully behind the scenes, another even more elite group of power brokers lent more legitimacy to the efforts taking place in the neighborhood. George Ranney—lawyer, industrialist, University of Chicago trustee, MacArthur Foundation board member, and civic planner—met monthly with other principals of the public and private sectors, including Valerie Jarrett, who had just been named the Commissioner of the Department of Planning and Development. They were "very interested in seeing this project succeed and felt that it was important to keep the city involved and keep the University [of Chicago] involved." Ranney saw himself as someone "that people could come to for support and advice, to provide the right contacts with foundations and the University."[66]

Back in the neighborhood, from August 1988 to March 1989, more than 200 residents busied themselves in nineteen community meetings of the Neighborhood Planning Committee and almost a dozen subcommittee meetings devoted to housing, community development, economic development, culture, education, recreation, health, and public safety. The Neighborhood Planning Committee—an official body sponsored by the Department of Urban Renewal—was the quintessential example of the series of "technical problems that should be treated with very specific practices" that Lester Spence highlights as how black urban residents have been incorporated into neoliberal forms of economics and governance. Alongside residents' work, the Community Assistance Panel, described as a group of "urban experts," was convened by the Chicago Department of Planning and Development. And the city's Department of Housing conducted its own study to make sure that the area could legally qualify as a Conservation Area, meeting such criteria as being larger than forty acres, predominately residential, and showing sufficient deterioration of the housing, infrastructure, or community facilities that it might become a slum.[67] Soon after the Department of Housing deemed the neighborhood eligible, the Department of Urban renewal accepted its recommendation and passed resolution 90-DUR-1 legally establishing North Kenwood–Oakland as a Conservation Area.

A Conservation Area required the creation of a Conservation Community Council (the CCC, or the Council), which would be the community voice in the creation of a Conservation Plan that would govern future development in the area. The Conservation Plan was about density, building heights, commercial versus residential uses, parking, and infrastructure. It was not about disrupting the system of uneven development across the metropolis, where investment in one area often coincides with disinvestment from another. It was not about challenging NKO's explicitly racist prehistory, which had impoverished it while enriching far-flung suburbs and their white residents. And it was definitely not about how black people, especially poor black people, were always and often on the losing end of the investment/disinvestment spectrum.

The Conservation Plan and the Council that would oversee it was, however, definitely about politics—but politics of the technical sort. Council members were appointed by the city's planning office and ultimately by the mayor; they were not elected by the community. The community's power was further attenuated by the legal fact that the Council was an advisory not a decision-making body. Nonetheless, with its ability to instantiate its vision in a Plan that would be made binding by a full vote of the city's leadership, the Council became a coveted appointment.

There were forty-three nominations for the fifteen positions, and residents scrutinized every step of the nomination and selection processes. Residents could nominate their neighbors, or themselves, and the roster would be presented to the mayor to make the final decision. Along the way, the list of possible candidates was filtered through a string of officials and city agencies, prompting criticism that such official oversight essentially undercut community control. "You do your job first," Harry Gottlieb from the Department of Urban Renewal Board instructed residents, "and I will assure you that we will try to do the best job of selecting as we can and support those selections as vigorously as we can as they're passed up the line."[68] As part of their job, community members coordinated letter-writing campaigns and petition drives to offer Council nominees. The debates over the Kramer Plan had clearly established camps of residents on the issues of public housing and community autonomy. These camps were reflected in the nomination and selection of

Council members. The anti–Kramer Plan forces put forth a slate of candidates endorsed by pages of signatures that excluded KOCO members and others who prominently supported the Kramer Plan.

The University of Chicago was not a neutral party, having invested time and energy and having lent its name to parts of the process. Jonathan Kleinbard was a strong advocate of a Conservation Area and a Conservation Community Council because it would "ensure over time that the people who live there and are invested in it have advised what happens. That they have a real voice and they can hold things up that they don't like." Looking back at the rapid transformation of the neighborhood, Kleinbard was most impressed by the strong resident leadership that guided it. While his respect for local control was obviously genuine, Kleinbard seemed less conscious of how instrumental the University was in promoting a particular leadership, one that had been willing all along to work collaboratively with the University. His celebration of the fact that the community had a "real voice" was preceded by his narration of the following chain of events:

> We submitted names and they [the Department of Housing] came up with this awful list. I mean I don't know where it came from. And so we had sort of an internal discussion/fight with the administration over that . . . So I said to [the mayor's chief of policy Frank] Kruesi, I want you to meet with [Shirley Newsome]. She ought to be chairman of the CCC and she ought to help you figure out who ought to be on it. She knows everybody. And if not everybody's going to vote for the way I wanted, but at least she'll get a sense of the community on this point. So they met . . . I arranged for all three of us to meet on 57th Street [in Hyde Park] there was some kind of a restaurant and Kreusi at that time lived in South Kenwood and I just introduced them and left. And he was very impressed. He had her in to see the Mayor.[69]

While Kleinbard had recurrent reservations that the University would be perceived as the heavy, this is an example of a lighter, more behind-the-scenes touch. Kleinbard championed community participation, but primarily of those deemed most appropriate to the University. Shirley Newsome had the cultural and social capital to impress the University and its officers. The University had the social, economic, and political clout to sway the decision-making process. The University was well within its bounds to make recommendations for the Council. The enabling legislation directs the Department of Urban Renewal to "cooperate and consult with public and private agencies and individuals interested in the area" when evaluating Council nominees. As long as its nominees lived within the Conservation Area, the University was an acceptable nominator.[70] The power imbalance occurred, however, when weighing the handwritten letters and un-notarized petitions that NKO residents sent to support their candidates against the phone calls and introductory lunches that Kleinbard arranged.

The scale of history shows that the University's candidate, Shirley Newsome, won the position of chairman of the Conservation Community Council. Having re-energized the block clubs and co-chaired the Neighborhood Planning Committee, she seemed to know the history of every parcel of land in the Conservation Area, and, just as important, was comfortable referring to people's homes and yards as "parcels." Her day job as a judge's assistant didn't hurt, either; her officiating style reproduced the decorum and precision of the courtroom. A testament to her skills of diplomacy, she gained the respect of even her most piercing critics, such as public housing activist Izora Davis.

> Shirley Newsome, at the first time, like I said, we didn't know each other. We only knew her through the newspapers and the things that she—that they were saying about us and what not. And at that particular time we didn't know her at all. She didn't know us. But it was very nasty. Very nasty. But throughout the years and once knowing each other and talking with each other, I think we gained a respect for each other and what not. I know she's a sweet person. You know. And she's a sweet person. But business is business . . . And that came to an understanding. Well we have to work together, you know, to try to build up this community and what not.[71]

Regardless of the deeply contested agenda or the issue, Davis recognized Newsome's commitment to working together. However, Newsome's willingness to collaborate, to be informed, to be influenced, and to compromise was exactly what concerned some of her detractors who saw such flexibility as cooptation.

Another controversy brewed over the first and most basic requirement for appointment to the Council—that a person reside within the
Conservation Area. Because of this legal stipulation, the public housing
residents—who had been moved out of the public housing projects but
who still hoped to return to rehabilitated apartments—were not eligible
to serve on the Council. Representing the public housing residents, John
Williams delivered the following impassioned statement at the public
hearing to gather nominations:

> Mr. Chairman and all those interested at this meeting, this is not actu-
> ally a question. It is also a statement similar to the one that was just read.
> But I have been on the Board of Directors of the Lakefront Community
> Organization. Since 1985, we have been involved in negotiations with the
> Chicago Housing Authority, HUD and contractors, and anyone that has
> an interest in seeing the rehabbing of the six buildings known as lakefront
> properties. WE are here as representatives of the 700 plus families. Notice
> I said "families" not "people that were forced to leave these six buildings."
>
> I now refer you to your letter dated May 23, 1990. This is a notice you
> sent to inform everyone of this meeting. In Paragraph 3, you stated that
> all members of this Council must reside within the North Kenwood–
> Oakland Conservation Area. You say that this is in compliance with the
> City of Chicago, Department of Urban Renewal Procedures and the Ur-
> ban Renewal Consolidation Act of 1961 as amended.
>
> We, the Lakefront Community Organization, strongly protest these
> procedures in this Consolidation Act. We feel that those that passed this
> Act 29 years ago could not have foreseen the unique situation we have
> before us now. It is unique because we have the 700 families who are resi-
> dents in absentia who have been guaranteed in writing the right to return
> to these rehab buildings if they choose to do so. Therefore, it follows that
> a resident of any of these six buildings that left the lakefront because of
> rehabbing of these buildings, must be afforded the same right to decide
> what happens to the area as those residents who remain in the area. The
> area to mean the same area as described in your notice.
>
> Mr. Vincent Lane, Chairman of the Housing Authority, when he
> appeared before you, he made you aware of this very situation that I
> speak of now. The memorandum before us sets forth in writing these
> guarantees. And we, the Lakefront Community Organization, as

representatives of these residents in absentia, must insist that they be fully allowed to participate in any and all decisions affecting this conservation area.[72]

Applause followed Williams's speech. But the reply from the public officials who were present was unyielding. The law was clear on the residency requirement and allowed no flexibility. Former residents of the now-empty public housing were just that—former residents—and thus not eligible for positions of community leadership.

The inability of public housing residents to serve on the Council returns the discussion to the Master Plan of 1943 that originally put forth the notion of Conservation Areas and the legislation that followed ten years hence. The goals were to "preserve" and "protect" "what is good," and to prevent the infiltration or preponderance of those things or people thought to inevitably lead to community decline. Public housing in North Kenwood–Oakland was on the list of things to prevent, not to protect, as it had been in the creation of the Hyde Park–South Kenwood Conservation Plan, and as had "families of lower economic status" in the Master Plan itself.[73] Public housing and, by extension, its residents had for so long been placed in the "bad" category that it soon had very few protectors. At the same time that debates raged in NKO about public housing, the US Congress was continuing to reduce the funding and authority of the Department of Housing and Urban Development.[74] The Quality Housing and Work Responsibility Act of 1998 rescinded one-for-one replacement rules that bound public housing authorities to maintain their public housing inventory, and repealed the priority given to the neediest families.[75] The officials who summarily dismissed NKO's poor, displaced families were not alone in challenging the entitlement of public housing residents to the buildings and neighborhoods they had long called home. Indeed, the entire language of entitlements had become anathema in the neoliberal era of the 1990s, from the federal government down to the neighborhood.

Conclusion

The ultimate irony of this story is actually its major takeaway. North Kenwood–Oakland's African American residents in the 1990s chose a neighborhood planning strategy—the Conservation Area—that in its first incarnation in the 1950s was utilized to keep black people out. Indeed, some black middle-class leaders even partnered with the same institution—the University of Chicago—that had worked to keep them out of South Kenwood and Hyde Park. There was no memory of the 1930s, which set in motion the impoverishment of NKO through the proto-neoliberal public/private partnerships that built the suburbs and public housing and undertook urban renewal. There was no critique of the growing privatization that single-family homes and individual mortgages engendered. Instead, the neighborhood planning process of NKO's black neoliberal urbanites became technical, with politics operating as individual power-brokering rather than collective organizing. NKO residents became part of the ownership society. They became entrepreneurial citizens. In so doing, they erected new barriers of exclusion, this time based on class, not race. They turned away from collective political mobilization toward the technical details of neighborhood planning. They fiercely claimed ideological allegiance to homeownership from which they had been so vehemently excluded during the New Deal and after. The North Kenwood–Oakland story shows both how the neoliberal city was forged in a past more distant than the 1970s, and, perhaps more worrying, how its future seems ever more secure as even those groups who had been excluded and maligned by it—as Newton Farr conveyed clearly in the 1940s—now utilize its technologies and forms of governance.

NOTES

1   Portions of this chapter have been previously published in Mary Pattillo, *Black on the Block: The Politics of Race and Class in the City* (Chicago: University of Chicago Press, 2007) and Mary Pattillo, "Race, Class, and Neighborhoods," in *Social Class: How Does It Work?* ed. Annette Lareau and Dalton Conley (New York: Russell Sage Foundation, 2008).

2   "South Side Leaders Consider New Approach to Blighted Area Problem," *Chicago Daily Tribune*, April 7, 1940, B11.

3   Richard Durham, "Farr of YMCA Calls 'Negroes Undesirable,'" *Chicago Defender*, February 17, 1945, 1.

4   For example, Brenner and Theodore write: "Faced with the declining profitability of traditional mass-production industries and the crisis of Keynesian welfare policies . . . neoliberal doctrines were deployed." Neil Brenner and Nik Theodore, "Cities and the Geographies of 'Actually Existing Neoliberalism,'" *Antipode* 34:3 (2002), 350.

5 Andrew J. Diamond, "The Long March Toward Neoliberalism: Race and Housing in the Postwar Metropolis," *Journal of Urban History* 36 (2010), 925.

6 Lester K. Spence, "The Neoliberal Turn in Black Politics," *Souls* 14:3–4 (2012), 145.

7 Monica Prasad, *The Land of Too Much: American Abundance and the Paradox of Poverty* (Cambridge, MA: Harvard University Press, 2012).

8 Jamie Peck, *Constructions of Neoliberal Reason* (Oxford: Oxford University Press, 2010), esp. chap. 3.

9 Wendy Brown, "Neo-Liberalism and the End of Liberal Democracy," *Theory & Event* 7.1 (2003). Project MUSE. Web. September 17, 2015, https://muse.jhu.edu/, para. 196.

10 Jacob S. Hacker, *The Great Risk Shift: The New Economic Insecurity and the Decline of the American Dream* (New York: Oxford University Press, 2006).

11 Jason Hackworth, "Progressive Activism in a Neoliberal Context: The Case of Efforts to Retain Public Housing in the United States," *Studies in Political Economy* 75 (2005), 35.

12 Gail Radford, *Modern Housing for America: Policy Struggles in the New Deal Era* (Chicago: University of Chicago Press, 1996), 1; Peter Dreier, John Mollenkopf, and Todd Swanstrom, *Place Matters: Metropolitics for the Twenty-first Century* (Lawrence: University Press of Kansas, 2004), 122.

13 O'Connor raises the contradictory nature of many housing policies over a longer historical period. Alice M. O'Connor, "Swimming against the Tide: A Brief History of Federal Housing Policy in Poor Communities," in *Urban Problems and Community Development*, ed. Ronald Ferguson and William Dickens (Washington, DC: Brookings Institution, 1999). Also, von Hoffman argues that there are deep contradictions *within* the mandates of the Housing Act of 1949 as it endeavored to build low-income housing while simultaneously providing for the destruction of thousands of other affordable housing units. See Alexander von Hoffman, "A Study in Contradictions: The Origins and Legacy of the Housing Act of 1949," *Housing Policy Debate* 11:2 (2000), 299–326.

14 For a discussion of the racist stipulations and rules in other federal programs during the New Deal, see Ira Katznelson, *When Affirmative Action Was White: An Untold History of Racial Inequality in Twentieth-Century America* (New York: W.W. Norton, 2005).

15 Kenneth T. Jackson, *Crabgrass Frontier: The Suburbanization of the United States* (New York: Oxford University Press, 1985), 209, 213; Thomas W. Hanchett, "The Other 'Subsidized Housing': Federal Aid to Suburbanization, 1940s–1960s," in *From Tenements to the Taylor Homes*, ed. John F. Bauman, Roger Biles, and Kristin M. Szylvian (University Park: Pennsylvania State University Press, 2000), 166.

16 Dreier et al., *Place Matters*, 116; Hanchett, "Other 'Subsidized Housing'"; Jackson, *Crabgrass Frontier*.

17 Radford, *Modern Housing*, tables 4.1 and 4.2; Jackson, *Crabgrass Frontier*, 224.

18 Jackson, *Crabgrass Frontier*, 224; also see Radford, *Modern Housing*, 200.

19 Alexander von Hoffman, "Why They Built Pruitt-Igoe," in Bauman et al., *From Tenements to the Taylor Homes*, 180–205; Devereux Bowly, Jr., *The Poorhouse: Subsidized Housing in Chicago*, 2nd ed. (Carbondale: Southern Illinois University Press, 2012).

20 Arnold R. Hirsch, "Searching for a 'Sound Negro Policy': A Racial Agenda for the Housing Acts of 1949 and 1954," *Housing Policy Debate* 11 (2000), 393–441.

21 Community Conservation Board of Chicago, *Save Your Neighborhood: The Chicago Conservation Program* (Chicago: Community Conservation Board, 1957), 10–11, 16; Arnold R. Hirsch, *Making the Second Ghetto: Race and Housing in Chicago, 1940–1960* (1983; repr., Chicago: University of Chicago Press, 1998), 136.

22 On distribution of urban renewal relocatees, see Scott A. Greer, *Urban Renewal and American Cities: The Dilemma of Democratic Intervention* (Indianapolis, IN: Bobbs-Merrill, 1965). On relocation in Chicago, see Community Renewal Program, *Relocation in Chicago* (Chicago: Community Renewal Program, 1964), table 2.

23 See Herbert J. Gans, *The Urban Villagers: Group and Class in the Life of Italian-Americans* (Glencoe, IL: Free Press, 1962), and Kevin Fox Gotham, *Race, Real Estate and Uneven Development: The Kansas City Experience, 1900–2000* (Albany: State University of New York Press, 2002).

24 Robert Gray and Steven Tursky, "Location and Racial/Ethnic Occupancy Patterns for HUD-Subsidized Family Housing in Ten Metropolitan Areas." in *Housing Desegregation and Federal Policy*, ed. John M. Goering (Chapel Hill: University of North Carolina Press, 1986), 235–52.

25 Radford, *Modern Housing*, 189.

26 von Hoffman, "A Study in Contradictions"; Radford, *Modern Housing*.

27 Monica Prasad, *The Politics of Free Markets* (Chicago: University of Chicago Press, 2006), 1.

28 von Hoffman, "A Study in Contradictions," 306.

29 Ibid., 305.

30 Charles J. Orlebeke, "The Evolution of Low-Income Housing Policy, 1949 to 1999," *Housing Policy Debate* 11:2 (2000), 493.

31 The Chicago Housing Authority had the exact opposite reasoning. They argued that building the Wells Homes would *ease* pressure on white neighborhoods by creating new housing within the black community, even though the Wells Homes rebuilt roughly the same number of housing units that had existed on the site previously. The CHA wrote: "One of the factors which has been most important in driving the Chicago Housing Authority to quick action on this South Parkway project has been the increasing tension in race feeling due to activities in deed restriction at the southern boundaries of the Negro areas. This report has amply indicated the extreme degree of overcrowding and doubling up in the Negro area. The map on deed restrictions indicates what has prevented the Negro from expanding into other areas. These two maps must be interpreted in terms of potential violent outbursts resulting from the efforts of the Negro to take over areas now reserved for whites. If there is not an immediate addition of dwelling units

to the Negro area, the section immediately south of Washington Park will be absorbed for Negro occupancy. This will not happen without warfare. The proposed
site will also serve to shift the center of Negro population to more nearly the
geographical center of the Negro area than it is at present. It will of course, to a
small degree, serve to check the flow of Negroes into white areas." Chicago Housing Authority, *Information in Regard to the Proposed South Park Gardens Housing
Project* (Chicago: Chicago Housing Authority, 1938), 64.

32 Al Chase, "Realty Board Raps Federal Housing Unit," *Chicago Daily Tribune*,
March 7, 1935, 23; William Flemming, "1 Voice of the People: The Bonus Com-
promise," *Chicago Daily Tribune*, December 1, 1934, 10; Bowly, *The Poorhouse*, 24.
Also see "Colored Area Residents Send Appeal to Ickes," *Chicago Daily Tribune*,
August 25, 1935.

33 Chicago Plan Commission, *Master Plan of Residential Land Use of Chicago* (Chicago: Chicago Plan Commission, 1943), 9.

34 Jackson, *Crabgrass Frontier*.

35 Chicago Housing Authority, *Mortgage Risk Classified by District* (Chicago: Chicago Housing Authority, 1938), 35.

36 David Wallace, *Residential Concentration of Negroes in Chicago* (PhD diss.,
Harvard University, 1953), 268–70. A study by the Chicago Housing Authority
(1955) about displacement from seven sites cleared to make way for new public
housing developments found that 18% of the sample moved to Oakland, Kenwood, and Washington Park. These neighborhoods were the destinations for
12% of the people displaced from the CHA developments on the near northwest
side—Cabrini, Abbott, and Horner. The study summarized: "The heaviest movement was directed to Oakland and Kenwood, where nonwhite occupancy has
increased substantially since 1950." See Chicago Housing Authority, *Relocation of
Site Residents to Private Housing: The Character and Quality of Dwellings Obtained
in the Movement from Chicago Housing Authority Slum Clearance Sites* (Chicago:
Chicago Housing Authority, 1955). A *Chicago Reader* article charts the journey to
North Kenwood of one family "whose two gray stone houses on Cottage Grove
had been seized by the city and demolished to make room for Lake Meadows."
See Robert McClory, "The Plot to Destroy North Kenwood," *Chicago Reader* 23
(1993), 16.

37 Hirsch, *Making the Second Ghetto*, 210; Peter Henry Rossi and Robert A. Dentler,
The Politics of Urban Renewal: The Chicago Findings (New York: Free Press, 1961).

38 A 1951 survey of Hyde Park, Kenwood, and Oakland gave its sponsors empiri-
cal justification for severing any connections to the areas north of 47th Street. It
found those areas had a higher percentage of substandard housing units, that one
of every four housing units was overcrowded, and that there was greater population turnover with the newcomers being in "the lowest income classification" and
black. "This sector," the report concluded about North Kenwood–Oakland, "is
moving downhill more rapidly than any other part of the Survey Area . . . [T]he
future of this sector is not bright." Quote from Hyde Park–Kenwood Community

Conference, *Community Appraisal Study: Report on Housing and Social Survey* (Chicago: Hyde Park–Kenwood Community Conference and South Side Planning Board, 1952), 32–33.

39 Federal Housing Administration, *Replacing Blight with Good Homes: FHA's Section 220, Mortgage Insurance for Urban Renewal* (Washington, DC: US Government Printing Office, 1956).

40 Kenwood–Ellis Community Center 1959, *North Kenwood–Oakland Planning Program: Report 5* (Chicago History Museum files), 26–27.

41 See, for example, Lisa Duggan, *The Twilight of Equality?: Neoliberalism, Cultural Politics, and the Attack on Democracy* (Boston: Beacon Press, 2003).

42 Bowly, *The Poorhouse*, 99.

43 Rudolph Unger, "CHA Helps Put Fresh Face on Old South Side," *Chicago Daily Tribune*, August 30, 1956.

44 Adam Cohen and Elizabeth Taylor, *American Pharaoh: Mayor Richard J. Daley: His Battle for Chicago and the Nation* (Boston: Little Brown, 2000), 184–85. At the national level, Hirsch, *Making the Second Ghetto*, 395, charts the discussions about race within the federal government at the time and illustrates the marginalization and ultimate dismantling of the federal Racial Relations Service (RRS) whose mission it was to "place race at the center of the postwar housing policy debate." Always in the service of "sound racial policy" as far as housing was concerned, Hirsch charts the progressive disillusionment that outraged RRS staff.

45 On OKPOA's plans, see "Lay Foundation for Controlling Growth of Area," *Chicago Daily Tribune*, December 19, 1948, and also see Oakland–Kenwood Planning Association, "A Report to the Oakland Kenwood Community: Digest of the Talk by Retiring Association President, Bradford W. Alcorn," 1952, Chicago Historical Society, Chicago, Illinois.

46 Kenwood–Ellis Community Center 1959, 3.

47 Kenwood Oakland Community Organization, *Alternatives for Planning Kenwood Oakland* (Chicago: KOCO, 1968), 27. Hereafter referred to as KOCO. The introduction to KOCO's 1968 plan read, "Knowing that the Negro community in this and most urban areas has been historically moved by the wishes and aggrandizement of non-residents, we of the Kenwood–Oakland Community Organizations propose alternative plans to the people of our community, and those responsible City, State and Government agencies and officials. The purpose of these plans is to take the offensive in an effort to see that this community along the lakefront is conserved and secured for the Negro people who presently reside here." KOCO, 3.

48 City of Chicago, *The Chicago Approach to Model Cities*, 1967, 8.

49 Chicago Plan Commission, *Master Plan of Residential Land Use*, 91.

50 OKPOA later redirected its energy to the issue of property maintenance, circulating Conservation Agreements to replace racial covenants. But while OKPOA's rhetoric claimed that the new "good" to be maintained was the neighborhood's low-density, clean streets, and well-kept homes, it is difficult not to assume a racial subtext to its conservation efforts.

51 KOCO, 21.

52 Illinois Compiled Statutes, http://www.ilga.gov/legislation/ilcs/ilcs3.
    asp?ActID=1447&ChapterID=30.

53 Hirsch, *Making the Second Ghetto*.

54 Metropolitan Housing and Planning Council, *Conservation: A Report to the Con-
    servation Committee of the Metropolitan Housing and Planning Council* (Chicago:
    Metropolitan Housing and Planning Council, 1953), 22. Another example of
    this convoluted language is the following: "As developed in this study, conserva-
    tion—in many areas, at least—must really mean maintenance of such communi-
    ties at roughly a middle-class economic level. This, of course, means de facto
    exclusion of certain groups on economic grounds." The suggestion here seems to
    be the acceptability or at least the unfortunate necessity of de facto exclusion. As
    long as it is not legally inscribed, then, exclusion is a reasonable strategy.

55 Hirsch, *Making the Second Ghetto*, 170, emphasis in original.

56 There were many other players involved in the establishment of Hyde Park–South
    Kenwood as a Conservation Area. The Hyde Park Kenwood Community Conference
    was a much more liberal organization than the University of Chicago and worked
    hard to keep the issues of racial and class integration on the table, but it was often
    overpowered by the University and its community development arm, the South East
    Chicago Commission. On this history, see Rossi and Dentler, *Politics of Urban Re-
    newal*, and Julia Abrahamson, *A Neighborhood Finds Itself* (New York: Harper, 1959).

57 On the role of universities in neoliberal development, see Sayoni Bose, "Univer-
    sities and the Redevelopment Politics of the Neoliberal City," *Urban Studies* 52
    (2015): 2616–32; Jason Hackworth, *The Neoliberal City: Governance, Ideology, and
    Development in American Urbanism* (Ithaca, NY: Cornell University Press, 2007).

58 Spence, "Neoliberal Turn," 150.

59 Author interview with Shirley Newsome, 2002.

60 Nevin Hedlund, "Too Good to Be True?" *Inland Architect* 33 (1989), 30. Kramer
    is listed as the first member of the ad hoc committee as follows: "Ferd Kramer,
    Draper and Kramer, Inc.—Catalyst." Also see Stanley Ziemba, "CHA Urged to
    Raze 4 High-Rises," *Chicago Daily Tribune*, November 24, 1987.

61 Roberts quoted in Stanley Ziemba, "Key Supporters Bolster Plan to Raze CHA
    Sites," *Chicago Daily Tribune*, November 25, 1987; Sawyer quoted in Stanley
    Ziemba, "There Are No Little Plans: Aging Kramer Pushes Kenwood Rebirth,"
    Chicago Daily Tribune, April 25, 1988.

62 Author interview with James Fitzhugh, 2003.

63 Letter dated September 8, 1989 to "Jim Macena" [misspelling of Mocena] from
    The Community Council of Kenwood and The North Kenwood Association, in
    Chicago Department of Planning and Development files (*DPD files*), author's
    archive. It is difficult to gauge the extent of support that this group had. The
    organizations that formed under various names occasionally submitted petitions
    with pages of signatures, but it is always difficult to know how people interpret the
    message or what people think they are signing.

64 Author interview with Robert Lucas, 2002.

65 Author interview with Jonathan Kleinbard, 2002.

66 Author interview with George Ranney, 2002.

67 Chicago Department of Housing, *Report to the Department of Urban Renewal Board on the Designation of North Kenwood–Oakland Conservation Area* (Chicago: City of Chicago, Department of Housing, 1990).

68 Transcript of public meeting regarding CCC nominations held June 6, 1990, 64, *DPD Files.*

69 Author interview with Jonathan Kleinbard, 2002.

70 Illinois Revised Statutes, from chap. 67 1/2, par. 91.121.

71 Author interview with Izora Davis, 2003.

72 Transcript of public meeting regarding CCC nominations held June 6, 1990, pp. 38–40, *DPD Files.*

73 On controversies over public housing in the Hyde Park Conservation Area, see especially Abrahamson, *A Neighborhood Finds Itself*, chap. 16, in which she states: "The question of public housing aroused some of the bitterest debate and soul-searching" (256). See also Chicago Plan Commission, *Master Plan*, 95.

74 Dreier et al., *Place Matters*, 138–46.

75 Quality Housing and Work Responsibility Act of 1998—Title V—"Public Housing and Tenant-Based Assistance Reform" of P.L. 105–276. Section 513 on income targeting establishes that no less than 40% of new public housing residents must have incomes below 30% of the area median income, i.e., be very poor families, but it also requires an "income-mixing by bringing higher income tenants into lower income projects." It further prohibits the concentration of poor families. Section 514 repeals federal preferences for very low-income or housing-challenged families in favor of a preference system created by the public housing authority. Section 531 eliminates the requirement that demolished public housing be replaced on a one-for-one basis.

2

"New Life, New Vigor, and New Values"

Privatization, Service Work, and the Rise of Neoliberal Urbanism
in Postwar Southern California

THOMAS ADAMS

Standing in the lobby of the Westin Bonaventure Hotel in Los Angeles some time in the early 1980s, the social theorist Frederic Jameson thought he glimpsed the preeminent representation of postmodernism, not solely as an architectural form, but as an encompassing politics of space. He mused, "the Bonaventure aspires to being a total space, a complete world, a kind of miniature city . . . it does not wish to be a part of the city but rather its equivalent and replacement or substitute."[1] Jameson's reading of the Bonaventure, as the pinnacle of the postmodern experience of space, of its "transcending the capacities of the individual human body to locate itself, to organize its surroundings perceptually, and cognitively to map its position in a mappable external world," has come to represent one of the key theorizations of the peculiar brand of spatial politics Los Angeles is said to exemplify.[2] For Jameson, "the Bonaventure is content to 'let the fallen city fabric continue to be in its being' (to parody Heidegger); no further effects, no larger protopolitical Utopian transformation, is either expected or desired."[3] In other words, the Bonaventure produces a new, idealized total space while simultaneously divesting itself from the larger city and community surrounding it as well as any notion of progress at the heart of urban modernity.

Jameson's reading of the Bonaventure inspired the "Bonaventure Debates" of the late 1980s.[4] Using Jameson's lack of a materialist ethics as a foil, Los Angeles's two leading social theorists of the last decades of the twentieth century, Edward Soja and Mike Davis, criticized Jameson's interpretation while further reifying the Bonaventure's place as a physical representation of some sort of new spatial world. For Soja, in contradistinction to Jameson, the Bonaventure is "postmetropolis, fragmented and fragmenting . . . seemingly open to presenting itself to view but constantly pressing to enclose . . . once inside . . . it becomes daunting to get out again without bureaucratic assistance."[5] Thus, for Soja, while the Bonaventure is representative of the new *postmetropolis*, it is not because of its totalizing character but rather its encompassing compartmentalization—once someone enters, she or he is sorted, fragmented, and metaphysically unable to leave.

For Davis, the Bonaventure is not so much a landscape where distinctions of space and time break down, but a physical representation of the carceral state. Its skyways, omnipresent surveillance, and enclosed parking lots remove it from the city, as Jameson argues. More important though, is its ability to keep the city out, rather than keep itself outside of the city. Thus, for Davis, while the largely black and brown proletarians of Los Angeles faced an increasingly militarized police force and spatial configurations meant to segregate and criminalize their movement, the Bonaventure, indeed the entirety of the broader neighborhood of Bunker Hill of which it is a part, represents society produced outside the walls of Davis's prison state. If Jameson and Soja see the Bonaventure as next to impossible to leave, Davis sees it as even harder to enter.[6]

The Westin Bonaventure, like all buildings of course, is the product of a specific history. Grounded in a particularly early reimagination of state-induced urban development as a privatized and service-oriented response to the flight of capital and the white middle class, Bunker Hill and the Bonaventure are indeed important physical representations of the late twentieth-century urban landscape. Without attempting to enter into the theoretical debates surrounding the Bonaventure, postmodernity, and the development of new urban forms, this chapter nonetheless argues that the history, politics, and political economy of the Bonaventure and Bunker Hill, while certainly not divorced from the building's peculiar and innovative design, are far more encompassing of the actually existing history of inequality than theoretical treatises have recognized. In the decades after World War II, a group of elite Los Angeles boosters, exemplified by the Chamber of Commerce, the *Los Angeles Times*, and the city's massive real estate lobby, created an innovative and peculiar tax plan as a means to defeat public housing. In so doing, they established a funding structure that demanded private service and commercial investment, paving the way for the redevelopment of Bunker Hill as one of the nation's most concentrated areas of service industries and service workers while simultaneously developing the tools that would become key in the growth of urban neoliberalism.[7] In the seven decades following World War II, city governments, private developers, and urban planners across the country combated the dispersal of capital and households by attempting to replicate the amenities, conveniences, services, and safeties central to the appeal of suburban life. Such replications, though, have been especially dependent on the maintenance of a low-wage service workforce to staff the concentration of hotels, office buildings, restaurants, and other urban enhancements meant to attract people and capital. Thus, aside from reorienting urban planning toward private development and turning key aspects of governance over to profit-driven sectors, such schemes saw the solution to urban crises in recruiting outside people and firms rather than producing political mechanisms that imagined good wages and working conditions for those who labored in the high-rise hotels and office buildings as the basis for a prosperous city.[8]

The redevelopment of Bunker Hill gained official imprimatur February 27, 1964, when the California Supreme Court released its ruling in *Community Redevelopment Agency v. Goldman et al.*[9] The case had worked its way up from two lower courts over the preceding seven years and concerned the legality of the City of Los Angeles's attempt to raze the Downtown Bunker Hill neighborhood. At issue was the Los Angeles Community Redevelopment Agency's ability to declare an entire residential area blighted, and in turn go forward with a plan to redevelop the area into a privatized, predominately commercial neighborhood. The redevelopment of Bunker Hill, through its emphasis on remaking urban space as private and service-centered—rather than public and industrial or housing-centered—its innovative use of tax law in order to push costs down the road, and its dependency on thousands of low-waged workers in hospitality, building services, and security provided a template model for American urban redevelopment. By the end of the twentieth century, as this volume suggests, such interrelated processes had become critical dimensions of urban neoliberalism.

Bunker Hill had been built as a residential suburb of Los Angeles in the late 1860s. Just five blocks northwest of the city center, bounded by

Figueroa Street on the West, First Street on the North, Hill Street on the East, and Fifth Street on the South, by the 1890s the neighborhood "had become a setting for authentic Victorian mansions in Queen Anne style or Italianate and Romanesque architecture."[10] In the early 1900s, Bunker Hill had become Los Angeles's most exclusive address, with ornate mansions and the opening of the Angel's Flight Railway, a two-block-long passenger funicular that ran up the steep hill. The neighborhood's opulence was demonstrated by a pigeon messenger service between the top of the hill and the wealthy vacation enclave of Catalina Island. As the city's official history of the neighborhood put it, "mainland bound pigeons would bring items for newspapers regarding social activities at Avalon on the island, 20 miles off the coast. Island bound pigeons would carry love notes to vacationing belles from their swains in workaday Los Angeles."[11]

The years after World War I saw the rise of the automobile and the subsequent dispersal of the wealthiest of Angelenos to Westside communities like Beverly Hills and Bel-Air.[12] Bunker Hill witnessed a rapid decline between World War I and World War II as the wealthy moved out and their old mansions were subdivided into small retirement housing developments, and increasingly, single-resident occupancy hotels for transients. As Yukio Kawaratani, the former head of the Community Redevelopment Agency (CRA), remembered it, "modest income families, single men, and transients found Bunker Hill a convenient place to reside in the center of town . . . by the 1940s, the housing stock had severely deteriorated and crime, fires, and health conditions worsened."[13] As the head of the CRA, Kawaratani had a vested interest in portraying the neighborhood as blighted. Others, though more philosophically sympathetic to the area's residents, could not help but reiterate Kawaratani. The famed noir writer and popular front sympathizer Raymond Chandler, in his 1942 novel *The High Window*, wrote,

> Bunker Hill is old town, lost town, shabby town, crook town . . . On the wide cool front porches, reaching their cracked shoes into the sun, and staring at nothing, sit the old men with faces like lost battles . . . And there are ratty hotels where nobody except people named Smith and Jones sign the register and where the night clerk is half watchdog and half pander. Out of the apartment houses come women who should be young but have faces like stale beer; men with pulled-down hats and quick eyes that

look the street over behind the cupped hand that shields the match flame; worn intellectuals with cigarette coughs and no money in the bank; fly cops with granite faces and unwavering eyes; cokies and coke peddlers; people who look like nothing in particular and know it, and once in a while even men that actually go to work.[14]

Kawaratani's and Chandler's depictions of the neighborhood were echoed by countless other mid-century films and pulp writers. Mickey Spillane and John Fante used Bunker Hill as a backdrop for their stories of corruption and the defeat of idealism. Indeed, the neighborhood and its rapid transition from opulent mansions and the cream of Los Angeles high society to single-resident occupancy (SRO) hotels for the derelict unemployed and criminals provided a perfect metaphor for the noirish sensibility of internal decay. Furthermore, Bunker Hill's relative population density made it the most East Coast–like of Los Angeles neighborhoods, a fact that provided writers and filmmakers the opportunity to use the area as a corrupt and rotten counterpart to the sunshine and good-life idyllicism that was the hallmark of Southern California's cultural image.[15]

During World War II the neighborhood witnessed a brief period of resurgence as heavy demand for housing brought migrants, soldiers, and war workers to Southern California in massive numbers.[16] Bunker Hill housed many of these war workers and Southern California newcomers as the defense industry morphed into the region's largest employer.[17] After World War II, Bunker Hill reverted to its interwar decline, as the wartime migrants began moving out to newly built suburbs in the Valleys and Southland.[18] Indeed, by the late 1940s the neighborhood reached its nadir in terms of crime and dilapidation. As the city's pro-redevelopment history put it, "the period between World War I and World War II saw a shift to . . . pensioners, derelicts, and transients. And the post–World War II era added a surge in problems in health, crime, and safety."[19]

The neighborhood's closeness to downtown combined with its rapidly decaying character made it ground zero for Los Angeles's version of urban renewal. A pamphlet intended for relocatees argued, "blighted conditions will be removed, thus permitting maximum use of this area . . . near the center of the city. Redeveloping Bunker Hill is a practical way to eliminate the blighted area . . . and produc(e) new tax revenue, to relieve all taxpayers."[20] As the urban planner Don Parson and the sociologist Janet Abu-Lughod have pointed out, as early as the late 1940s, Los Angeles adopted what can best be described as a privatized vision of urban redevelopment.[21] Unlike Northeastern and Midwestern metropolises or even San Francisco to the north, from the immediate postwar years onward the way Los Angeles envisioned urban renewal and redevelopment was about private, commercial, and service development instead of housing. The redevelopment of Bunker Hill, and later, areas like the Latinx, working-class Pacoima neighborhood in the San Fernando Valley and the African American middle-class Crenshaw neighborhood, as well as projects in the largely white exurban community of Lancaster, reflected a reimagination of the metropolitan economic landscape oriented toward corporate and private spaces of service and dependent on service laborers, thus dually contributing to urban growth through producing low-waged jobs and gifting public land to private interests that profited from the existence of these jobs as poorly paid.

The legal context for urban renewal in Los Angeles began with the 1945 passage by the State Assembly of the Community Redevelopment Act. As the bill stated,

> The decay of large areas in American cities, notably in the central sections, is one of the major problems of today. Blight and slums have spread throughout an estimated one-fourth of . . . urban America. The deterioration of property originally assessed at an estimated $40 billion has destroyed a large part of the tax base of our cities.[22]

California's bill was the first in the nation that allowed municipalities to establish public-private partnership agencies and grant them the power of eminent domain in order to redevelop various areas that were defined as blighted. In the case of California, blight was defined as including four major characteristics: defective design and overcrowding, economic disuse, "a prevalence of depreciated values, impaired investment, and social and economic maladjustment," and "a total lack of proper utilization."[23]

Mayor Fletcher Bowron appointed a five-member, public-private Los Angeles Community Redevelopment Agency in 1948 to guide this process, defining its objectives in the following terms:

Urban blight and slums today constitute one of the greatest problems facing American municipalities. To maintain an attractive and an economically sound city it is essential that we eliminate the slums and develop the
blighted areas to their best social and economic use. Community redevelopment in Los Angeles means new life, new vigor, and new values.[24]

In redeveloping Bunker Hill, along with other "blighted" neighborhoods such as Chavez Ravine north of downtown, Pacoima in the San
Fernando Valley, and Watts, Bowron and his allies on the city planning
committee envisioned remaking Los Angeles as a more affordable housing destination for the thousands of families flocking to Southern California in search of high-paying industrial jobs after the war's end.

The biggest proponent for a public housing–focused redevelopment
in Los Angeles was Robert E. Alexander. Alexander was a leading Los
Angeles architect and Bowron's appointee as the head of the City Planning Commission. A former popular front fellow traveler and supporter
of Upton Sinclair's End Poverty In California Plan, Alexander envisioned remaking Los Angeles into a mecca for public and mixed-income
housing. He was thus a perfect example of similar mid-century urban
planners who attempted a democratic remaking of public space.[25] As he
recalled,

> I got to know the real scene of the way people were living at that time.
> And even though the slums of New York were famous as slums, we had
> slums right here right next to the city hall—within view of city hall. I got
> grand tours of these places and talked to the people. And nothing was
> being done to ameliorate that situation, so I just became a part of the
> movement to get something done.[26]

The Community Redevelopment Agency enlisted Henry A. Babcock,
a structural engineer and urban planner, as the city's lead engineer on
Bunker Hill Urban Renewal. Babcock's earlier claim to fame was a defeated plan in 1948 to build a comprehensive subway system in Los Angeles and, it was hoped, manage the area's already pronounced tendency
toward sprawl.[27] Babcock was a liberal and imagined the area would
become a mixed-income neighborhood of thirty-seven 13-story apartment buildings. For Babcock, the plan made sense in terms of both ar-

chitecture and land use. As Alexander, a Babcock admirer, put it, the Babcock Plan wanted to "bulldoze the whole thing down and make it honest and level with the rest of the downtown city."[28] For Babcock, even more important than Bunker Hill architecturally matching the rest of downtown was his strong belief that only exclusively residential-based development made sense.

> The physical characteristics of the site, its location, topography, and lack of highway and railroad facilities make it entirely unsuitable for manufacturing and industrial use . . . any attempt to establish department stores, commercial office buildings, banks, or theatres on the hill would result in failure because of the difficulty of access and the inability to meet the competition . . . consideration was given to the inclusion of one or more high-priced luxury hotels of the type found on Nob Hill in San Francisco. It is our conclusion, however, that such enterprises would not be successful because so much of the night-life activity of the Los Angeles Metropolitan area has developed away from the Central Business District, particularly to the west, along Wilshire Boulevard, Hollywood, and the western suburbs.[29]

Babcock was adamant that the only sensible development for Bunker Hill was housing. Los Angeles was too physically spread out to make commercial development worthwhile. Its cultural and entertainment centers were far removed from downtown, so building hotels, restaurants, or cultural attractions would make poor use of the site. The growing car culture of the region made Bunker Hill's downtown location a hindrance for commercial office space, since including the necessary parking would be too problematic.

For Babcock and Alexander, the only real issue with turning the blight of Bunker Hill into a sparkling mixed-income area of housing was relocating the neighborhood's roughly 15,000 residents, a diverse mix of working-class Angelenos, recently migrated families, and long-time transient singles. In Alexander's proposal for the neighborhood, he suggested that the city could kill two birds with one stone by building mixed-income housing in nearby Chavez Ravine and relocating Bunker Hill's residents there while developing Bunker Hill as affordable housing.[30] Chavez Ravine was a largely Latinx neighborhood approximately two miles north of downtown. As Alexander described the neighborhood,

> it was all one story shacks . . . people living in old chicken coops, it was squalor of the worst kind. But, you know, children growing up in that area must have had an enchanted life, in a way. I mean, they were surrounded by Elysian Park. Their ravine itself had not very many trees in it, but it was country living, as if it were a little place in Mexico. It wasn't all that bad from the standpoint of living conditions. From the standpoint of sanitation and so on, not too hot. The housing was not the greatest. There was no toilet or bathtub in every unit, you know. The housing criteria devised by the census bureau to define whether the housing was safe and sanitary, as they say, don't tell the whole story. In a way it was an idyllic situation, in spite of its squalor.[31]

Alexander's plan to build mixed-income public housing and sanitary facilities in Chavez Ravine largely garnered support from the neighborhood. As the CHA told residents in 1951, "this project is going to be built for you . . . you'll have first priority, you can do whatever you want."[32] For Alexander, and much of the left-liberal city planning establishment in Los Angeles, the redevelopment of Bunker Hill and Chavez Ravine, the two most "blighted" neighborhoods in central Los Angeles, would work together symbiotically to ensure central, affordable, low-cost, and safe housing for the city's growing working-class populations, a plan that found support among Latinx people, African Americans, and unions.[33]

These plans for housing and urban redevelopment became the key issues in Los Angeles's municipal politics in the early 1950s. For Babcock, Alexander, and their supporters in civil rights organizations and unions, housing-centered urban renewal in Los Angeles would run directly against a rising tide of anti-communism and real estate privatism. As Don Parson has amply demonstrated in his detailed study of the red scare and public housing in Los Angeles, the city's powerful real estate lobby was able to use cries of Bolshevism directed against Bowron, Alexander, and others in order to discredit their plans for housing-centered urban redevelopment.[34]

It is important to understand that the anti–public housing advocates in Los Angeles were not against urban renewal per se. While they saw taxpayer expenditure for public housing and the general principle of a right to housing as incipient socialism, they were in favor of slum clearance and the private, commercial development of land. Indeed, they saw urban redevelopment as a key instrument in establishing Los Angeles as a world-class city and a center of the growing economy. Hollywood placed Los Angeles at the center of American culture, and its location on the edge of the Pacific Rim gave it a growing centrality in world trade and finance. Moreover, its rapidly expanding industries ensured its place as a center of production. Finally, its booming population was quickly making it one of the world's largest metropolitan areas. The single thing the city was missing in the eyes of its economic elite was a concentrated core of service, finance, and commerce that could attract capital in the form of investment, global FIRE industries, tourism, and conventions.[35] As a Chamber of Commerce publication put it, "the missing element that critics of the city have noted is its lack of a center, a concentration of culture and commerce."[36] The instrument of this elite group's redevelopment strategy was put forward that summer in the form of an innovative new state ballot measure that became the first law in the nation to allow what would come to be known as tax increment financing (TIF). Indeed, the success of Proposition 18 proved to be one of the most underappreciated innovations in Los Angeles history, as its passage and usage preceded the rest of the nation by at least two decades.[37]

The innovation behind TIFs was twofold. First, the law allowed redevelopment projects to be paid for by the collection of assumed growth in future tax revenues based on redevelopment. Thus, a redevelopment agency could eschew federal funding or municipal bonds in favor of using the promise of future tax revenues to pay for the project. Second, TIFs pushed municipalities toward private, commercial development rather than public, residential development. The future tax revenue model was based on the development and gifting of razed land to private interests. As the urban historian Colin Gordon has noted, "TIFs depend upon dramatic increases in property value, and as a result, are geared more toward new commercial investment."[38] In practice, as Gordon and a host of social critics have commented, TIFs tended to spend public money to clear and raze "blighted" areas and then sell the land to private developers at a cheap cost in order to guarantee better tax returns. Effectively then, TIFs led to commercial and service-based development and real estate land speculation as industrial development tended to lower surrounding property values. As Robert Alexander wrote in his criticism of the law, "the community in effect has paid through the nose for acquiring land substandard in some way . . . the community should retain title to it forever and simply lease that land. Eventually that might mean that all cities would be leased land, which I think would be good. I think the major curse of the cities is caused by land speculation."[39]

Tax increment financing–based development was the perfect antidote to the specter of Bolshevism that critics charged was inherent in public housing. In practice and conception it was market-based and privatized rather than entitlement-based and socialized. Municipalities and the public would not be taking social responsibility for the poor or turning housing into a right. Redevelopment funds would be removed from direct democratic control and profit incentivization would be used to produce their desired outcome. Finally, they would not be creating an entitlement, but rather, would utilize their power of eminent domain as an investment in the future growth of a given neighborhood and the city as a whole by razing "slums," combating "blight," and subsequently turning the land over "for redevelopment by private enterprise to better the whole community."[40]

The legality of tax increment financing and what it portended for the future of urban redevelopment would eventually be decided in *C.R.A v. Goldman*. By the time the ruling in the case was released in 1964, the scope of the Bunker Hill plan contained a major shift that separated Los Angeles's biggest urban renewal project from the projects of other urban areas. In 1956, the CRA scuttled Babcock's previous mixed-income residential plan in favor of a private-commercial development of hotels, shopping, dining, nightlife facilities, office buildings, and cultural and tourist attractions. The main thrust was

the creation of a plan of land use of great benefit to the people of the entire Los Angeles metropolitan area . . . facilities will be constructed for trade expositions, industrial fairs, and cultural gatherings . . . for shoppers and business persons.[41]

The new plan contained no provisions for low-income or public housing, and instead devoted two high-rise buildings to luxury housing for
downtown office workers, complete with convenient shopping, high-
end recreational facilities, and abundant parking.[42] The rest of the land
use was taken up by "a commercial plaza containing office buildings and
a major hotel . . . with service stores in the plaza," additional hotels, and
office plazas with ground- level shopping malls.[43] The use of Proposition
18 and the TIF was instrumental in the new project's financing. Simply
put, the agency was going to borrow money from the federal government and repay it through "proceeds of land sales . . . and principally,
through increased tax revenue from the project."[44] On November 7, 1956,
the City Council approved the new plan by a vote of twelve to two.[45]

The crown jewel of the revised 1956 Bunker Hill plan was the development of two 1,500-room hotels along with a convention center,
numerous restaurants, and an indoor shopping mall. Since the revised
Bunker Hill plan's approval in 1956, building destination and convention hotels was considered the key ingredient in the redevelopment of
downtown space. Babcock and Alexander were both convinced that
hotels would be superfluous in downtown Los Angeles—a place often
mistakenly referenced by Gertrude Stein's "there's no there, there" quote
about Oakland.[46] But the Community Redevelopment Agency, Chamber of Commerce, and *Los Angeles Times* had other ideas. Bunker Hill
provided Los Angeles a chance to remake the urban landscape, to produce an urban core ideally suited to an increasingly dispersed postwar
world. Bunker Hill would provide Los Angeles the perfect opportunity
to mimic the good parts of financial capitals like New York and Chicago,
while disavowing the ugly parts—namely poor residents and socially
integrated streets. In a 1949 *New York Times* article entitled "Los Angeles Has It, But What Is It?" on the phenomenonal postwar growth of
Los Angeles, reporter Sam Boal expressed typical East Coast derision of
the city, a derision of which those on the Chamber of Commerce were
hyperconscious.[47] As Boal put it,

> It is hard to access Los Angeles as a city because it isn't a city. It's a col-
> lection of some 145 suburbs, or developments which are grouped vaguely
> around the "city" of Los Angeles, the word city meaning in this sense
> merely an administrative center . . . Many residents never go into Los An-

geles, and it is a local joke that nobody—nobody—lives in Los Angeles, any more than anyone lives in Wall Street.[48]

Bunker Hill would represent the perfect counterargument to the critics who saw Los Angeles as simply one massive suburb. Bunker Hill was nothing less than a planned downtown ideally suited to the twin pillars of late twentieth-century economics and urban growth—service and finance. It would provide the institutional loci and density to develop Los Angeles into a leading international finance center. It would also attract tourists, business travelers, and conventions, while providing the city with a sorely missing cultural center. With hotels, restaurants, raised skyways and sidewalks, shopping malls, office buildings, cultural attractions, and parking lots, the newly planned neighborhood would concentrate development in a central downtown neighborhood, cater to automobile-based consumers and office workers, and through its sanitized and controlled landscape, remove the specter of urban mixing and diversity traditionally associated with dense urban cores.[49]

The one remaining obstacle to the revised Bunker Hill plan was a series of lawsuits filed by small downtown property owners immediately after the approval of the new plan. The cases were consolidated under the name of Henry Goldman, a retired teacher, and his wife, owners of a small Bunker Hill apartment building.[50] Two lower courts ruled in favor of the CRA, but with little comment as they knew the case would eventually be decided in the California Supreme Court.[51] The Goldmans put forward a whole series of objections to the plan, ranging from the assessed value of their land to CRA chair William Sesnon's possible conflict of interest as a downtown property owner to the number of days the CRA held community hearings.[52] Tellingly though, the court took seriously only two of the concerns of the Goldmans and their co-appellees: the CRA's legal authority to use eminent domain for the express purpose of turning a neighborhood from predominately residential to predominately commercial, and the constitutionality of tax increment financing.

As the Goldmans and their co-appellees argued to the California Supreme Court, the redevelopment plan was

in violation of the Fourteenth Amendment of the United States Constitution, and constitutes an unlawful delegation of legislative power in that, no ascertainable standard has been prescribed to enable a determination to be made by the agency as to whether the land may be acquired by condemnation in furtherance of a redevelopment project, which land is predominantly residential in character, for the purpose of converting the area into a predominantly commercial area.[53]

For the Goldmans, the City Council's delegation of authority to the CRA to decide whether a given neighborhood was residential or commercial represented an anti-democratic breach of power, both in terms of the delegation of authority *and* its ability to turn an area from predominately residential to predominately commercial. The court seriously considered this claim and noted that the two instances when redevelopment plans had been overturned in other states resulted from some question about the legality of land resale for commercial purposes.[54] In the end, though, the court argued that there was no express delegation of authority to the CRA to make such a decision, as the plan was eventually confirmed by the city council. In effect, the city council had made the decision to turn the neighborhood from a residential one into a commercial one, something the court argued was, while perhaps unprecedented, and possibly illegal in other states, not prohibited by any local, California, or federal law.[55]

The second argument that the court seriously considered, though eventually dismissed, concerned the legality of tax increment financing and Proposition 18. The argument that the Goldmans put forward was that because a TIF mandates a certain percentage of future tax revenue to be redirected to the city, it could be construed as "permitting a municipal legislative body to deprive other taxing agencies of taxes without their consent."[56] The court admitted that this could be legally problematic, as Proposition 18 did not require the permission of other taxing agencies to go ahead with a given plan. Taking a pragmatist line, the court deferred to an *amicus curiae* brief from the state Attorney General, the representative of the most concerned taxing agency, who argued that the plan was fine; nothing in California's Constitution could be construed to imply that a municipal authority needed the consent of other taxing agencies.[57]

It is a testament to the newness of the Bunker Hill plan that the California Supreme Court looked hardest at its two most innovative aspects. The court's affirmative ruling on the ability of legislative bodies to transform a residential neighborhood into a commercial one effectively legitimized the key development goal of the Bunker Hill plan. Similarly, the process by which the CRA hoped to achieve commercial redevelopment, the use of the TIF, was also upheld due to a lack of any legislative decree on the need for consent by other interested taxing parties. In the end, the CRA's victory in the case and the court's legal legitimization of the plan's two most foreshadowing aspects destroyed the final roadblock to the new, private, and service-oriented reimagination of the political economy of urban redevelopment.[58]

The Bonaventure was, and remains, the crown jewel of the new Bunker Hill. Throughout the 1960s, it went through various stages of planning and development, as it was always considered to be the key to Bunker Hill's success. The CRA envisioned that having a destination hotel was critical to drawing people and capital downtown. If the city wanted to attract concentrated high finance and consumers, it needed a project with the magnitude and symbolism that the Bonaventure would come to represent. Lowell Dillingham, the high-end developer who purchased the land on which the Bonaventure would eventually be built, noted in 1968, "we feel downtown Los Angeles—the renewal site—has the greatest potential of any area in the Los Angeles region . . . whoever thought up the concept of urban renewal was a mastermind, our cities are rotting at the core."[59] What Dillingham did not mention in his triumphalist view of downtown L.A.'s urban renewal as the antidote to the city's decay was the profit he stood to make. Indeed, the preceding quote is from the day after he bought a parcel of the most central land in the region from the city for a mere $3 million and the promise of a future hotel.[60]

Dillingham would never build a hotel on the site, and instead he sold the lots for a healthy $2.5 million profit to the developer that eventually did, the influential Atlanta architect and developer John Portman.[61] Indeed, Alexander's warning that Proposition 18 and the TIF would lead to rampant land speculation seemed to be coming true.[62] For his part, Portman built a hotel, the Bonaventure, which opened to much fanfare on New Year's Eve 1976. The hotel's official guide drew the connection between the hotel and the city at large:

Los Angeles, super city and trendsetter for the nation has done it again. The City of Angels has created a splendid new Downtown at historic Bunker Hill. Where stately Victorian mansions once stood, shining towers now rise, connected by soaring skybridges. In the renaissance of Downtown, the city introduces a totally new, 21st century brand of elegance . . . Los Angeles, with its lively new downtown, has become the financial, business and cultural center of the West.[63]

The connection between the hotel's success and that of the reinvigorated downtown was explicit. The *Los Angeles Times*'s revered architectural critic, Ray Hebert, noted, "A 110 million dollar complex composed of five bronze glass cylindrical towers jutting 35 stories above Fifth Street . . . already a city landmark . . . it is said to be the costliest hotel ever built."[64]

The hotel offered guests as well as locals unparalleled amenities. "In food, drink, atmosphere, and service the Bonaventure caters to every taste."[65] An enclosed six-story atrium centered on a 2-acre lake, indoor and outdoor swimming pools, lounges virtually everywhere, along with five restaurants, and two 24-hour coffee shops. The hotel provided convention and meeting space with the capacity for at least twenty thousand people.[66] Finally, guests and locals alike were to be attracted by "five levels of the most exciting shopping in Southern California . . . shops at the Bonaventure offer the essentials, the luxuries, and the just plain frivolous."[67] Indeed, as Jameson argued, the Bonaventure aspired to be a totalizing space. But the hotel's totalization was not embedded in its cylindrical postmodern architecture. Rather, food and drink, shopping and scenery, luxuries and essentials, business and leisure, all the frivolity of modern consumption combined with all the weight of a city's development could be found at the Bonaventure.

While the Bonaventure was certainly Bunker Hill's crown jewel, it was not alone. Four years after its opening it was followed by an utterly similar hotel, located a block away, the Sheraton Grande (now the Marriott). In describing the growing attraction of the site, the hotel-planning firm MAT Associates stated the enormous transformation that the Bunker Hill Plan had achieved downtown.

The financial center of the city has moved to Bunker Hill . . . the result of this growth has been a wholly new, modernized downtown . . . with the advent of the present freeway system, the city's economic activity has become highly dispersed; a similar pattern has resulted in the supply and demand for hotel accommodations . . . until recently there has been no downtown center."[68]

Led by the Bonaventure, office buildings, shopping, and cultural attractions sprang up in Bunker Hill and Los Angeles finally developed a concentrated core of "commercial, service, financial, and professional establishments."[69] MAT Associates estimated that the demand for services similar to those the Bonaventure offered would only grow, thus necessitating a hotel-entertainment complex with one thousand rooms, seven restaurants, four bars, and 35,000 feet of retail space.[70] While not as gargantuan as the Bonaventure, the architecturally significant Sheraton Grande, which opened in 1981, mimicked the Bonaventure's emphasis on an enclosed and self-contained site of service. Guests would not have to leave the hotel for anything, while the emphasis the complex placed on food and beverage service, shopping, and business facilities would attract visitors from across the region.

The Bonaventure, the Sheraton Grande, and the rest of the Bunker Hill project represented the transformation of urbanity into enclosed, service-producing private spaces. The model for urban vibrancy was private capital-producing services of convenience, luxury, and frivolity for the betterment of the entire metropolitan area. Through tax increment financing, Los Angeles attempted to use private investors, who in the 1970s were increasingly based in Japan, in order to create a modern cityscape with the centralized amenities of older European and eastern cities, while distancing the rotten and problematic aspects of public space from its new city center through private control.[71]

What neither the celebratory boosters of downtown revival nor critical theorists like Jameson, Soja, and Davis noticed was that such developments depended inordinately on securing cheap service labor. There was no shortage of people willing to work such jobs during the economic crises of the 1970s. Indeed, in the months before its opening, the Bonaventure accepted more than ten thousand applications for its two thousand positions—the majority of which were for maids, busboys, and cleaning personnel. As a *Los Angeles Times* caption stated two months before the opening, "lines form everyday outside the new Los Angeles Bonaventure Hotel where thousands are seeking jobs."[72] The Bonaventure did not skimp on training its massive new workforce, as all employees were put through weeks-long training courses.[73]

Similarly, labor costs were key to the success of the Sheraton Grande. MAT Associates estimated that based on 72% occupancy, the hotel could expect to pay out approximately 60% of its $6 million annual operating costs in wages.[74] With 500 estimated employees, that cost worked out to an average annual wage of approximately $7200 a year, barely 50% of the 1981 national average wage.[75]

The work of maids in these hotels was particularly demanding and low paid. As one advocacy organization put it in the 1980s,

> A maid's workday, after she has prepared the cleaning area and cart, includes—for each room: changing the beds, vacuuming the rugs, cleaning the bathroom (scrubbing the toilet, tub, sink and floor), supplying the room with fresh linens, and washing windows and mirrors "as needed." Often there is a drunkard's sickness to clean up and always maids are subject to insults from male customers.[76]

Besides the poor and often physically grueling working conditions, the wage structure for hotel maids was designed to ensure that the maximum number of rooms were cleaned with as little labor cost as possible. Maids worked on a modified piece schedule, getting paid an hourly wage to clean a quota of two to three rooms an hour, depending on the hotel and type of room. If the rooms were not cleaned, the work still had to be done, thus ensuring high productivity at relatively low cost to the hotel.[77]

African Americans, who seem to have been initially relegated to the jobs of table bussers and doormen at the Bonaventure, found the hotel a particularly poor employer. The *Los Angeles Sentinel* quoted Lang as saying that the Bonaventure "is like a plantation. It's not that they overtly show racial prejudice, but it is the condescending attitude they show when dealing with the black employees."[78] Lang was particularly upset that the hotel had happily hosted a series of black professional conventions yet continued to relegate African Americans to low-paying and untipped positions.

The importance of labor costs to the success of this model of service was demonstrated immediately upon the opening of the Bonaventure. Before its opening, the Bonaventure had joined the Restaurant-Employers Council of Southern California, the industry conglomeration of hotels and restaurants that used economies of scale to get better prices on goods and collectively bargain with the Hotel Employees Restaurant Employees Union (HERE). Upon staffing the hotel, various bargaining units were formed and HERE asumed that they were covered under the master industry bargaining unit. But the Bonaventure had other ideas, and after the National Labor Relations Board ruled that "as a member of Council the Employer became part of the multi-employer unit and agreed to be bound by negotiations in such unit," it proceeded to leave the Council in favor of creating a single bargaining unit, thus, in effect, deunionizing.[79] Indeed, the importance of low-wage service to the success of Bunker Hill cannot be dramatized in greater detail by the number of people who worked in the neighborhood by the end of twentieth century. Of roughly fifty thousand employees who worked in the two zip codes in Bunker Hill in 1997, somewhere around a third to a half could be classified as low-wage service, mostly working in food and beverage, cleaning, security, retail, and parking.[80] Indeed, one would be hard pressed to find a better spatial representation of how low-waged service based redevelopment is a key context for the nation's growing economic inequality. While bussers, parking attendants, and maids labor for wages lower than the federal poverty line, the hotels, FIRE industry offices, and high-end stores of Bunker Hill earn profits in the billions annually.

While Bunker Hill redevelopment centered on transforming the urban core of Los Angeles into a place of immense profit dependent on service consumption, and less apparently, of low-wage service employment, twenty miles northwest of Bunker Hill, on the outer edge of municipal Los Angeles, the 1970s and 1980s witnessed a similar transformation through similar means. The neighborhood of Pacoima rapidly grew during World War II as a housing destination for workers at Lockheed Martin's main plant in nearby Burbank. The federal government helped solidify this growth by building the San Fernando Gardens housing project in Pacoima. The result of San Fernando Gardens was that Pacoima was to become the most, and for years the only, Latinx, black, and white integrated neighborhood in the San Fernando Valley. By the end of the war, Pacoima was also the densest neighborhood in the

Valley.[81] Through much of the immediate postwar decades, the residents of Pacoima who lived outside of the San Fernando Gardens got by on small-scale household production. As Mary Helen Ponce has demonstrated in her memoir of childhood in a Mexican American section of Pacoima, most families in the neighborhood cobbled together odd jobs and services in order to make a living. Home ownership was high, and the houses, while dilapidated, helped forge a strong local community. Many of the families had migrated to the area from Central Valley farming communities. Most families acquired their food primarily from large backyard gardens, and raised their own chickens. Fathers and children earned cash by performing odd jobs. For instance, Ponce's dad collected scrap wood from dumpsters across the valley and turned his neighborhood lot into a de facto community lumberyard.[82]

By the middle of the 1970s, as the rest of the San Fernando Valley boomed around it, Pacoima, always a working-class neighborhood, experienced substantial disinvestment and white flight.[83] Its schools had some of the highest dropout rates in the city, unemployment in the neighborhood was considerably higher than the Los Angeles average, and it was made up of disproportionately single-parent households.[84] As a city report summed it up, "most observers tend to associate negative images with the name 'Pacoima.'"[85] Indeed, Pacoima, on the edge of the San Fernando Valley section of the city of Los Angeles and miles from downtown, seems an odd locale to mimic Bunker Hill. Yet, as the public-private tax increment financing–based partnership, Pacoima Revitalization Inc., demonstrated, by the early 1980s, the service-centered private redevelopment of which Bunker Hill was in the vanguard had become increasingly hegemonic across Southern California and was spreading across the nation as a whole.

Pacoima Revitalization Inc. (PRI) was formed as a public-private partnership in 1977 by City Councilman Rob Ronka, the CRA, and the Los Angeles City Council. While PRI had no illusions that it was going to turn Pacoima into an international hub for services and a modern city center attractive to finance capital, it nonetheless saw redevelopment as dually centered on TIFs and services. Omega Research Associates, a development accounting firm contracted to assess the neighborhood, argued that PRI would essentially have to give land away to entice developers because of the neighborhood's disrepair and reputation, but once the development occurred, the increased tax revenue would make up for PRI's initial outlay.[86] The proposed development included two restaurants, a cocktail lounge, bowling alley, movie theater, discount store, and roller-skating rink.[87] It would draw customers from Pacoima as well as from decidedly whiter and more affluent neighborhoods and towns like San Fernando, Mission Hills, Lakeview Terrace, Sylmar, Tujunga, Arleta, and Sun Valley.[88] The major selling point for the project though was that, upon completion, the project could expect to produce more than three hundred jobs, most of which would be in low-wage service work; the shopping and entertainment center would become Pacoima's largest employer.[89]

The Pacoima Center opened in 1984 with an initial three hundred employees as expected. It was hardly the success that PRI envisioned, though, and by the early 1990s, only a Thrifty Drug Store and a Trak Auto supply store remained.[90] The center's undoing was likely its location in racially tainted Pacoima. Whether a success or failure, the emphasis that the PRI put on using a TIF to develop a service-based center of consumption as the solution to Pacoima's ills was demonstrative of the degree to which the Bunker Hill model of urban redevelopment was becoming increasingly standard.

Two other examples from the 1990s further demonstrate the growing postwar connection between service development, tax increment financing, and the reimagination of successful and profitable urban space. In the middle of the 1980s, the far exurban Los Angeles County community of Lancaster used a TIF and a questionable application of "blight" to give land to Wal-Mart, Costco, and 99 Cent Stores in an effort to develop service facilities in the bedroom community.[91] Power Center, as the development became known, took off, so much so that Costco desired a massive expansion. As the US Court of Appeals described the situation: "viewing Costco as a so-called 'anchor tenant' and fearful of Costco's relocation to another city, Lancaster began . . . a 'friendly' eminent domain proceeding" against 99 Cent Stores in order to give the newly "blighted" land to Costco and produce more tax revenue.[92] Lancaster had taken the logic of tax increment financing and service development a step further to not simply moving a neighborhood from unwanted housing or industry to service and commerce, but toward pushing a neighborhood from undesired service business to desired service business.

Less egregious in some ways than Lancaster was the redevelopment of the Baldwin Hills Shopping Plaza in Los Angeles in the 1980s. Built in 1948, Baldwin Hills was one of the nation's first outdoor shopping malls. It initially served a large area of South Los Angeles, but as the surrounding Crenshaw neighborhood became increasingly African American in the decades after World War II, it became known as the "black mall," and its clientele became more and more limited.[93] Following on the heels of its racial marking in the 1960s and 1970s, Baldwin Hills suffered when many of the area's residents, like countless other Angelenos during these years, began to commute to more suburban indoor shopping malls.[94] By the early 1980s, the mall had become largely vacant, prompting the CRA to declare it blighted in order to offer private developers incentives through the establishment of a TIF. Eventually in 1982, Haagen Development, a Manhattan Beach firm, signed a contract with the CRA to redevelop the mall and receive $51 million in public financing.[95] Over the course of the next decade and a half, the mall slowly redeveloped, attaining flagship stores such as Gap and Macy's. For its part, Haagen sold the mall to a private investment trust, which eventually sold a large interest to Magic Johnson Enterprises (MJE). MJE succeeded in getting city funding for theater construction in 1995, and again in 1998 for the leasing of big box retail stores.[96] In the end, as the Los Angeles Alliance for a New Economy has pointed out, the CRA and the city provided an outlay of more than $60 million for the various Baldwin Hills projects. By the end of 2000, it had received roughly $4.2 million in additional tax revenue from the TIF, while MJE had sole ownership of one of the three most lucrative theaters in America and a controlling interest in the rent on a popular shopping mall and center.[97]

From Bunker Hill to Baldwin Hills, postwar Los Angeles has been at the forefront of the urban neoliberal project. This chapter has placed the developments that fall under the rubric of this term in a more historical and specified context as well as shown their close connection to a redevelopment vision founded on service-centered urban revitalization through the transfer of public land to commercial developers. Since its inception out of the ashes of Los Angeles's anti-public housing politics of the early 1950s, tax increment financing has been closely tied to a reimagination of healthy, vibrant urban space centered around private services rather than housing or industrial development. In the end, state and especially municipal policy and politics were not just simply super-structural phenomena controlled by a macro-level transition from New Deal to neoliberal, Fordist to post-Fordist, and industry to service, but were important reasons for this shift through their conception of what constituted an ideal urban redevelopment. This transformation was integral to the disestablishment of public goods like low-cost housing as the key to stemming the tide of fleeing people and capital and establishing a new, privatized thrust of state-sponsored urban redevelopment that not only transformed the urban landscape into a particularly profitable locale for profit-making but was also dependent upon the labors of tens of thousands of low-wage service workers.

NOTES

1 Frederic Jameson, *Postmodernism, or, the Cultural Logic of Late Capitalism* (Durham, NC: Duke University Press, 1991), 40.

2 Ibid., 44, 38–55.

3 Ibid., 41.

4 In the 1980s, the Bonaventure was *the* place for high social theorists to congregate and glimpse the future. As Soja writes, "in 1984 . . . Jameson, Lefebvre, and I wandered through the Bonaventure, rode its glass-encased elevators, and had some refreshments in the rooftop revolving restaurant overlooking downtown. In 1989, I took much the same trip with Robert Manquis and Jean Baudrillard." See Edward Soja, *Thirdspace: Journeys to Los Angeles and Other Real and Imagined Places* (New York: Wiley-Blackwell, 1996), 196, n. 8.

5 Edward Soja, *Postmodern Geographies: The Reassertion of Space in Critical Theories* (New York: Verso, 1989), 243–44.

6 Mike Davis, "Urban Renaissance and the Spirit of Postmodernism," *New Left Review* 151 (May–June 1985), 106–13. Mike Davis, *City of Quartz: Excavating the Future in Los Angeles* (New York: Verso, 1990), 221–64.

7 While not overly concerned with origin stories of neoliberalism, this chapter nonetheless suggests that the close focus on the early 1970s by scholars like David Harvey has missed key historical developments, particularly in the way city governance responded to postwar metropolitanization that occurred much earlier, if in piecemeal fashion. For a recent study that offers a similar perspective on the evolution of neoliberalism over the twentieth century, see Andrew J. Diamond, *Chicago on the Make: Power and Inequality in a Modern City* (Oakland: University of California Press, 2017).

8 This argument meshes with Wendy Brown's suggestion that neoliberal governance produces a logic that devolves authority over social problems to bodies that are both capable of addressing them and incentivized through profit rather than mandated to produce particular outcomes. See Wendy Brown, *Un-*

doing the Demos: Neoliberalism's Stealth Revolution (Cambridge, MA: MIT Press, 2015), 131–42.

9 In the Matter of the Redevelopment Plan for Bunker Hill Urban Renewal Project 1B of the *Community Redevelopment Agency of the City of Los Angeles v. Henry Goldman et al.*, Supreme Court of California, 61 Cal. 2d 21; 389 P.2d, 538. Hereafter cited as *C.R.A. v. Goldman*.

10 Bergen and Lee Inc., "100 Years (And More) of Bunker Hill History, Prepared for the City Reconstruction Corporation," 1967, 5, Box 13, Bunker Hill Redevelopment Project Papers (hereafter referred to as BHRP), Department of Special Collections, University of Southern California Libraries, Los Angeles.

11 Bergen and Lee Inc., "100 Years (And More) of Bunker Hill History, Prepared for the City Reconstruction Corporation," 1967, 7, Box 13, BHRP, Department of Special Collections, University of Southern California Libraries, Los Angeles.

12 Scott L. Bottles, *Los Angeles and the Automobile: The Making of the Modern City* (Berkeley and Los Angeles: University of California Press, 1991), 52–92; Robert M. Fogelson, *The Fragmented Metropolis: Los Angeles, 1850–1930* (Berkeley and Los Angeles: University California Press, 1993), 85–108, 137–64.

13 Yukio Kawaratani, "The Evolution of Bunker Hill," *LA Downtown News*, August 3, 1998.

14 Raymond Chandler, "The High Window," in *Raymond Chandler: Stories and Early Fiction* (New York: Library of America, 1995), 1002. For a discussion of Chandler's political sympathies, see Dennis Broe, "Class, Labor, and the Home-Front Detective: Hammett, Chandler, Woolrich, and the Dissident Lawmen in 1940s Hollywood and Beyond," *Social Justice* 32:2 (2005), 167–99.

15 On Bunker Hill as Los Angeles's most dense neighborhood, see Robert E. Alexander and Drayton S. Bryant, *Rebuilding a City: A Study of Redevelopment Problems in Los Angeles* (Los Angeles: John Randolph and Doris Haynes Foundation, 1951), 44. For literary examples, see Mickey Spillane, *Kiss Me Deadly* (New York: Dutton, 1952); John Fante, *Ask the Dust* (New York: Harper Collins, 1939); Fante, *Dreams from Bunker Hill* (New York: Harper Collins, 1982); Charles Bukowski, *Longshot Pomes for Broken Players* (Los Angeles: Seven Poets Press, 1962). For film examples, see Robert Aldrich's adaptation of Spillane's *Kiss Me Deadly*, 1955; Robert Siodmak, *Criss Cross*, 1949; Kent McKenzie, *The Exiles*, 1962. For a similar analysis of the role that a broader swath of decaying Los Angeles neighborhoods, exemplified by Bunker Hill, played in postwar film, see Eric Avila, *Popular Culture in the Age of White Flight* (Berkeley: University of California Press, 2005), 72–81. On the "sunshine and noir" typology of the depiction of Los Angeles, see Davis, *City of Quartz*, 15–98.

16 For a general history of the War years in Southern California, see Kevin Starr, *Embattled Dreams: California in War and Peace* (New York: Oxford University Press, 2002), 66–95.

17 Donald Parson, *Making a Better World: Public Housing, the Red Scare, and the Direction of Modern Los Angeles* (Minneapolis: University of Minnesota Press, 2005), 103–37.

18 For the most comprehensive and broadest consideration of Los Angeles urban flight and its relationship to war work, see Greg Hise, *Magnetic Los Angeles: Planning the Twentieth-Century Metropolis* (Baltimore, MD: Johns Hopkins University Press, 1997), 86–153.

19 Bergen and Lee, "100 Years and More of Bunker Hill History," 11, BHRP.

20 Community Redevelopment Agency, "You and the Bunker Hill Urban Renewal Project," 1961, 4, Box 12, BHRP.

21 See Don Parson, *Making a Better World*, especially, 137–63; Janet Abu-Lughod, *New York, Chicago, Los Angeles: America's Global Cities* (Minneapolis: University of Minnesota Press, 1999), 259–63. While Abu-Lughod's analysis is primarily derived from her reading of Parson's 1985 UCLA urban planning dissertation, she is much more explicit in reading Los Angeles's experience in public-private urban renewal partnerships and general spatial privatization as anticipatory toward future national and international urban experiences.

22 California State Assembly, Community Redevelopment Act, 1945, quoted in Robert E. Alexander and Drayton S. Bryant, *Rebuilding a City: A Study of Urban Redevelopment Problems in Los Angeles* (Los Angeles: John Randolph and Doris Haynes Foundation, 1951), 36–37.

23 Ibid.

24 Fletcher Bowron, quoted in "City Launches Drive on Slums," *Los Angeles Times* (hereafter *LAT*), October 24, 1948, 1, 6.

25 This urban planning impulse had a much longer lineage, dating back to the Progressive Era; see Daniel T. Rodgers, *Atlantic Crossings: Social Politics in a Progressive Age* (Cambridge, MA: Belknap Press of Harvard University Press, 2000) 112–59. Similar progressive urban planners would include Robert Rochon Taylor and Elizabeth Wood in Chicago, and Catherine Lansing in New York. See Arnold R. Hirsch, *Making the Second Ghetto: Race and Housing in Chicago* (1983; repr., Chicago: University of Chicago Press, 1998), 212–39; Nicholas Bloom, *Public Housing That Worked: New York in the Twentieth Century* (Philadelphia: University of Pennsylvania Press, 2009).

26 Robert E. Alexander, transcript of oral history interview with Martin Laskey, 1986, Oral History Program, Young Research Library, University of California, Los Angeles, 71.

27 Henry A. Babcock, *Metropolitan Area Passenger System Proposed for the Los Angeles Area* (Los Angeles: Metropolitan Area Passenger System, 1948).

28 Alexander, Oral History transcript.

29 Henry A. Babcock, *Report on the Feasibility of Redeveloping Bunker Hill* (Los Angeles: Henry A. Babcock, 1951), 2–3.

30 Alexander and Bryant, *Rebuilding a City*, 45–46.

31 Alexander, Oral History Transcript, 337.

32 City Housing Authority Pamphlet, quoted in Avila, *Popular Culture in the Age of White Flight*, 156.

33 See Parson, *Making a Better World*, 173–254. The transition of Chavez Ravine from working-class "slum," to proposed public housing, to suburbanized landscape

of entertainment with the construction of Dodger Stadium and the movement of the Brooklyn Dodgers baseball team to Los Angeles, along   with the Chicano resistance to this transition, is not a subject of this chapter, though its trajectory in many ways mirrors that of Bunker Hill. For a detailed study of Chavez Ravine as a site of Chicano resistance, see Ronald William Lopez II, "The Battle for Chavez Ravine: Public Policy and Chicano Community Resistance in Postwar Los Angeles, 1945–1962" (PhD diss., University of California, Berkeley, 1999). For an analysis of the creation of Chavez Ravine as a suburbanized landscape of popular culture, see Avila, *Popular Culture in the Age of White Flight*, 145–84.

34 Parson, *Making a Better World*.

35 Southern California Research Council, *The Los Angeles Economy: Its Strengths and Weaknesses* (Los Angeles: Haynes Foundation, 1954).

36 Chamber of Commerce brochure, "LA Alive Again," 1963, Box 12, BHRP.

37 As Colin Gordon points out, only five other states had TIF laws by 1970, and California and the Bunker Hill project in particular were by far the heaviest users of the law. In the late 1970s, as federal money for urban renewal began drying up, states began to rapidly pass TIF laws in order to combat the so-called growing urban crisis. See Colin Gordon, "Blighting the Way: Urban Renewal, Economic Development, and the Elusive Definition of Blight," *Fordham Urban Law Journal* 31 (2004), 305–37.

38 Ibid., 5.

39 Alexander Oral History, 232.

40 "Recommendations on Propositions," *LAT*, November 2, 1952, B1.

41 C.R.A., "Bunker Hill Urban Renewal Project, Tentative Plan," June 1956, 14, Box 12, BHRP.

42 Ibid.

43 Ibid.

44 Ibid.

45 "Bunker Hill Plan OK'd by Council," *LAT*, November 8, 1956.

46 Stein's quote is often misreported as referring to Los Angeles rather than Oakland. See for instance Thom Anderson's documentary film, *Los Angeles Plays Itself* (2003). Also, Margie Busch, quoted in John Pomfret, "Downtown Los Angeles Gets a $10 Billion Remake," *Washington Post*, January 2, 2006, A3.

47 See, for instance, Minutes, April 13, 1950. Box 29, Los Angeles Chamber of Commerce Papers, University of Southern California. The Boal article inspired particularly heated discussion at the Chamber of Commerce.

48 Sam Boal, "Los Angeles Has It, But What Is It?" *New York Times* (hereafter *NYT*), September 4, 1949, 95.

49 C.R.A., "Bunker Hill Urban Renewal Project, Tentative Plan," June 1956, 3–8, Box 12, BHRP. The argument here regarding the spatial politics of downtown Los

Angeles mirrors those of Mike Davis, Reichard Weinstein, and Edward Soja while providing more historicity and context. See Davis, *City of Quartz*, 221–48; Weinstein, "The First American City," and Soja, "From Crisis Generated Restructuring to Restructuring Generated Crisis," in *The City: Los Angeles and Urban Theory at the End of the Twentieth Century*, ed. Allen Scott and Edward Soja (Berkeley: University of California Press, 1996), 22–46, 426–62.

50 "Suit Filed to Prevent Project on Bunker Hill," May 26, 1959, *LAT*, 21.
51 See one of the consolidated cases argued before the District Court of Appeals, *Frank W. Babcock v. Community Redevelopment Agency of the City of Los Angeles*, 148 Cal. App. 2d 38, 1957.
52 *C.R.A. v. Goldman*, 17–33.
53 Quoted in ibid., 31.
54 Ibid. The two cases were *Adams v. Housing Authority of City of Daytona Beach* (Fla. 1952) 60 So.2d 663, and *Housing Authority of City of Atlanta v. Johnson* (1953) 209 Ga. 560.
55 *C.R.A. v. Goldman*, 30–32.
56 Ibid., 29.
57 Ibid., 28–29.
58 Roger Arnebergh to Samuel Yorty, "Report RE Conclusion of Bunker Hill Redevelopment Project Litigation," March 3, 1964, Box 12, BHRP.
59 Lowell Dillingham, quoted in Ray Hebert, "Hotel Planned for Bunker Hill Area," *LAT*, September 13, 1968, B2.
60 Ibid.
61 Ray Hebert, "Team Named to Build L.A. Convention Hotel," *LAT*, August 19, 1971, B6.
62 Indeed, much of the backlog on Bunker Hill development has been the level at which speculators have purchased lots from the city with promises to build a hotel, office building, etc., only to turn around a few years later and sell the lots and the promises to other developers.
63 Western International Hotels, Los Angeles Bonaventure Guide, 1977, 2, Box 1, BHRP.
64 Ray Hebert, "Hotel a Turning Point for Bunker Hill Program," *LAT*, December 12, 1976, A1.
65 Western International Hotels, Los Angeles Bonaventure Guide, 1977, p. 4, Box 1, BHRP.
66 Ibid., 8–11.
67 Ibid., 13.
68 MAT Associates to Americana Hotels, "Report of Potential Market Demand and Statement of Annual Operating Results for a Proposed Hotel on Parcel 'C' in Proposed Bunker Hill Redevelopment Area," March 1977, II-4, Box 1, BHRP.
69 Ibid.
70 Ibid.
71 See Nicholas Kristoff, "Los Angeles: Money Center," *NYT*, March 26, 1986, D1.

72 Margaret Kilgore, "Bonaventure: Reflection of Things to Come," *LAT*, November 7, 1976, F1.

73 Ibid.

74 "Report of Potential Market Demand," BHRP, X-4.

75 Ibid. The poverty level that year was approximately $4,620, so it stands to reason that management wages, factored into the hotel's total labor outlay, drove the average costs way up. Thus, it seems safe to assume that for most Sheraton Grande employees, their individual yearly wage put them right at the poverty level.

76 Jesse Larsen, "Maids," n.d., Folder 6, Box 17, Union Women's Alliance to Gain Equality Records, California Labor Archives, San Francisco State University.

77 Ibid.

78 Mary Thompson, "Employee Charges, Hotel Answers," *Los Angeles Sentinel*, March 30, 1978, A3.

79 Quoted in "Los Angeles Bonaventure Hotel and American Federation of Guards, Local," No. 1, Case 21-RC-15279, March 18, 1978, *Decisions of the National Labor Relations Board* (Washington, DC: US Government Printing Office, 1978), 97. The hotel would reunionize upon Westin's takeover in the early 1990s.

80 US Census, "Zip Code Patterns," 1997.

81 City Planning Commission, *Planning for the San Fernando Valley*, City of Los Angeles, 1945, 93.

82 See Mary Helen Ponce, *Hoyt Street: An Autobiography* (Albuquerque: University of New Mexico Press, 1993). See "General Facts on San Fernando Valley," Folder 10, Box 12, "Industrial Zoning and Development of San Fernando Valley," Folder 16, Box 12, "Destination 90," Folder 38, Box 11, all Valley Industrial and Commerce Association Papers, Urban Archives Center California State University Northridge. "Pacoima Neighborhood Report," Folder 8, Box 5, Pacoima Revitalization Inc. Papers (hereafter PRI), Urban Archives Center, California State University Northridge. Ponce's remembrances also conform to the social history of the similar edge-urban community of South Gate that Becky Nicolaides brilliantly documents in *My Blue Heaven: Life and Politics in the Working-Class Suburbs of Los Angeles* (Chicago: University of Chicago Press, 2002), 65–183.

83 Omega Research Associates, "Feasibility Study," 5, Folder 12, Box 4, PRI.

84 Ibid.

85 "Comprehensive Community Development Program-Pacoima," I-1, Folder 19, Box 5, PRI.

86 "Feasibility Study," 1–4.

87 Ibid., 6, 10, 27, 46, 68.

88 Ibid., table X.

89 Ibid., 6, 10, 27, 46, 68.

90 "Area's First Major Shopping Center," *LAT*, October 9, 1983. Ironically, in August 2008, the City Council recommended another TIF for a retail development in Pacoima, this time centered around a Best Buy and Costco. See "L.A. City Councils Oks $18.7 Million for Plaza Pacoima," *LAT*, August 13, 2008.

91 *99 Cents Only Stores v. Lancaster Redevelopment Agency*, 60 Fed. Appx. 123 (9th Cir. 2003).

92 Ibid., 7.

93 On the development of Crenshaw as a renowned middle-class black neighborhood, see Josh Sides, *L.A. City Limits: African-American Los Angeles from the Great Depression to the Present* (Berkeley: University of California Press, 2004), esp. 95–130, 161–98. On Baldwin Hills as the "black mall," see, for instance, Karen Robinson-Jacobs, "Noticing a Latin Flavor in Crenshaw," *LAT*, May 2, 2001.

94 See Los Angeles Alliance for a New Economy (LAANE), *Who Benefits from Redevelopment in Los Angeles? An Analysis of Commercial Redevelopment Activities in the 1990s* (Los Angeles: UCLA School of Public Policy and Social Research, 1999), 19.

95 Ibid.

96 Ibid.

97 Ibid.

3

The Politics of Austerity

The Moral Economy in 1970s New York

KIM PHILLIPS-FEIN

The fiscal crisis that nearly sent New York City into bankruptcy in 1975 continues to reverberate in the city's dominant mythology. Ever since the 1970s, urban economists and people in the upper echelons of the city's political life have seen the crisis as an inevitable consequence of lax spending, unrealistic expectations of city government, and absence of oversight. The resolution of the crisis through the adoption of budget cuts that shrank the public-sector workforce by about 60,000 people has therefore often been viewed as a moral and political victory for the leadership of the city. As Lazard Freres investment banker Felix Rohatyn (who played a leading role in negotiating the deals that kept the city out of bankruptcy court) put it in an essay in the *New York Review of Books* about the fiscal crisis a few years after its resolution, "The people of the city were willing to make real sacrifices as long as they believed that those sacrifices were relatively fairly distributed, that there was an end in sight and that the result would be a better city, a better environment, and a better life."[1]

Although the real causes of the fiscal crisis were more complex than this moralistic interpretation indicates, aspects of this narrative of common sacrifice are persuasive. The city's major public-sector labor unions, and most of its leading Democratic politicians, quickly came to consensus that there was little point but to acquiesce to retrenchment. Fearing that bankruptcy might mean the loss of their contracts and could endanger the very practice of collective bargaining, most of the city's public-sector unions agreed to wage cuts and freezes and a policy of shrinking the city government through attrition and layoffs. They used the pension funds of their members to purchase hundreds of millions of dollars of city debt in order to help the city avoid declaring bankruptcy, making them literal participants in the new order of the city. The politicians at the city's helm, all of them Democrats, were the ones who enforced and created the austerity regime. Despite some initial objections and rebellions against the new order, it grew increasingly difficult for any mainstream political leader to propose a real alternative and remain within the framework of accepted discourse—as became clear in the mayoral election of 1977, when even candidates who might have seemed open to more radical approaches (such as former Congresswoman Bella Abzug) adopted programs that had much in common with the business-oriented platforms of Congressman Ed Koch and incumbent mayor Abraham Beame. Thus, the turn toward a framework for governance in the city that emphasized the primacy of the private sector and the weakness of the public can seem inevitable, as though most people in the city came to believe that this was the only real way forward.

But despite this rapid consensus at elite levels, the working-class response to the fiscal crisis was far more ambivalent than this capsule summary suggests. The cutbacks and retrenchment of the fiscal crisis era set off a wave of protests in working-class neighborhoods—demonstrations of resistance that have been almost entirely neglected in most treatments of the crisis. Many of these were focused on the protection of public services—schools, fire stations, colleges, hospitals—that were important both materially and symbolically. They delivered real benefits to the various neighborhoods of the city, but they also represented the inclusion and incorporation of its residents into the city as a whole. These struggles suggest that the turn in New York politics was deeply contested, that it was not accomplished easily, and that efforts to shrink local government met with substantial difficulty and friction.

Accounts of the rise of neoliberalism at times make it sound as though this epochal shift was accomplished fairly easily, as though the elite program was developed and imposed from above on a population that had little real capacity to articulate alternatives. The story of New York City during the fiscal crisis, though, suggests an alternative way to approach both the politics of crisis and that of neoliberalism. The city's economic and political elites abandoned older ways of organizing social life in the city only with difficulty. Although many shared a general sense that the city's government was too large and expensive, taxes too high, and social provisions too generous, they did not have a clear or coherent policy alternative at hand before the crisis began. And when they finally were able to impose a set of budget cuts, these cuts met with substantial critique and resistance, so much so that at times city elites had to make real concessions and preserve services. Far from being a straightforward, easy process, then, the shift in the city's governance at the end of the 1970s took place haltingly and slowly, and the transition was far from complete even at its conclusion.

Recognizing this does not mean that we should overstate the nature of the resistance. This had an intensely local focus, as people in particular communities sought to preserve their services and their neighborhoods. It was defensive in nature, seeking to hold on to what had existed—even though local activists had previously been critical of the various racial and economic inequities in the city's public sector. During the crisis, there was no organization from the left that was capable of mounting a substantive political challenge to the basic logic of the fiscal crisis or proposing an alternative future for the city's public sector. Those who opposed austerity were not capable of uniting different groups throughout the city into a coherent mass movement. Nonetheless, this neighborhood orientation, with all its limitations, did not mean that the politics of resistance to the fiscal crisis was simply framed in terms of protecting services in particular communities. On the contrary, the fiscal crisis was intensely charged with symbolic meaning. It came to represent the withdrawal of public resources from these poor and working-class neighborhoods and their redirection to other constituencies in the city, most notably the corporate sector and those who worked within it.

Throughout the 1960s, New York's local welfare state—already more extensive by far than most municipal governments—had expanded in response to the political protests of the era and in particular those mobilizations that had been animated by the civil rights movement. The fiscal crisis marked the end of this period of growth and became part of a broader social conflict extending back to the 1960s and into the 1980s over the question of for whom and in whose interests the city government would run. Many causes of the crisis were rooted in the underlying structure of city finances: the dependence of the city on Albany to raise taxes; the funding formulas for welfare and Medicaid that left New York responsible for a full quarter of the payment of these social programs; the constitutional limits on the city's property taxes; the divide between the city and its suburbs, which meant that people who earned their incomes in the city and whose wealth depended on New York could evade paying taxes to the city government; the trends undergirding the migration to the suburbs and the departure of industry from the city.

The climate of emergency during the 1975 fiscal crisis and the real risk that the city would go bankrupt effectively reframed all these issues in the much more restricted and highly moralistic rhetoric of budgetary responsibility. The city's problematic accounting practices, its raiding of the capital budget to pay for expenses, and the high level of disorganization that had made it possible for New York to borrow hundreds of millions of dollars guaranteed by funds that might never appear without anyone really acknowledging that this was happening all came under scrutiny and criticism as the crisis unfolded. The larger reasons the city government remained perennially short of funds disappeared.

Recalling the resistance to the budget cuts can be a reminder that not everyone in the city forgot about these structural problems. Although historians have frequently seen the urban populist uprisings of the 1970s as racially antagonistic and fiercely local (especially the white working-class efforts to resist the integration of public schools), the fiscal crisis in New York was met by a vision of the city centered on debates over its economic restructuring.[2] The working-class and middle-class people (white, African American, and Latinx alike) who protested the shutdown and retrenchment of local institutions were driven by a sense of the broader organization of the city and the role of their neighborhoods within the polity as a whole. They came to view the city government and the financial elites of the city—rather than other racial groups—as the primary threats to their autonomy and their continued presence in the city. In their response to the crisis, they insisted that social considerations should be paramount over narrowly fiscal logic. What might have appeared to be neutral, technocratic, and uncontroversial concerns about budgets, taxes, revenues, and accounting practices actually hid a level of fierce engagement and struggle over the nature of the city, the questions of who the city government ought to serve and to whom it should be accountable, and whose voices mattered in determining the future direction of the common metropolis.[3]

* * *

"New York City is in a far greater state of disarray than appears from the crises which erupt from day to day or week to week," wrote lawyer and Democratic Party activist Edward Costikyan in a *New York Times* op-ed in August 1971. "Western Electric is leaving town one day. American Telephone & Telegraph the next. A public strike takes place a week later. It is or will be followed by a police scandal and then perhaps by a jail riot or a total court breakdown. And so it goes."[4]

Costikyan spoke for a group of people in the city's economic and political elite who were becoming increasingly concerned in the early 1970s with the intensifying conflicts that appeared to be engulfing New York. On one level, these problems could be summed up in terms of the white flight and deindustrialization that plagued so many northeastern and midwestern cities at this time. Both were real issues in the city: New York's population declined by 10% (more than 800,000 people) during the 1970s. Most of those who migrated away from the city were white; the city's Latinx and African American population actually rose slightly over the decade.[5] At the same time, the city lost more than half a million jobs between the late 1960s and late 1970s. While the city's diverse, small-scale manufacturing base comprised of medium or small factories in a wide range of industries had long been different from that found in many industrial cities such as Detroit, Youngstown, or Chicago, dominated by a single industry or a few large plants, it was affected no less than these manufacturing behemoths by intensifying competition from low-wage regions (especially in the garment trade) and the migration of plants to the south and overseas.

City leaders tried to meet the decline of industry by articulating a vision of New York City as a service-centered metropolis and by using city government to actively retain both industrial and other firms. In the mid-1960s, Mayor John Lindsay had envisioned a post-industrial future for New York as a white-collar city of executives and professionals. But by the end of the decade, the very corporate headquarters that were the centerpiece of Lindsay's vision were departing the city as well, prompting leaders in real estate (the least mobile of industries) to start a new organization, the Association for a Better New York, to try to woo companies to stay through use of public relations campaigns, efforts to market the city, and attempts to create a "better business climate" in New York. All these issues and the mounting anxiety about business leaving the city gave a sharply political cast to questions about spending and taxation, limiting the sphere of action available to the city's leaders in the years leading up to the fiscal crisis.

On the other side, rising unemployment in the city and the social desperation of the urban poor created an intense political atmosphere. Throughout the postwar years the city had been defined in part by its extensive public sector—its network of municipal hospitals, colleges, libraries, parks, public housing, and transit that set New York apart from other American cities. The very terms of this urban "social democracy" (as historian Joshua Freeman has described it) were being called into question in the late 1960s and early 1970s.[6] Public services were often at the heart of political struggles, as the Young Lords (working in the Puerto Rican community) and the Black Panthers frequently challenged the substandard public institutions that served people of color in New York.[7] In 1970, for example, the Young Lords led a takeover at Lincoln Hospital in the South Bronx, objecting to the unsatisfactory care delivered there—which even the hospital itself described in an internal memo as "a completely inappropriate place to care for the sick."[8] The activists wanted to return the hospital to "community control," echoing the fight over public schools in the late 1960s. Meanwhile, welfare rolls in the city expanded to about 1 million people, not only because people were losing jobs as industry departed but also because welfare rights organizers encouraged women to know their rights to collect benefits and facilitated their signing up. Activists staged protests at welfare centers to demand "special grants" to pay for such necessities as beds, dust mops, telephones, new clothing for kids to wear to school; when the state government tried to limit such grants, welfare recipients took over buildings and sat in for hours—hundreds were arrested.[9] Black and Puerto Rican students took over the City College campus in 1969 and demanded the expansion of the enrollment of students of color at the flagship four-year schools in the city system.[10] Inmates at the Men's House of Detention—the city jail in Lower Manhattan known as the "Tombs"—rioted to protest their conditions, which Congressman Charles Rangel likened to those in Con Son, the South Vietnamese prison where political inmates were kept in cages the size of chicken coops.[11] At the same time, there was an upsurge in unionization campaigns among public-sector workers—who were inspired by the spirit of the movements for racial equality—in New York City as across the entire country at this time.[12]

This atmosphere of social and political struggle was the backdrop to the expansion of the city government and of spending in the late 1960s. It brought the needs of the city into fierce competition with the imperative to reduce spending and taxation to lure investment, as business people feared that they would bear primary financial responsibility for the growth of government programs that served poor people. In 1966, for example, the New York Stock Exchange flirted with the idea of moving out of New York to Connecticut or even California after the city gained permission from Albany to enact a stock-transfer tax. Mayor John Lindsay set up a special commission to try to keep the stock exchange in New York. But this did not mollify the representatives of the NYSE, who wrote in their final report, "The fiscal and political pressures on the City Administration are so great we can look for no tax relief whatsoever from the City of New York." The city was too committed to keeping its cheap transit and to providing welfare to let go of an available tax source. In fact, it seemed far more likely taxes would be raised again in the future than that they would ever be cut. Given this, the Board of Governors should proceed "with all deliberate speed" to relocate the NYSE beyond the city limits.[13]

Even before the fiscal crisis began, different classes and social groups within the city were struggling over resources through the city budget. This would only intensify once the city's banks ceased to roll over its debt in the spring of 1975, so that the city could no longer access the credit it needed to finance everyday operations. The result was that New York was left near bankruptcy—a condition that endured through most of 1975, and was only resolved once the city had agreed to enact extensive budget cuts; public-sector workers had accepted wage freezes, attrition, and layoffs; and the federal government, banks, and the city's labor unions had agreed to extend loans to New York to help it avoid bankruptcy court. But the settlement of the budgetary aspects of the crisis did not mean that social peace had been restored to the city. On the contrary, the conflicts that had fueled the spending crunch to begin with continued and even gained momentum as the city enacted a sweeping program of cuts in the years that followed the crisis: cutbacks that affected the school system, fire protection, sanitation, higher education, police protection, infrastructure and maintenance, the city's criminal justice system, and the daily experience of life in the city as a whole.

* * *

The protests against the budget cuts of the era were framed rhetorically in a variety of ways. One line of argument emphasized that service cuts would imperil the future of the middle class in New York City. The city was becoming increasingly dangerous, and the local state no longer seemed capable of offering protection—especially to its productive, virtuous citizens. One person who self-identified as a businessman wrote to Mayor Abraham Beame to warn that "without sufficient police protection this city will become a jungle."[14] Another wrote the mayor to complain that anyone with the resources to flee New York would do so, leaving the city destitute: "Someday not too far off in the future, someone will make a study on how NEW YORK CITY became a GHOST CITY. He will find that it became that way because the Middle Class residents that lived there had been chased away . . . by having to pay taxes, and little by little being deprived of all public services."[15] Another Bronx woman wrote to her state senator: "CAN YOU PLEASE HELP? Mayor Beame has put our lives in jeopardy" (she objected to "reckless" cuts to the fire department).[16]

This set of arguments implicitly contrasted a respectable, worthy middle class with an image of the "undeserving poor," suggesting that the city's cuts meant abandoning the former and allowing the city to be overwhelmed by the latter. However, this conservative framing was not the only source of resistance to the cuts. Equally important was the idea that the city government had taken sides: that it had chosen to favor groups other than the working-class residents of the city, and that the cuts reflected an underlying logic that was intended to actively drive these unwanted New Yorkers away.

This sensibility came to the forefront in struggles over fire protection. Fire service in the city had been the subject of fierce contention even before the fiscal crisis. In the late 1960s, the Lindsay administration had contracted with the RAND Corporation to study the fire department and suggest ways that the city could improve its services. Based on analysis of the amount of time it took a fire company to get to the fire, and on dividing the city into different "hazard categories" determined by the likelihood of fires, the RAND researchers proposed closing or relocating thirty-five fire companies between 1972 and 1976.[17] Over the course of the 1970s, thirty-two of the city's 114 fire companies were disbanded (seven of them after the fiscal crisis became common knowledge).[18] Lindsay's Fire Commissioner, John O'Hagan, prided himself on the idea that he could increase the efficiency of the department, running it more safely despite having fewer resources. The RAND analysis also advocated replacing the old alarm boxes with telephone-style alarms so that the person calling in could actually speak to the dispatcher—an idea that might have been helpful, but which led in practice to a dramatic rise in the number of false alarms, and which encouraged RAND to argue that a single truck should be sent whenever the dispatcher could not make out what the person on the other end of the phone was saying.

The RAND reforms did not reduce fire in New York. Instead, over this same period of time the number of serious fires in the city rose from 160 per year in the mid-1960s to 500 in the late 1970s.[19] Fire, as one retired fire chief put it, had become "a metastasizing cancer on the city."[20] Because the consequences an increase in fires could have on a neighborhood were so severe, almost every one of the RAND-driven proposals to close or relocate a fire company between 1972 and 1976 met with intense resistance and protest, both from neighborhoods and from firefighters themselves. "Fires in the Bronx mean empty firehouses in Queens, Brooklyn, Manhattan and Staten Island," read a 1975 full-page ad taken out by the fire officers' union in the *Daily News*, objecting to the RAND-endorsed strategy of closing firehouses in areas with a high incidence of fire and servicing them with units from elsewhere in the city.[21] When the onset of the fiscal crisis brought a new wave of threatened closures in the summer of 1975, there were protests at nearly every one of the endangered firehouses. But the most dramatic of these came in the Northside neighborhood of Greenpoint-Williamsburg in Brooklyn, where local activists and families took over their 112-year-old firehouse and staged a sixteen-month-long sit-in to keep the engine from being moved out, desperately trying to save fire protection before their entire neighborhood was condemned.

For the activists involved in trying to keep Engine Company 212 open, the city's desire to close it seemed to reflect an underlying hostility to their presence in the neighborhood overall. Many feared that the plan to shutter Engine 212 was part of a larger plot by the city to withdraw services, drive residents away, claim the waterfront land of the neighborhood and turn it over to industrial businesses to keep them in New York.[22] They found it impossible to accept the city's rhetoric of fiscal necessity at face value. "We believe that the fiscal reforms adopted by the City Government are an attack against the poor and working people," read one editorial in the newsletter of a community development organization.[23] The firehouse activists described themselves as hardworking members of society who fulfilled their obligations and were deserving of services: "They took the truck we paid for through taxes," one speaker at a rally said.[24] The "working people" of the Northside—blue-collar, middle-class, and poor alike—wanted their due respect as "taxpayers."[25] People reasonably feared that the closure of Engine 212 would lead to more abandonment of buildings, more redlining by banks, more expensive fire insurance policy rates. Thus, it might actually lead to an increase in fires in the neighborhood, tipping Greenpoint-Williamsburg toward becoming a neighborhood, like Bushwick, that was completely decimated by fire. The physical destruction caused by fire mirrored the underlying hostility they believed the city's leaders felt toward them. They framed their struggle in the terms famously laid out by the city's housing commissioner in the mid-1970s, Roger Starr. One banner hanging in the firehouse read, "Planned Shrinkage Means Planned Genocide," and another pronounced: "Planned Shrinkage Stops at Northside."[26]

The fight over the firehouse was waged in a white working-class neighborhood inhabited primarily by people of Polish and Italian descent who feared that their social place within the city was slipping. Equally intense, however, were the conflicts over the City University of New York, which had long provided a vision of upward mobility and intellectual uplift that was widely celebrated in the city as a whole. CUNY had been transformed in the early 1970s to grant African American and Latinx New Yorkers a new measure of inclusion. The adoption of "open admissions" in 1970—whereby any high school graduate in the city could attend a city university—increased the size of the university system from 118,000 students in 1969–70 to 212,000 students in 1974–75.[27] This expansion strained both its physical capacity and its faculty. In 1970, the first year after open admissions began, teachers held classes in coat rooms, copy centers, an indoor ice skating rink, a bingo hall, and a synagogue. One campus president set up his office in a campus trailer.[28] Some faculty members resented open admissions, arguing that it degraded the quality of education possible within the system overall. But the expansion of CUNY also offered great hope to those who were able to benefit from the changes. CUNY's growth in the early 1970s also reflected the opening of several new campuses, including Hostos Community College in the South Bronx.

Hostos was an unusual educational experiment. Opening in 1970, the college was designed for a bilingual population, offering classes in Spanish alongside instruction in English. The students were older than traditional college age, and they included many single mothers and others for whom access to higher education was hardly a given. From its earliest days, people saw Hostos as a rare example of city investment in the South Bronx. As such, the college commanded an intense loyalty from the broader community.

In the fall of 1975, the president of City College, a chemist named Robert Marshak, introduced a plan to rationalize CUNY by closing and merging several campuses into each other. (The idea was to model CUNY on the University of California system—to create some flagship campuses such as City College that would serve as "research centers" while making others into teaching institutions.) Hostos, he proposed, might be joined to Bronx Community College—a move that would take it out of the South Bronx and also end the distinctive bilingual programming at the school. When people on the campus and in the neighborhood heard that Hostos might be closed as a result of the fiscal crisis, it seemed an unconscionable withdrawal of city resources from a neighborhood and a community that was starved for them already. The Hostos Community College Senate formed a Save Hostos Committee, to "mobilize the forces of the students, faculty, staff and community" to guarantee that the school would survive as a "separate entity," not closed or "absorbed into any other institution."[29] Letters from Hostos professors began to appear in the *New York Post*, the *Daily News*, and eventually the *New York Times*.[30] Congressman Charles Rangel pledged his support for the school, and a group of Latinx state politicians wrote a letter to the Board of Higher Education: "No budget crisis can ignore the devastating impact which the closing of this college would have on the

Puerto Rican population which has received the least services from the public education system of this city."[31] Even the head of the Manhattan/ Bronx division of Bankers Trust wrote to the CUNY Chancellor to express his hope that the "imminent state of crisis" facing New York would not mean the "complete abandonment" of Hostos.[32]

Meanwhile, more radical student organizations were less focused on organizing through the electoral system, viewing the city's political leaders as impotent and arguing that the only way to pressure the city successfully was to target the banks. As one early flyer put it, "the banks, through 'Big MAC,' are responsible for all the cutbacks which threaten to close all the services that our community needs." One group held a late November demonstration at Chase Manhattan Bank: "Join your neighbors in the struggle to protect our right to a better life."[33] The chair of the Social Sciences Department at the school penned a furious letter to deputy mayor John Zuccotti: "Why close the only college in the economically depressed area of the South Bronx?"[34] In a subsequent letter, he wrote that the creation of Hostos had been a major victory for the people of the South Bronx and Harlem. "When their interests are so callously cast aside, the city loses, and our precious democracy and equality become empty symbols. Our future lies in opening such colleges, not closing them."[35] Stephen Berger (executive director at the Emergency Financial Control Board) noted that he had received 400 letters in support of Hostos, while one state senator wrote: "The mail on Hostos is so heavy that it is impossible to answer each letter personally."[36] The efforts to protect Hostos culminated in a student-led three-week-long takeover of the school in the spring of 1976, which brought many community people into the mobilization. One day neighborhood parents brought more than 500 children to encircle the school, chanting: "Save Hostos, we too want to go to college!"[37]

In Greenpoint-Williamsburg and in the South Bronx, the neighborhood mobilizations were to some degree successful. The city relented and withdrew its plans to close Engine 212, reorganizing fire service in Brooklyn in order to keep it open. (At first the Fire Commissioner proposed closing a fire station in mostly African American Fort Greene to move the resources to North Brooklyn—a suggestion that the activists at Engine 212 vetoed.) When the Board of Higher Education voted in the summer of 1976 to impose tuition at CUNY in return for receiving additional aid from New York State (money it badly needed, as the university had been forced to shut down for lack of funds before even finishing the spring semester), Governor Hugh Carey permitted Hostos and the other campuses threatened with closure to remain open. Neither of these victories was unambiguous. Keeping Engine 212 open meant shifting resources for fire prevention around Brooklyn and Queens, not restoring the money given to the fire department in the budget overall. Preserving Hostos (and the other CUNY campuses threatened with closure, including John Jay and Medgar Evers) was possible, but preventing the imposition of tuition for CUNY alongside budget cuts to the system as a whole was not. The logic of the fiscal crisis meant that it was easier to keep specific and beloved institutions open than it was to maintain public spending overall. Nonetheless, that the city changed its direction with regard to both Hostos and Engine Company 212 was a sign that protests could make a difference: that community resistance to austerity could change the options available to the city overall.

Five years later, the fight over Sydenham Hospital in Harlem suggested the limits of this kind of neighborhood resistance. Sydenham Hospital was a historically African American hospital, once among the few places where black doctors and nurses could practice medicine in New York City. Throughout the postwar years, it had provided care to the Harlem community, as well as offering a secure place of employment for African American medical professionals and hence a foothold for the African American middle class in the city. During the fiscal crisis, however, the city's municipal hospitals came under fire, both from the Beame administration and from the Emergency Financial Control Board, the state agency that had been created to oversee the city's budget and guarantee that it was making progress toward balance. Many of New York's hospitals, city officials argued (with the support of the EFCB), were poorly staffed and badly run, providing substandard care and failing to meet basic health standards while also draining the city's financial resources. The only reason to keep them open was as a source of jobs—they no longer functioned to provide decent care. The head of the Health and Hospitals Corporation—an African American doctor named John Holloman who had a background in the civil rights movement and a politically radical approach to health care, viewing it as a fundamental human right—was publicly and fiercely critical of this stance, and of the city's insistence on closing hospitals in order to balance the budget. He was ultimately forced to resign his position. Several hospitals were closed in late 1975 and 1976, and Mayor Beame's office proposed shutting Sydenham as well—a suggestion that was withdrawn after it became clear that it would be met by an uproar.

By 1980, however, Ed Koch was the mayor. Koch's electoral coalition joined white ethnic New Yorkers with members of the city's business elite, and he had something to gain from showing each of these groups that he was willing to shutter popular public institutions over community objections and pressure if it was necessary to meet budgetary objectives after the fiscal crisis. Koch insisted that it was necessary to close Sydenham. The plan met with approval from the city's leading media institutions: as the *New York Times* editorial page put it, "[The] decrepit facility should be closed down, beyond doubt."[38] Koch suggested that instead of continuing on as a hospital, Sydenham should be refitted as a drug and alcohol treatment center.

The suggestion met with outrage from the Harlem community. Whatever the problems with Sydenham might be, the withdrawal of resources from a neighborhood that seemed in the grip of real health crises seemed unconscionable. Harlem had been designated a federal "medical disaster area" in 1977, with infant mortality rates that were much higher than in the rest of the city and tuberculosis rates more than twice as high—how could closing a hospital be justified?[39] "Harlem Hospital is always crowded, and our only alternative is to go downtown for treatment. But they don't want poor or black people down there in their hospitals," one patient told the *Daily News*. As a public hospital, Sydenham treated people without insurance, and it was unclear what would happen to these patients without the hospital. "I guess a lot of the people around here are just going to die," said one nurse, a Harlem native.[40] Beyond this, the hospital represented the hard-fought efforts of African American doctors and nurses to carve out a space where they could practice their skill and receive respect and a sense of dignity. Closing the hospital would make it impossible to maintain an African American middle class in the neighborhood at all. One *Daily News* columnist wrote that Sydenham was one of the forces that "keeps the junkies from taking over this neighborhood."[41] The hospital was already surrounded by empty and deserted buildings. For it to be closed, or turned into a facility for treating addicts, suggested the broader impoverishment of the neighborhood. As one woman put it, "It seems to me they're closing down Harlem."[42]

When the closure of Sydenham began in September 1980, protesters quickly gathered in the streets outside. One small group of protesters—including the Reverend Herbert Daughtry of the Black United Front and the House of the Lord Church in Brooklyn, which had been a center for organizing the opposition to budget cuts in the black community throughout the 1970s, and Cenie Williams, the president of the National Association of Black Social Workers—initiated a sit-in in the hospital administration's offices. Staff doctors kept treating patients, saying that they would go to jail to keep the hospital open.[43] Over the next few weeks, the hospital was a center of protest. One Sunday saw a demonstration of several thousand people who came dressed in their church clothes, as though to show the respectability of the neighborhood, marching past rows of mostly white police officers decked out in riot gear.[44] There were also open skirmishes with the police—some said that these began when crowds charged wooden barricades, while others alleged that the police were the ones who had attacked the protesters, running into a group of demonstrators with their batons swinging.[45] Police cut the phone lines to isolate the group of occupiers and prevented food from being brought into the building, leaving those conducting the sit-in to rely on what remained in hospital storerooms for sustenance. After eleven days, the police entered the hospital to remove those sitting in, saying that there were rumors that the Communist Workers Party planned to bring in guns and that they had to act to forestall violence. The protesters went limp and were carried out of the facility. Despite several more months of daily demonstrations, Sydenham was closed at the end of the fall.

The Sydenham protest was the last of the major upheavals related to closing public institutions in the wake of the fiscal crisis: Koch was able to defeat a challenge from the left (by state assemblyman Frank Barbaro, who explicitly criticized Koch's approach to the fiscal crisis) and win re-election in 1981. When his administration shut down two more neighborhood hospitals in Brooklyn in the early 1980s, there was little in the way of public criticism.[46] For Koch, the entire episode was an opportunity to prove his tough resolve and unwillingness to concede to popular political pressure—the more opposition there was, the more determined he was not to give in. As he told the press, "Am I supposed to give in to mob rule just because it's a black mob? I'll never give in to unreasonable demands or threats by any group."[47] But the underlying pessimism of Koch's approach was evident in the fate of the old Sydenham building, which stood vacant and abandoned for years, even as AIDS and tuberculosis ravaged the city and took an especially severe toll in Harlem.

The revival of the city's economy later in the 1980s meant the restoration of much of the spending that had been cut during the crisis. But other measures—such as the hospital closures and the introduction of tuition—were never undone. In the decades that followed, the city would expand its subsidies for corporate investment and real estate development. Efforts to harness private wealth to fund city services— such as park conservancies to raise money for specific parks, or parent-teacher associations taking on major fund-raising responsibilities—grew dramatically, with the effect of generating substantial inequality in the funding of parks and schools.[48] While the protests associated with the fiscal crisis and the attendant budget cuts subsided, they nonetheless remain important for what they can tell us about working-class politics in the 1970s. They suggest the deep social and political meaning that New Yorkers attached to public institutions at this moment in the city's history. Schools, hospitals, colleges, fire stations, sanitation—these were not simply city services that people were entitled to because they paid taxes. They were a marker of who the city valued, a symbol of the city government's commitment to the different communities of the city, a way of ensuring respectability and progress or of demonstrating neglect that could lead to catastrophic neighborhood decline. The residents of Harlem who protested the closure of Sydenham, the people of the South Bronx who pushed to maintain Hostos Community College, and the residents of Greenpoint-Williamsburg who occupied their fire station articulated what we might think of as a moral urban economy, to paraphrase the great British social historian E. P. Thompson. They explicitly rejected the arguments of the city, the state, the federal government, and the financial community (as well as business in the city more broadly) about the primacy of fiscal norms and the needs of urban bondholders. Instead, they argued that this emphasis was one that undermined the social claims of urban citizens—and they suggested that it might be possible to preserve the communal institutions of the city while at the same time adopting policies that preserved its fiscal integrity. Their protests marked the assertion of social needs against fiscal and economic logic in an era that is largely associated with the opposite trend, suggesting the difficulties and resistance that the new economic rationales encountered, the lingering importance of the protest movements and conflicts of the 1960s, and the gradual ebbing of earlier approaches to policy and urban life as a new era defined by fiscal austerity came into existence.

NOTES

1 Felix Rohatyn, "The Coming Emergency and What Can Be Done About It," *New York Review of Books*, December 4, 1980.

2 For examples of these approaches to the working-class politics of the 1970s, see Michael Stewart Foley, *Front Porch Politics: The Forgotten Heyday of American Activism in the 1970s and 1980s* (New York: Hill & Wang, 2013); Ronald Formisano, *Boston Against Busing: Race, Class and Ethnicity in the 1960s and 1970s* (Chapel Hill: University of North Carolina Press, 1991); Jonathan Rieder, *Canarsie: The Jews and Italians of Brooklyn Against Liberalism* (Cambridge, MA: Harvard University Press, 1984).

3 The fiscal crisis that nearly sent New York City to bankruptcy court in 1975 has been described by various different social theorists, most notably David Harvey, as the opening move in an era of neoliberalism. The crisis, as Harvey puts it, became an opportunity for New York City to radically shift its spending and social priorities, so that these no longer were focused on economic redistribution but instead on economic development. Driven by a vision of the reorganization of public life in the city to conform more closely to the idea of the free market as popularized by economists such as Friedrich von Hayek and Milton Friedman throughout the postwar years, elite social groups in the city took advantage of the crisis to reinforce their own priorities for the future development of New York. My chapter builds on this analysis, but I see the response to the crisis as more fragmented and less ideologically coherent than Harvey might suggest. David Harvey, *A Brief History of Neoliberalism* (New York: Oxford University Press, 2007).

4 Edward Costikyan, "Needed: A New Committee of 100," *New York Times*, August 20, 1971.

5 John Mollenkopf, *A Phoenix in the Ashes: The Rise and Fall of the Koch Coalition in New York City Politics* (Princeton, NJ: Princeton University Press, 1994), 58.

6 Joshua Freeman, *Working-Class New York: Life and Labor Since World War II* (New York: New Press, 2001).

7 Johanna Fernandez, "The Young Lords and the Postwar City: Notes on the Geographical and Structural Transfigurations of Contemporary Urban Life," in *Afri-*

can American Urban History Since World War II, ed. Kenneth L. Kusmer and Joe W. Trotter (Chicago: University of Chicago Press, 2009); also see Alondra Nelson, *Body and Soul: The Black Panther Party and the Fight Against Medical Discrimination* (Minneapolis: University of Minnesota Press, 2013).

8 "Report of the Ad Hoc Committee on Lincoln Hospital," quoted in Merlin Chowkwanyun, "The New Left and Public Health: The Health Policy Advisory Center, Community Organizing and the Big Business of Health, 1967–1975," *American Journal of Public Health* 101:2 (February 2011).

9 Premilla Nasaden, *Welfare Warriors: The Welfare Rights Movement in the United States* (New York: Routledge, 2005), 82, 98.

10 Sandra Shoiock Roff, Anthony M. Cucchiara, and Barbara J. Dunlap, *From the Free Academy to CUNY: Illustrating Public Higher Education in New York City, 1847–1997* (New York: Fordham University Press, 2000), 114–22.

11 New York State Senate Committee on Crime and Correction, *The Tombs Disturbances: A Report*, October 5, 1970, City Library. Also see Heather Ann Thompson, "From Researching the Past to Reimagining the Future: Locating Carceral Crisis, and the Key to Its End, in the Long Twentieth Century," http://www.havenscenter.org/files/Thompson.ResearchingtoReimagining.pdf.

12 Bernard Bellush and Jewel Bellush, *Union Power and New York: Victor Gotbaum and District Council 37* (New York: Praeger, 1984).

13 Henry Harris, George Leness, and Henry Watts to Board of Governors, Subject: Final Report on the Mayor's Committee to Keep the New York Stock Exchange in New York City, March 8, 1967. G. Keith Funston Papers, Box 6, Folder 6. NYSE Archives.

14 R. M. Campbell, vice president of Roan Industries, to Abraham Beame, January 20, 1975. Roll 12, Abraham Beame Papers.

15 Chana Klajman to Abraham Beame, May 9, 1975. Roll 12, Abraham Beame Papers.

16 Nilda Ortiz to Senator Isabel Ruiz, January 31, 1975. Roll 12, Abraham Beame Papers.

17 Joe Flood, *The Fires: How a Computer Formula, Big Ideas and the Best of Intentions Burned Down New York City—And Determined the Future of Cities* (New York: Riverhead, 2010); Rodrick Wallace and Deborah Wallace, *Studies on the Collapse of Fire Service in New York City 1972–1976* (Washington, DC: University Press of America, 1977), 48.

18 "Disbanded Companies," FDNY. Copy in possession of the author.

19 Rodrick Wallace and Deborah Wallace, *A Plague on Your Houses: How New York Was Burned Down and National Public Health Crumbled* (New York and London: Verso, 2001), 66.

20 Ibid., 47.

21 Advertisement, *Daily News*, June 15, 1975.

22 This fear was animated in part by the Lindsay administration's efforts to use the power of eminent domain to claim the land occupied by ninety-seven working-class homes and turn it over to a corrugated box–making company that threat-

ened to move to New Jersey—an attempt at industrial retention that was bitterly fought in the neighborhood for years before the last holdouts were forcibly removed from their apartments. People in Greenpoint-Williamsburg would have been surprised to see luxury high-rises, not industrial companies, sprouting up at the water's edge years later.

23 *Onward*, vol. 1, no. 1, November 1976. In Frances McCardle Subject Files, Box 9, Folder 165, Municipal Archives.

24 City-Wide Fire Protection Coalition Meeting and Rally Notes, Ida Susser, Ida Susser Collection.

25 Thomas Raferty, "Residents Sound Alarm at Phasing Out of Firehouse," *Daily News*, November 24, 1975.

26 See photograph accompanying Denis Hamill, "A Brooklyn Neighborhood Battles City Hall," *Village Voice*, December 6, 1976.

27 "CUNY's Budget Has Grown Rapidly," in American Federation of Teachers, Professional Staff Congress, Local 2234 Papers, Box 58, Folder 231. Tamiment Library.

28 Leonard Buder, "Open-Admissions Policy Taxes City U. Resources," *New York Times*, October 12, 1970.

29 "Save Hostos Committee Formed," Gerald Meyer Papers, Box 1, Save Hostos Committee. Hostos Community College Archives.

30 "Save Hostos Committee Update," December 5, 1975. Gerald Meyer Papers, Box 1, Save Hostos Committee.

31 "Save Hostos Committee Update," December 22, 1975; letter from elected officials to Alfred Giardino, November 3, 1975; both in Gerald Meyer Papers, Box 1, Save Hostos Committee.

32 Michael Gill to Robert Kibbee, December 8, 1975. Gerald Meyer Papers, Save Hostos Committee, Correspondence.

33 Open Letter to Our Community, from the Coalition to Save Hostos. Gerald Meyer Papers, Box 1, Community Coalition to Save Hostos, Save Hostos Committee.

34 "Why Close It?" Peter Roman, *New York Amsterdam News*, March 6, 1976 (the letter was reprinted in the newspaper).

35 Peter Ronan to John Zuccotti, April 28, 1976, Gerald Meyer Papers, Save Hostos Committee, Correspondence. Zuccotti had responded to Ronan's earlier note in his standard formula: "Unfortunately the City must set priorities for its dwindling resources. Basic protective and health services and elementary education must be the City's first regard." John Zuccotti to Peter Ronan, March 10, 1976. Gerald Meyer Papers, Save Hostos Committee, Correspondence.

36 Gerald Meyer, "The Save Hostos Committee: A History," Gerald Meyer Papers, Save Hostos, Writings.

37 Ramon Jimenez, "Hostos Community College: Battle of the Seventies," *Centro Journal*, 15:1 (Spring 2003) 107.

38 "Cooling Off at Sydenham Hospital," *New York Times*, September 27, 1980.

39 Ebun Adelona, "Sydenham: Politics vs. Health Care," *City Limits*, February 1983.

40 Ron Howell, "Sydenham Employees: Sad, Angry and Confused," *New York Daily News*, September 16, 1980.

41 Earl Caldwell, "A Fight for Survival on a Battlefield Called Sydenham," *New York Daily News*, September 20, 1980.

42 Wista Johnson, "The Sydenham On-Lookers," *New York Amsterdam News*, October 4, 1980; also see Cenie Williams, Jr., "The Battle for Black Dignity," *New York Amsterdam News*, October 11, 1980.

43 Cynthia R. Fagen and Eric Fettmann, "Rebels at Sydenham Defy Court Order," *New York Post*, September 17, 1980.

44 Paul Meskil, "3,000 Hold Nonviolent Sydenham Demo," *New York Daily News*, September 22, 1980.

45 Paul L. Montgomery, "30 Hurt as Police and Protesters Clash Outside Sydenham," *New York Times*, September 21, 1980; Ron Howell, "Cops Battle Sydenham Protesters," *New York Daily News*, September 21, 1980.

46 Michael Spear, "The Struggle to Build a Progressive Urban Politics: Frank Barbaro's 1981 New York City Mayoral Campaign," *New York History* 91:1 (Winter 2010), 45–69.

47 Paul L. Montgomery, "1,000 Rally at Sydenham to Back Protesters Inside," *New York Times*, September 22, 1980.

48 Kyle Spencer, "Way Beyond Bake Sales: The $1 Million PTA," *New York Times*, June 1, 2012; Suleiman Osman, "'We're Doing It Ourselves': The Unexpected Origins of New York City's Public-Private Parks During the 1970s Fiscal Crisis," *Journal of Planning History* 16:2 (May 2017), 162–74.

4

Doing Business New Orleans Style

Racial Progressivism and the Politics of Uneven Development

MEGAN FRENCH-MARCELIN

On a warm September afternoon in 1982, Joseph Canizaro—resembling a successful used-car salesman—addressed a crowd of downtown business and real estate executives who had gathered from the far corners of the nation. In the decade prior, the developer, a Biloxi, Mississippi native, had made a fortune as one of those who invested in the first wave of downtown New Orleans growth. Now he spoke of the city's future. The time had come, he noted, to accept the futility of progressive tax measures that fell victim, one by one, to a constituency accustomed to low taxes as well as the reality made clear by President Reagan's most recent cuts to urban aid that help would not come from the federal government. New Orleans, like cities across the nation, faced massive budget deficits that the fixes of yesteryear could no longer confront, he said. The solution was then found in fortifying the private sector. If businesses were to stay and cities were to grow, local officials would need to pursue the "use of investment tax credits, tax increment financings, industrial revenue bonds, abatements, [and] land swaps," making "these tools . . . available for private use," the developer stated. What he called for, an economic program wherein the cardinal function of local government was to facilitate private profiteering and promulgate the market as the arbiter of thriving cities, was a nascent iteration of neoliberalism. In Canizaro's assessment, this system represented the future of all American cities. And it was New Orleans, where such strategies had been the bedrock of the city's political economy for nearly a decade, that would lead the way.[1]

The policies and programs that developed in New Orleans over the course of the 1970s and 1980s now associated with urban neoliberalism responded to broad transformations wrought by national economic shifts and nearly half a century of government-sponsored hollowing out of cities through highway subsidies, suburbanization, and capital flight.[2] In New Orleans, a touristic economy and regressive state tax laws only exacerbated the crisis that most cities were dealing with by the mid-1970s.[3] Yet, policies that marshaled public resources toward private ends—under the premise that generating growth and jobs were commensurate enterprises—were also shaped by the willingness of liberals, white and black, to subordinate appraisals of structural inequality to pro-growth visions of progress.

In New Orleans, development had long been stymied by a politics of insularity that buttressed power among the city's segregationist social elite and curbed the evolution of capital investment channels necessary for speculative growth. Thus, those that led the growth regime gained both power and legitimacy among newly mobilized black voting constituencies through their efforts to maintain the synchronicity between civil rights goals and the development agenda *as well as* vice versa, positioning growth as the liberal economic alternative to the Jim Crow economy.[4] Indeed, the vitriolic racism of the city's elite that persisted long after bureaucratic integration lent ironic credibility to the representation of the growth regime as progressive if not singular in its commitment to racial equality. Given that growth was heralded as a salve to a panacea of socioeconomic ills, the economic inequalities inherent in its speculative program were thus shrouded within a socially progressive lexicon of new freedoms.

In New Orleans, the willingness of new liberals to overlook the limitations inherent to speculative growth stemmed not only from the desire to insure stability within the alliances between developers and emerging black political organizations with working-class constituencies, though this was true and helped maintain the fallacy of inclusiveness amid rising unemployment.[5] Yet more broadly, and increasingly over the course of two decades, for those anointed as leaders of the new South, notions of equality conformed to and coalesced under market rules—privileging property rights and profit as a means to consolidate, if not extend, black social and political authority. Though black leadership in New Orleans was not homogenous in its consent to a program of downtown growth (as city officials, black and white, claimed it to be), it was those who accepted progress through expansion of the private-sector marketplace that attained access to and alliance with the local state.[6] Thus, fortifying an interracial middle class was increasingly presented as *the* yardstick by which equality would be measured—even as such rhetoric normalized and justified class differences. In step with white counterparts, black leadership defined racial progress by the capacity of those who constituted a "natural" elite—doctors, lawyers, social service professionals—to attain equal middle-class status.[7] As the leaders of the growth coalition willingly challenged those facets of institutional racism that hampered middle-class market participation, they invoked their efforts to gain new forms of access as if it would shore up redistributive results for working-class black residents as well.[8] A visible share in the apparent spoils of growth was thus the measure of inclusion and defined the terms (and limits) upon which interracial neoliberalism would thereupon flourish.

While most readily characterized as interracial neoliberalism, by the post–Civil Rights era, the point to be made here is that neoliberalization at the municipal level was inherently interracial. This reality was the result of a powerful if not readily recognized coupling: the claims of moneyed interests to the spoils of a civil rights movement that had not, in fact, shifted the economic reality of most New Orleanians, and an emerging interracial elite who assumed roles in the growing trend of privatization as if participation would manifest itself as civil rights. The result was programs of development that reinforced the inequalities that had preceded them—if with new players.

Over the course of two decades, however, the constraints of such strategies for producing economic equity, let alone challenging the racism that further denied the black working class equitable access to jobs, housing, and schools, became more and more apparent. In an era of retrenchment, as the aid that had long served as a stopgap measure in low-income neighborhoods disappeared, liberal leadership increasingly relied on ideology that linked poverty and unemployment to base assumptions about cultural pathologies. In line with their economic agenda, the city's leadership conveniently discounted structural change (not to mention their development program) as a reason for black unemployment, focusing instead on the perceived individual choices of low-income residents themselves.[9] Such explanations undercut critiques that linked growing inequality to the locally sanctioned, public subsidization of speculative forms of development, thereby circumscribing and redirecting resident demands for redistribution.

While this chapter is by no means a comprehensive account of early neoliberal development in the Crescent City, it demonstrates the ways that initial proponents of such strategies mobilized narratives of racial progressivism and inclusiveness to underwrite uneven growth, even as the outcomes led increasingly to an even more unequal city. Invariably, the leaders of two city administrations—both of which maintained rhetorical commitments to working-class black voters—were attuned to the uneven nature of development they underwrote. Nevertheless, they committed to political economic ventures that augmented and reproduced working-class socioeconomic precarity to reimagine the city as a middle-class playground of sorts. If the origins of neoliberal urban development grew out of bipartisan political imperatives, as was true in cities across the United States where Democratic mayors wholeheartedly embraced speculative real estate in the face of fiscal insolvency, in New Orleans, this coalition was also interracial, where a rationalization of pro-growth strategies was necessarily rooted in tying uneven economic development to the expansion of black (middle-class) opportunity.[10]

The Landrieu Years: Getting above the Broom and Shovel

The city's first racially liberal, pro-growth mayor, Moon Landrieu, was elected in 1970 on a platform that committed his administration to incorporating the newly enfranchised black near-majority into the growth machine. In a campaign financed by freshman developers, Landrieu delineated the expansion of development as a civil rights issue—the opportunity to reimage New Orleans as the interracial cosmopolitan center of the new South.[11] Over the course of his tenure, Landrieu sought to remake the city over and over again in ways that reflected the demands of the new speculative economy—marshaling local and federal funds to bulwark the nation's first business improvement district and deploying public investment to maintain the sovereignty of new private-sector interests in shaping the city's economic development strategy. In turn, the liberal mayor would make good on promises to civil rights leaders through patronage expanded first under antipoverty programs and then by the devolution of federal urban aid in the form of

Community Development Block Grants (CDBGs), all of which gave the mayor added flexibility to award contracts and appointments as well as leverage symbolic development in low-income neighborhoods. Where civil rights victories coalesced with the expansion of new patronage channels, black political leadership was professionalized by a coalition heretofore organized around growth.[12]

Landrieu undoubtedly took office amid broad structural economic changes that circumscribed his capacity to pursue meaningful forms of redistribution. Early reports predicted a $45 million deficit by 1975, and the mayor's initial attempts to steer a municipal income bill through the state legislature backfired, resulting in the punitive constitutional amendment that effectively barred the city from initiating income levies in perpetuity.[13] Middle-class and capital flight only further narrowed the prospects of a redistributive program, restricting the already negligible capacity to marshal property taxes toward public service delivery as a result of a $50,000 homestead exemption.[14] Nevertheless the mayor, bankrolled by real estate interests, was uncompromisingly committed to a program of speculative growth aimed at re-creating the Central Business District (CBD) as a center for high-end consumers. Leveraging a myriad of public resources to create enclaves of economic authority over which the real estate community would then preside, the administration subsidized the building of hotels and tourist attractions—including diverting nearly $19 million in federal revenue sharing to support capital improvement projects that buttressed tourism—thus building his power base around downtown interests.[15] In the early years of his administration, Landrieu, using sheer force of will, steered a land swap through the city council that gave riverfront land to a young Canizaro at just a fraction of its original appraisal price. The swap facilitated the massive development of Canal Place—a behemoth, three-phase project replete with corporate offices, retail space, and luxury housing.[16]

Where this kind of growth seemed mismatched with the broader socioeconomic issues facing much of the city's low-income population, Landrieu carefully articulated the urban crisis as having origins in issues of solvency rather than economic inequality, utilizing the specter of New York's fiscal meltdown to further circumscribe conversations of the inequity built into the landscape of speculative development.[17] In making growth a fiscal issue, the administration distanced what was essentially a framework upon which to extend the primacy of the tourism industry from the uneven consequences of the service economy. Instead, top officials in the administration insisted that where official unemployment rates approached 10% for black workers, growth was the only means by which to create and sustain jobs.[18]

Black representation in the growth machine was therefore critical to upholding a fantasy where a future of minimum-wage, contingent employment could allegedly enhance mobility for black residents. Rewarding the black political organizations that had indubitably secured his election, Landrieu formalized the bureaucratic place of former civil rights and antipoverty warriors through appointments to his cabinet. In a matter of years, the face of city government was radically different: Clyde T. J. McHenry, a leader of Community Organization for Urban Politics (COUP), a black political machine out of the Seventh Ward, took the helm of the city's housing authority, unseating the nearly forty-year reign of Gilbert Scheib; Terrence Duvernay became the city's first black Chief Administrative Officer; Robert Tucker, another COUP leader, was to serve as Landrieu's executive housing aide; and the list went on of patronage appointments that tied black political leadership to growth.[19] As one reporter scornfully remarked, Landrieu had effectively used patronage arrangements to make former civil rights activists into "the coat and tie men of black power."[20] In New Orleans, this had often been the reigning definition of black power to begin with. Moreover, the mayor used appointments and contract awards to legitimize specific growth projects, most controversially around the Superdome. By the early 1970s, the Dome was still unfinished and bad press abounded regarding the economic impact it would likely have on surrounding black neighborhoods. Behind closed doors, the mayor's executive staff conceived of Superdome Services, Inc. (SSI)—a management firm to be run by Sherman Copelin, the outspoken leader of the Southern Organization of Unified Leadership, better known as SOUL—and positioned Copelin to launch a formal bid on a lucrative contract to manage janitorial and security services for the new arena.[21]

While local media questioned the city's clear intention to circumvent the bidding process, despite other competitive offers, Landrieu once again effectively framed the arrangement as a civil rights issue, and an authoritative government response to discrimination at the Dome. Depicting opposition to Copelin's bid as nothing more than abject racism, Landrieu told the press that "the furor arose only when some blacks got involved," a line he would use over and over as the council debated the merits of SSI's bid. Contrary to those that came before him, his was an administration that was "going to bend every which kind of way to get minority participation in the stadium," Landrieu stated.[22] Where the mayor deployed charges of racism and "won," the SSI contract became, for Landrieu and SOUL alike, a sort of political shorthand for black economic inclusion.[23] In step with the mayor, Copelin took to framing the contract as one that offered real economic power to black working-class residents.

While these appointments were certainly base patronage, local officials mobilized these efforts to recast segregation as if it were intrinsically tied to stagnation, and not the overarching Jim Crow regime for which stagnation was simply one tool. Circuitously then, growth—in short-circuiting institutionalized racism (albeit only from a middle-class metric) could provide a means for racial redress. Landrieu emphasized time and time again that the city needed to nurture an environment where a man could "go as far as his talents will carry him," reiterating liberal claims to racial mobility through market participation that appealed to middle-class sentiment among black leadership.[24] Buoyed by depictions of homogeneity within black socioeconomic interests and buttressed by theories that linked poverty to the cultural pathologies of the poor, both black and white leadership articulated the growing presence of black participation in governance as indicative of democracy expanding for all.[25] Where this paradigm prepared leadership to make demands through the market, it interpreted and emphasized minority set-asides and black representation, as with SSI, as meaningful interventions in a former Jim Crow city where the growth machine produced the golden brick road of opportunity.

Landrieu was adept at mobilizing symbolic capital around controversial battles that extended his image as an ardent civil rights supporter while preserving the sanctity of the growth coalition. Early in his mayoralty, he aligned himself with civil rights leaders to fight a proposal to locate a new bridge in an all-black uptown neighborhood. Originating with the state, the plan would displace almost 7,000 residents.[26] The controversy followed in the wake of the city's decision to raze hundreds of homes in Tremé, a black neighborhood that bordered the French Quarter, first to construct an interstate that extended downtown access to the suburbs and then to build Louis Armstrong Park with the hopes of developing it into a new tourism site.[27] Landrieu's opposition to the bridge's location came with relatively low political stakes, providing an opportunity to raise the specter of racism alongside black activists without sacrificing city dollars or his position vis-à-vis city developers. Where it combated displacement of a propertied black area, his bridge opposition doubly furnished tremendous symbolic clout which the city then committed to protecting black middle-class families. Even as the city dialed back antipoverty programs and committed city machinations to uneven development, the mayor supported charges of racism with regularity when they did not implicate his own administration, though remaining quick to sidestep issues of job and housing discrimination, which working-class residents confronted daily. To call out abject racism, in the mind of the mayor, was a commitment to a city wherein growth would flourish alongside the commitment that all were welcome who could pay to play.

Thus during Landrieu's tenure, low-income residents were increasingly swept aside or alternatively addressed through the sole apparatus of federal urban aid to make room for growth to continue unabated.[28] Where, under the transition to CDBGs, decentralized urban aid was largely narrowed to physical development programs, it too translated neatly into rhetoric that speculative growth was intrinsic to fighting economic ills. Simultaneously, it allowed the chosen black leadership to produce figurative victories for their constituencies—a new playground, paved streets, recreational centers.[29] Black and white leaders alike indicated that new channels for community participation that linked constituencies to an array of black political representatives ensured programming that was more responsive to actual community need—Potemkin development with representation.[30] Therefore, while CDBG aid had few redistributive properties given the program's focus on physical development, officials in the growth regime nevertheless characterized representative *access to power* as a *say in power*.

Narrowed to a neighborhood-level focus, "antipoverty" responses were calibrated through a partition from the broader growth project that, unlike in low-income areas where power diminished by treating neighborhoods with like problems as discrete, drew strength from being articulated as a "neighborhood project."[31] Centering growth on the Central Business District, the administration won business improvement district status for the area, which allowed real estate not simply to authorize new taxes but to exercise broad control over how capital investment projects were implemented. By 1973, a substantial portion of the city's capital budget was no longer subject to voter approval—the result of decentralized funding and the consolidation of authority under the newly formed board of the Core Area Development District (later known as the Downtown Development District).[32] While the area-controlled growth had in one sense been a response to preservationist interests that wielded significant power in elite city circles, it also legitimized downtown sovereignty as nonpolitical—simply another neighborhood project. In the months and years that followed, economic development was generated as a program of speculation that made little effort to disguise the leadership's exclusion of the city's low-income residents.

Nevertheless, by the mid-1970s, though the impact of uneven growth was already remarkably apparent, liberal leadership bowed to the private sector on questions of economic development. Those black leaders once critical of the city's uneven development scheme, like Clarence Barney—the fiery head of the Urban League who argued that downtown growth exacerbated an economy where the market "flows not freely but unfairly"—nevertheless had to genuflect to the Canizaros and the Lester Kabacoffs[33] of the city if they were to gain access to even modest funding for community-level economic development projects and social service allocations.[34]

Though reports admonished the city for its evasion of downtown growth's impact on low-income residents and for habitually releasing overly optimistic job reports to cast current development trends as positivistic for all residents, growth leadership continued to extol downtown development as the single most important indicator of urban progress.[35] Growth, the mayor noted, had actually led to a "more legitimate, honest integration and mutual respect in government between blacks and whites and other minorities than any other place in the United States."[36]

It was a sentiment echoed by black political leaders who aimed to represent progress to a constituency now subject to the effects of deepening economic inequality. Jim Singleton, president of the Central City

Economic Opportunity Corporation (CCEOC)—a neighborhood that sat on the edge of the CBD and whose rates of unemployment and sub-employment reached nearly 40%—praised the administration's focus on downtown economic development.[37] Depicting growth as evidence of the city's expanding racial progressivism, Singleton affirmed that the singular focus on speculative development was "deeper than changing the skyline of the city." It was "developing a pride" in the racially diverse spirit of that growth.[38] Where measures that sought racial equality were regularly conflated with those that could facilitate economic equity, city officials held up the black representation in the growth regime as defini-tive proof.

Yet, increasingly, middle-class integration did not suffice as an ex-planation for the lack of trickle-down benefits, resources, and jobs for working-class residents in low-income neighborhoods. In the same years of the building boom (1970–1976), the number of unemployed New Orleans residents rose from twenty thousand to thirty-two thou-sand.[39] By some estimates, nearly 30% of black residents were unem-ployed and many more were underemployed.[40] The same leadership that alleged that eradicating barriers to middle-class mobility could, in fact, diminish the impact of racism also willfully ignored the struc-tural impediments to broad economic equity and rampant racism that originated in and was reproduced by the market.[41] Landrieu, facing a room of working-class residents, retorted, "Four years ago there were no blacks in city government above the broom and shovel level. This, in a city that is 50 percent black. I've changed that."[42]

By some measures, Landrieu was right: During his tenure in office, black municipal employment had more than doubled, creating unprec-edented opportunities for black residents in civil service—a trend that was occurring nationally, but held far more significance in a city that re-mained de jure segregated through 1970.[43] In contrast to the administra-tion of Landrieu's predecessor, the changes at City Hall appeared radical indeed and, in many circles, were represented as a meaningful commit-ment to expanding opportunity. Yet critics challenged the impact of such positions, noting that new access to municipal jobs was equally the result of an expanding antipoverty bureaucracy as it was the product of aggres-sive executive action.[44] As they pointed out, new municipal employment was, for black residents, clustered in "soft jobs." These positions, funded through federal aid, would surely disappear as soon as cutbacks occurred and thus remained a manifestation of new channels of patronage opened by an expanded federal role in municipal governance.[45] Moreover, where the mayor portrayed such achievements as demonstrative of black working-class mobility, the broader political economic strategies set forth by the administration, which necessitated a system of precarious, non-unionized labor, undermined this assessment. Municipal employment could not alone support the working class, while leadership continued to place a premium on speculative growth, critics argued.[46]

In less than five years, their critical assessments would bear out as the city's economy crumbled under cutbacks. By the early 1980s, those municipal jobs, nearly two thousand of which were funded through the Comprehensive Employment Training Act of 1973, had evaporated.[47] In the wake of the layoffs, the consequences of tourist-centered speculative growth would become ever more stark.

The Dutch Years: Go Out and Look for a Job!

Campaigning on a brash agenda that denounced earlier patronage-driven arrangements with black political organizations and economic strategies that formulated growth of any sort, irrespective of impact on working-class families, Ernest "Dutch" Morial appeared to be a different kind of progressive altogether. Local media had been quick to point out that despite the efforts of the Landrieu administration to forge an interracial city hall, the chances of a black candidate winning a mayoral election were negligible. Yet, Morial, as the first black member of the state legislature since Reconstruction and the first black judge in the Louisiana Court of Appeals, had made a name for himself as someone emphatically committed to a program of civil rights and launched a campaign aimed at working-class black voters. Appealing to those marginalized from the speculative downtown boom, Morial campaigned on a program of unwavering social and economic justice. He stunned white voters and black political organizations alike when he won by a narrow margin, defeating Councilman Joseph DiRosa, who had been favored in the polls, to become the first black mayor of the Crescent City.[48]

The mayor's inaugural speech was filled with the promise of a more equitable city, appealing to visions of racial egalitarianism that appeared radical in a city defined by its racist past. Articulating a future distinguished by a break from the past order marked more by cronyism than actual progress, he presented his administration as one that could bring "direct relief [to] all New Orleanians."[49] Over and over again, members of the Morial administration distanced their economic platform from the "one trick pony" efforts that invested solely in downtown touristic development. At town halls and council meetings, residents were assured of the administration's commitment to job creation and their intent to "open the door to socioeconomic advancement."[50]

Based on initial assessments, the city's Comprehensive Economic Development Strategy rolled out in the spring of 1979 appeared to do just that. The new economic strategy was imperative amid growing fiscal insecurity that, despite the efforts of tourism's boosters, resembled the budget deficit the Landrieu administration faced eight years prior: growing unemployment, increased reliance on federal urban aid to cover basic city operating expenses, and cuts to municipal employment.[51] Thus, significantly, the report focused on efforts to diversify the economy, including plans to drain a section of New Orleans East for the purpose of new industrial development.[52] The Almonaster-Michoud Industrial District (A-MID) would mobilize federal and state funding as well as an array of local incentives to attract industry that promised both blue-collar jobs and a more stable economy. Ignoring reports that cautioned investment in high-tech industries without corresponding subsidies for education and infrastructure, the mayor reiterated that with "thousands below the poverty level," growth in New Orleans must not simply extend the city's skyline, but "bring jobs to this community."[53]

While the administration's rhetoric made observers question what would become of downtown developers, in reality, the report reinforced a steadfast commitment to private-sector sovereignty. While enumerating a long list of impediments to low-income economic mobility—education, transportation, access—the report nonetheless upheld assumptions that the broader city was best served by investment in the market economy. Outlining an approach that included issuing some $15 million in industrial revenue bonds for corporate development, as well as experimenting with new forms of tax abatements, tax-incentivized zoning practices, and extending the now habitual diversion of federal urban aid to the private sector, the mayor's agenda looked ahead not to some more egalitarian socioeconomic vision, but rather to an increasingly formalized approach to public-private development.[54] Behind closed doors, members of the mayor's core team admitted that even the infrastructure needed for A-MID foregrounded a private sector–led approach—most notably by enabling Canizaro to lead efforts to entice new business—that "in a vacuum" could not "solve the City's unemployment and/or revenue problems."[55]

There was no confusion among developers, whose campaign contributions only further secured the mayor's allegiance, about what the administration's economic strategy entailed. Privately, Morial assured them that his "administration [was] strongly supporting the tourist industry," a promise he soon made good on.[56] In the opening months of his tenure, Morial announced a project called MEGALINK—a $436 million Central Business District revitalization scheme that represented the largest government investment in the city's downtown ever. Introduced by the mayor as the "most dramatic and comprehensive development concept proposed for our business district," MEGALINK was to provide cohesion to the last decade of real estate development in the city. The project called for constructing a pedestrian mall that would stretch from the Superdome to the foot of Canal Street, and thus link new corporate headquarters with new hotels, tourist attractions, and a brand new convention center.[57] The administration recommended that project financing—nearly half of which came from public funds—could additionally support existing projects, including Canizaro's Canal Place and the construction of a new Sheraton Hotel.[58] Seeking some $96.7 million in federal funds, to match $40 million in revenue from municipal bonds, the mayor's commitment to speculative development as a mainstay of his economic strategy was on full display.[59]

Before long, Morial was publicly boasting that businesses had learned that "they [could] get a better deal locating in Orleans Parish because of our many public assistance programs."[60] Where the mayor clearly overlooked the hypocrisy of corporate welfare in a time of fiscal austerity and federal cutbacks, businesses could in fact get a better deal. In 1979, the administration authorized the city's Industrial Development Board (IDB) to issue more than $8.5 million in revenue bonds to finance the reconstruction of a French Quarter hotel. In 1981, the city's Office of Economic Development was charged with coordinating "financial aid" efforts for businesses either expanding or relocating to Orleans Parish so that in the following year, the IDB had issued nearly $144 million in tax-free, interest-free revenue bonds.[61] By his second term, Morial had won approval to deploy federal funds—largely in the form of Community Development Block Grants—to underwrite "struggling" businesses, thus allowing the city to "become an active partner" in private-sector growth.

In his second term, the mayor continued to divert support and public resources to uneven development projects. In a particularly controversial exchange, Morial replicated the Canal Place land swap, negotiating a deal between the city and department store giant Edward J. DeBartolo.[62] Under the terms of their 1983 arrangement, negotiated in secrecy, the city would buy state-owned land to add to DeBartolo's preexisting property and contribute more than $500,000 to the purchase of an additional site. Additionally, the arrangements gave local businessman Jerome Glazer, a close friend of the Morial family, a 20% share in the profits for an upfront contribution to development costs. The result would be Poydras Square, a $300 million complex with a new hotel, office space, and a luxury shopping center.[63] As the deal went public, Morial, ever the astute politician, pivoted rhetoric to job creation for residents, chastising the project's critics for undermining the benefits it could bestow on working-class black families.[64]

Though the deal appeared to be on a continuum of public subsidization of speculative projects, it nevertheless represented a departure from the Landrieu years in that it sought to replicate national urban development models in New Orleans. While the majority of young entrepreneurial developers aligned with Landrieu's City Hall were transplants, most of them lived and worked in and around Louisiana. In contrast, the DeBartolo project opened a pathway for mega-developments that were not only financed from outside the city, but whose developers were in the process of transplanting models of speculative growth from city to city. These developers, like DeBartolo and the infamous James Rouse,[65] were chosen specifically because of their perceived ability to reproduce formulaic results across time and space. In New Orleans, the DeBartolo deal paved the way for national developers to stake claims in the city's burgeoning real estate market. Where these companies brought international capital and relationships with federal offices, their potential mobility urged local government to utilize a broad array of zoning and incentivizing powers to keep developers in place, only further eroding a public base capable of supporting working-class residents.

Thus, because such a focus did little to attenuate the power of speculative real estate interests and those building profit from the burgeoning tourist industry, the benefits of supporting the growth program were more dubious for working-class residents.[66] To be sure, federal cutbacks to the Comprehensive Employment Training Act (CETA) undercut the administration's capacity to operate specific employment programs aimed at circumventing prejudicial hiring practices of private employers, which continued despite government efforts to boost an image of diversity. Federal retrenchment had strained the mayor's capacity to place even allocational correctives—job training, employment programs, and youth services—on the downtown development program. In 1981, facing reductions in federal aid for a broad spectrum of employment-support programs, the mayor announced his intention to eliminate 1,500 municipal jobs, reducing the public workforce—a mainstay for black working-class employment—by 14%.[67] Official estimates placed unemployment officially at 7%, and nearly 10% among black residents; unofficially, unemployment was estimated to be much higher.[68]

However, in reality, the city had long supported a program of growth over job creation and that was better equipped to integrate black entrepreneurs into a system of uneven development than it was in fostering true economic equity. An exposé of the mayor's first term suggested that he had simply fueled class divisions, entrenching a system of "subsidized home loans and supported condominium conversions by middle-class settlers—measures that do nothing to limit rampant displacement of the poor" or address demands for economic equity.[69] In 1982, renowned Dillard University sociologist Daniel C. Thompson echoed this sentiment, casting shadows over the administration's efforts to depict downtown growth as a means to socioeconomic opportunity. Economic development aimed at utilizing city government to expand opportunities for the black middle class had succeeded, he acknowledged. To be sure, in slightly more than two decades, the black middle class had grown from a mere 5% of the city's black population to substantially more than 25%.[70] But for working-class black New Orleans, Thompson noted, the future was less rose-colored: The boom had actually narrowed the market for low-skilled, well-paying jobs, and exacerbated working-class insecurity already prevalent in the tourist industry. To the mayor's consternation, Thompson fired shots at the administration's promise of industrial development as well, suggesting there was little reason to hope that A-MID would provide employment opportunities to those most in need if the administration did not take broader aim at the structural inequalities that barred low-income residents from skilled labor from the start. Jobs would inevitably "go to people from out of town unless [the city] vastly improve[s] our public schools," the professor concluded.[71]

In response to the lack of mitigating correctives, the mayor, once critical of the use of minority contracts and set-asides, embraced with full force their symbolic potential to suggest that downtown growth did indeed offer redistributive benefits to black residents. In Morial's first term, his administration financed a $79 million set-aside program for minority contractors and utilized CDBGs to launch a program that had the potential to bond more black contractors.[72] By his second term, the mayor committed to an aggressive affirmative action program, pledging 20% of public contracts to black and female contractors without an open bid, and telling black businessmen, "You have to get a piece of the rock."[73] Exhibiting a political genius for doublespeak, the mayor subtly wove a future that articulated interracial leadership in these projects as the linchpin to new economic opportunity: "Now in constructive racial and ethnic communion, the economic salvation which has been the unfulfilled heritage of the city for more than 100 years is within our reach."[74] Given that such policies were actually redistributive for the growing black middle class, they shored up an important buy-in for the city's broader economic development program.

However, the administration capitalized on battles over set-asides and affirmative action to characterize these gains as advancing black mobility irrespective of class. Amid preparation for the privately operated 1984 World's Fair, the mayor berated the fair's leadership for its lack of black involvement. Speaking at a luncheon for Jesse Jackson's Operation PUSH, Morial made his disapproval clear.[75] Minority set-asides "ought to be the minimum goals in a community that is 55 percent black."[76] In the months following, which coincided with his reelection bid, Morial would repeatedly invoke the need for set-asides, telling the press that he would "not allow the opportunity for . . . minority economic development to pass."[77] Though grandstanding on issues of racial equality in public, the mayor worked quietly to negotiate with World's Fair leadership while extending local subsidies and federal funding to support the exposition, including a $14 million Urban Development Action Grant.[78] When in the following year the mayor announced that the city had struck a deal to set aside a minimum of 20% of all fair contracts for black businesses, Morial insisted it was a victory.[79] For those contractors who won contracts, it may have been; however, the administration's posturing ignored the structural inequalities embedded in the World's Fair, including the public subsidization of private profit and the fact that the fair would help build an infrastructure for further real estate speculation. Nonetheless, the public battle offered symbolic fodder to attenuate focus on the program's clear privileging of middle-class interests, instead depicting the negotiations as an effort to achieve racial equality.

Some believed this had been the mayor's vision all along, characterizing him as committed to racial equality, but economically "at home with the Chamber of Commerce, *The Wall Street Journal*, and the U.S. Stock Exchange."[80] It was no surprise then that the mayor retreated from the most aggressive critiques of narrow working-class opportunity at the end of election cycles. Though fraught with essentially contradictory sentiment, the mayor's commitment to racial progress was fundamentally bound to middle-class ideals. Throughout his tenure, Morial maintained the frank belief that racial injustice—and discrimination of any sort—limited the virtues of democracy and undermined the system of meritocracy upon which capitalism would best function. But if this genuine commitment to eradicating racially based discrimination defined an indubitably noble ideal for his administration, it was nevertheless expressed in rhetoric that was attenuated by market-centric ideology. Thus, the mayor bypassed proposals that linked public investment in equitable economic development to meaningful redistribution and evaded concerns that tied diminishing opportunity to private-sector sovereignty.

Where Morial viewed racism as an impediment to some sort of equalizing market logic, he narrowed discussions about poverty to past inequalities and present-day requisites of expanding the purview of capitalism. Indeed, he reiterated what has now become a mantra of neoliberalism: "You have to be willing to work, the government can't do it for you."[81] Inasmuch as his commitments clearly prioritized the private sector, the administration conformed its antipoverty approaches to strategies that sought to, on the one hand, reform poor people's places in the market and, on the other, eliminate the visible marker of poverty so destructive to enticing capital to central cities. While there was little doubt that local administrators were constrained by federal cuts and the broader transformations in the national economy, a vision of racial justice unattached from economic analysis was indeed compatible with the uneven consequences of touristic development.

In step with other liberals, black and white, the Morial administration accepted the conclusion that, barring the very real effects of racism on employment, poverty was just as much a product of individual decisions as it was the consequence of speculative development.[82] At a town hall meeting in Desire, an area with the city's largest public housing complex, residents challenged the mayor's narrative of progress. By 1983, residents were disillusioned with what some saw as the false hope of industrial jobs and demanded public accountability for the rising unemployment rates in low-income neighborhoods.[83] One resident, commenting on the slow advancement of A-MID, noted that when the complex was finally complete, the high-tech jobs would probably not even be given to low-income residents. The mayor, resorting to a lingo of self-determination, berated the group of residents: "You can't get trained for those jobs, my brother, by standing around hanging on the corners saying, 'I want a job.'"[84] He continued, "I ain't carrying a job in my pocket . . . You can't hoot and howl with the owls at night and soar with the eagles in the morning." The inherent implications—that residents had chosen failing schools, to not apply for jobs that did not exist, to live in substandard housing—cast unemployment as a lack of personal initiative rather than the result of government sponsorship of private-sector growth.

Time and time again, Morial retreated to a defense that bracketed working-class insecurity with cultural pathologies in an effort to attenuate criticism of the city's tourism-centric economic development strategy. In another instance, for example, he shouted back at youths protesting cuts to government-sponsored summer employment to "get up early, put on a clean white shirt, and go out looking."[85] As the mayor cast personal ambition as means to overcome economic exclusion, he underscored, reflected, and reproduced an image of poverty disconnected from state-sponsored uneven development. If the mayor's concurrent commitments to racial justice and speculative development as well as his reliance on culturalist explanations of poverty appeared to bring to pass a series of ideological contradictions, for Morial there were none. Unwaveringly committed to capitalism as both economic system and social order, Morial sought every opportunity to remove barriers to the market that were constituted by racial and other forms of discrimination. Yet, where capitalist economies, particularly in their nascent neoliberal form, produced unequal results for working-class residents, Morial pivoted culpability to residents themselves—a narrative that insulated both the speculative economy and black governing officials from charges of exacerbating working-class exclusion. For the mayor, racial justice was consummated through equal, but not equitable, market access.

This logic was also used to discount reports that revealed just how profound economic inequality in the city had become. A report by the University of New Orleans castigated city leadership for creating what could only be described as economic apartheid. The study reiterated Thompson's findings that more than ten years of racial liberalism had dramatically expanded opportunities for black professionals to gain affluence within certain professional sectors of the New Orleans economy. In fact, in just fifteen years from 1970 to 1985, the black middle class expanded from 10% to nearly 31% of the total black population of the city.[86] Yet, alongside the remarkable gains of black professionals, black working-class residents were—as other reports suggested repeatedly— faced with a far bleaker future. Moreover, local government did little to confront the duplicitous nature of trickle-down economic theory upon which support for speculative development was constructed. Federal aid cutbacks and the loss of employment and job training programs combined with the reduction of new affordable housing plans and the government-sponsored shoring up of public-private partnerships to cripple the city's working class. New Orleans remained, for most low-income residents, simply "a poverty-ridden city where as much as 40 percent of the potential workforce is either unemployed or underemployed."[87]

Conclusion

In 1987, Morial's successor, Sidney Barthelemy—a former COUP member and city councilman—proclaimed that strategic economic development was best devised by the private sector, effectively eliminating economic decision making from the public domain. In the subsequent months, commentators were quick to depict the new mayor, who had as a councilman routinely clashed with Morial, as likely to be more favorable to development interests.[88] Their predictions pivoted on comparisons between the freshman mayor's conservative, pro-business tone and the "combative" posturing of his predecessor, conflating style with substance and consequently obscuring the shared commitment to neoliberal urban development that, contrary to reporting, had remained remarkably consistent across nearly two decades of liberal administrations.[89] Liberals had in fact repeatedly cast their lot with private-sector interests. If for racially progressive leadership this evolved from a sort of Faustian bargain, it was one that surrendered redistributive socioeconomic ideals to maintain a share in the profits and thereby assured further disinvestment from working-class black neighborhoods. Yet, if leadership characterized such action as necessitated by fiscal insolvency, the growth regime's capacity to reproduce its own stability derived from the collective understanding that the pathway to middle-class incorporation was not all-inclusive. Indeed, where civil rights egalitarianism propelled the formation of an interracial coalition, there were few in that circle that assumed black middle-class incorporation would give rise to working-class mobility. The city's leadership had thus made neoliberal economics axiomatic to governance; Barthelemy's openly private-sector-first approach simply reduced the distance between rhetoric and reality.

Hence, neoliberalism in New Orleans flourished where racially egalitarian politics and public subsidization of speculative consumption intersected—its members united by a shared belief that a better city was inherently a more middle-class one.[90] Where this compact narrowed economic growth strategies to privately led, publicly subsidized development in the decade *before* federal cutbacks and corporate deregulation, it ensured that as transformations in the global economy took hold, the city would be increasingly dependent on neoliberal economic models. Consequently, long before the election of Ronald Reagan, New Orleans residents who had imagined a more equitable future had already been defeated.

More than thirty years later, in the aftermath of Hurricane Katrina, an older but no less slippery Canizaro diagnosed the catastrophe as an opportunity for a "clean sheet."[91] If the crisis created by governmental mismanagement led to confusion as to what a clean sheet entailed, swift local state action that barred residents from returning home, condemned structurally sound buildings, eliminated whole units of the municipal workforce, and hired an array of private consultants to direct the city's reconstruction made it plain: Private-sector sovereignty was to reign supreme in the "new" New Orleans. Within months, city officials took aim at critical public resources, utilizing disaster to demolish the vast majority of the city's remaining public housing and force the implosion of the public school system by firing nearly 7,500 school employees.[92] In turn, the city propped up a network of charter school corporations, technology and entertainment outfits, and new developers as the harbingers of recovery. With stunning alacrity, the city furnished the public sector as the sacrificial lamb upon which new growth could flourish. Yet, the effect of government-sponsored uneven redevelopment has been to recreate a city of stark polarities: Today, in percentages that mirror those during the Landrieu administration, the lowest two earning quartiles make just more than 7.5% of the city's total income, and nearly 27% of families remain below the poverty line.[93] As leadership continues to privilege the market over people, New Orleans has become the most neoliberal city in the nation.

NOTES

1 Joseph Canizaro, "Speech to International Downtown Executives Association," September 18, 1982, Box J6, Folder Mayor's Policy Statements, Ernest N. Morial Mayoral Collection, New Orleans City Archives, New Orleans Public Library, New Orleans, LA.

2 Thomas J. Sugrue, *The Origins of the Urban Crisis: Race and Inequality in Postwar Detroit* (Princeton, NJ: Princeton University Press, 2005); Jason Hackworth, *The Neoliberal City: Governance, Ideology, and Development in American Urbanism* (Ithaca, NY: Cornell University Press, 2006); Robert O. Self, *American Babylon: Race and the Struggle for Postwar Oakland* (Princeton, NJ: Princeton University Press, 2005; Kenneth T. Jackson, *Crabgrass Frontier: The Suburbanization of the United States* (New York: Oxford University Press, 1985); Arnold R. Hirsch, *Making the Second Ghetto: Race and Housing in Chicago 1940–1960* (Chicago: University of Chicago Press, 1998).

3 In New Orleans, state constitutional amendments undermine the power of its largest city. A 1974 law prohibits the use of municipal income taxes at the same time that other legislation, dating back to the years of Huey Long, has entitled homeowners to a homestead exemption that, since 1982, has amounted to $75,000. Where state legislation undermines progressive taxation, the city government—wary of aggravating its development class—has enacted a system that is at its core regressive. The combined state-city sales tax, almost 9% (which when enacted in 1984 made it the highest in the country), permits no exceptions for medication or groceries, making it punitive for working-class families.

4 Civil rights leaders in the city used a strategy that linked the city's tourism brand to Jim Crow to gain support for integration. J. Mark Souther, *New Orleans on Parade: Tourism and the Transformation of the Crescent City* (Baton Rouge: Louisiana State University Press, 2006), 74; see also Anthony J. Stanonis, *Creating the Big Easy: New Orleans and the Emergence of Modern Tourism, 1918–1945* (Athens: University of Georgia Press, 2006).

5 Pro-growth leaders understood integration as a tourism-centric imperative, particularly after unfavorable press emerged about the city's backward Jim Crow government. In the late 1960s, black National Football League (NFL) players were denied service in one of the city's most famous hotels, which led to national criticism.

6 Though the local chapter of the Urban League has been written about as a puppet of New Orleans local government, there is much evidence to the contrary. In fact, the president of the Greater New Orleans Urban League, Clarence Barney, was among the most strident critics of downtown growth as *the only* model for urban redevelopment. In the mid-1970s, he declared, "We side with Julian Bond and Coretta King in calling for an expanded innovative role for the national government in attacking urban problems and financing urban renewal . . . All employable citizens should be able to meet their daily needs and make some provisions for their future through work or other income generating activities." See Clarence Barney, Economic Development, Box 31, Folder 5, Greater New Orleans Urban League Papers, Amistad Research Center, Tulane University, New Orleans, LA.

7 Preston H. Smith II, *Racial Democracy and the Black Metropolis: Housing Policy in Postwar Chicago* (Minneapolis: University of Minnesota Press, 2012), 8.

8 Adolph Reed, *Stirrings in the Jug: Black Politics in the Post-Segregation Era* (Minneapolis: University of Minnesota Press, 1999), 101; see also Smith, *Racial Democracy*; N.D.B. Connolly, *A World More Concrete: Real Estate and the Remaking of Jim Crow South Florida* (Chicago: University of Chicago Press, 2014); Cedric Johnson, *From Revolutionaries to Race Leaders* (Minneapolis: University of Minnesota Press, 2007).

9 See Touré Reed, "Why Moynihan Was Not So Misunderstood at the Time: The Mythological Prescience of the Moynihan Report and the Problem of Institutional Structuralism," *Nonsite* 17, September 2015, http://nonsite.org/issues/issue-17-the-moynihan-report-and-the-crescent-city.

10 See Cedric Johnson, ed., *The Neoliberal Deluge: Hurricane Katrina, Late Capital-ism and the Remaking of New Orleans* (Minneapolis: University of Minnesota Press, 2011); John D. Arena, *Driven from New Orleans: How Nonprofits Betray Public Housing and Promote Privatization* (Minneapolis: University of Minnesota Press, 2013); Adolph Reed, "Three Tremés," *Nonsite*, July 4, 2011, nonsite.org/edito-rial/three-tremes.

11 Landrieu had long been a lone voice of racial progressivism in a state whose politics were rooted in a "segregation forever" mandate. As a junior state legisla-tor, he had been the only member of the Legislature to oppose new segregation measures. Landrieu understood integration as a moral necessity and vital to a functioning free market. See "Landrieu Is New Mayor after 'Vote of the Century,'" *Times-Picayune*, April 8, 1970, 1; "Orleans Lack of Planning," *Times-Picayune*, March 14, 1971, 54; Kent B. Germany, *New Orleans After the Promises: Poverty, Citizenship, and the Search for the Great Society* (Atlanta: University of Georgia Press, 2007), 247.

12 For an in-depth narrative of how block grants diminished the redistributive ca-pacity of federal urban aid, see Megan French-Marcelin, "Community Underde-velopment: Federal Aid and the Rise of Privatization in New Orleans," (PhD diss., Columbia University, 2014).

13 The growth of suburban constituencies further undermined the power of the city within the legislature. As changes to the city's tax program had to be approved by the state legislature, this system privileged suburban voters who wanted to avoid paying levies on their income earned in New Orleans. See Matteson Associates, *Dimensions and Solutions of New Orleans' Financial Dilemma: Report of a Recon-naissance Study* (New Orleans, LA: Bureau of Governmental Research, 1966).

14 "Tax Setup Bars Progress—Davis," *Times-Picayune*, December 15, 1966, 4; "PAR Says CC-73 Could Be Vital," *Times-Picayune*, August 2, 1973, 18; Matteson As-sociates, *Dimensions and Solutions of New Orleans' Financial Dilemma: Report of a Reconnaissance Study* (New Orleans, LA: Bureau of Governmental Research, 1966), iii.

15 See French-Marcelin, "Community Underdevelopment"; Megan French-Marcelin, "Boosting the Private Sector: Federal Aid and Downtown Development in the 1970s," in *Remaking New Orleans: Beyond Exceptionalism and Authenticity*, ed. Thomas Jessen Adams and Matt Sakakeeny (Durham, NC: Duke University Press, 2019), 241–60.

16 His dealings with Canizaro would resurface when Landrieu left office. In 1979, President Jimmy Carter appointed him as secretary of the Department of Housing and Urban Development. The confirmation hearings for Landrieu's new gig with HUD even further revealed the degree to which the mayor had extended his role as executive to conduct favors for real estate. The Canal Place land swap was indeed only the tip of the iceberg. In the previous year, Canizaro had sold a tract of land with little value to the city for more than half a million dollars. Further, while in office, Landrieu had made a profit on shares in another

Canizaro project. Unrelated to Canizaro, the committee found that Landrieu provided legal advice to a tourism company that then won bids with the city. As the head of the Committee on Banking, Housing and Urban Affairs, Senator Proxmire summarized, "What we have is the appearance of favors being done by the city for a major developer, and in turn, by that developer for the mayor, and possible quid pro quos." See Report, Issues in New Orleans 1985, Box 1, Folder Issue in New Orleans, John Pecoul Papers, Amistad Research Center, Tulane University, New Orleans, LA.

17 Alluding to the New York City fiscal crisis, Landrieu remarked on the similarities of the situations in the two cities. New York City was losing jobs and its middle class; it was becoming increasingly poor, old, and reliant on an ever-growing sales tax. "Does that sound familiar?" the mayor enjoined. "You leave the 'New' and replace 'York' with 'Orleans' and it all sounds very familiar. Interestingly, at the time New York City declared bankruptcy, Landrieu was the president of the US Conference of Mayors. As such, he was at the forefront of lobbying President Ford to provide the city with financial relief., "Landrieu Tells Conference of Problems," *Times-Picayune,* November 18, 1975, 1.

18 US Census Bureau, "Unemployment Rates, New Orleans 1960–1990" (Washington, DC: US Government Printing Office, 1990).

19 See Jack Davis, "Faust Revisited: Is SOUL for Sale?" *New Orleans Magazine* (1973); Charlotte Hayes, "Black Power for Sale," *Vieux Carre Courier,* August 31, 1972; "Black Politics 11: The Neighborhoods: Grass Roots Go Deep," *New Orleans States Item,* February 26, 1973; "Black Politicos Have Come a Long Way," *Times-Picayune,* September 26, 1976, 54. For a comprehensive list of black political leadership appointed to city government, see the appendixes in Kent B. Germany, *New Orleans After the Promises: Poverty, Citizenship, and the Search for the Great Society* (Atlanta: University of Georgia Press, 2007).

20 Following the Voting Rights Act, black political organizations discovered that their power to bring out the vote could be monetized. In the election cycles following Moon Landrieu's election, rumors abounded that SOUL and COUP, among other black political organizations, were receiving exceptionally high sums to "bring out the vote." There were whispers that candidates could actually buy this loyalty irrespective of whether they were the best option for black working-class voters. This is not to say that Landrieu's commitment to integration, nor SOUL's to the mayor, was disingenuous. Rather, this assessment explains the ways in which race, class, and patronage functioned in complicated and often contradictory ways in the post–Civil Rights era. Hayes, "Black Power for Sale." See also Germany, *New Orleans After the Promises.*

21 Arnold R. Hirsch, "Simply a Matter of Black and White: The Transformation of Race and Politics in Twentieth-Century New Orleans," in *Creole New Orleans: Race and Americanization,* ed. Arnold R. Hirsch and Joseph Logsdon (Baton Rouge: Louisiana State University Press, 1992), 300; "Contracts for Dome Said Hit After Blacks, Politicos Got In," *Times-Picayune,* March 30, 1974, 1.

22 "Contracts for Dome." See also "Which One of His Many Hats Is Arata Wearing Today," *Times-Picayune*, March 22, 1974, 1.

23 Within a year, both SSI and Copelin himself were subject to charges of corruption, mismanagement, and mishandling of funds. Copelin, tied as well to the antipoverty Family Health Foundation, was indicted on charges of accepting payoffs. Amid this scandal, Landrieu was sure to distance himself from the SOUL leader who had once been the top beneficiary of the mayor's patronage chain. See "Landrieu Sees Alleged Payoffs as 'Despicable,'" *Times-Picayune*, November 18, 1975, 1.

24 Betsy Halstead, "Candidate Landrieu Calls for Society 'Open to All,'" *Times-Picayune*, June 29, 1969, 17.

25 "Moon Looks Back at Last 8 Years," *Times-Picayune*, March 12, 1978, 1; see also "Mid-city Demos Hear Hopefuls," *Times-Picayune*, October 26, 1973, 43; Germany, *New Orleans After the Promises*, 267.

26 See Marlene Keller and Michael Peter Smith, "'Managed Growth' and the Politics of Uneven Development in New Orleans," in *Restructuring the City: The Political Economy of Urban Redevelopment*, ed. Susan Fainstein and Norman Fainstein (New York: Longman, 1986), 138. See also "Guste Favors Moon Landrieu," *Times-Picayune*, March 14, 1970, 1.

27 For more on these controversies, see Christine C. Cook and Mickey Lauria, "Urban Regeneration and Public Housing in New Orleans," *Urban Affairs Review* 30:4 (1995), 538–57.

28 For a discussion of how low-income neighborhood issues were relegated to the realm of federal aid, see Megan French-Marcelin, "If You Blight It, They Will Come: Moynihan, New Orleans, and the Making of the Gentrification Economy," *Nonsite* 17 (September 2015), http://nonsite.org/article/if-you-blight-it-they-will-come.

29 French-Marcelin, "Community Underdevelopment"; French-Marcelin, "Boosting the Private Sector: Federal Aid and Downtown Development in the 1970s," in Adams and Sakakeeny, *Remaking New Orleans*. For an overview of the legislation, see Robert Fishman, "Title I of the Housing and Community Development Act of 1974: New Federal and Local Dynamics in Community Development," *Urban Lawyer* 7:2 (1975).

30 Report, *OPPA Process Critique*, Box 17, Folder OD-PLPR-74: Planning process critique and recommendations (AIME-1974), OPPA Files, New Orleans City Archives, New Orleans Public Library, Louisiana.

31 For a longer discussion of the effect of neighborhood-level planning, see French-Marcelin, "If You Blight It, They Will Come"; see also Curtis and Davis Architects and Planners, "New Orleans Housing and Preservation Study" (New Orleans, LA, 1974); J. E. Bourgoyne, "History N.O. Areas to Vanish," *Times-Picayune*, March 24, 1974, 6.

32 Report, Analysis of the Non-Bond Portion of the City's 1973 Capital Budget, Box 7, Folder ED: Revenue Sharing, Office of Policy Planning and Analysis Papers,

City Archives of New Orleans, New Orleans Public Library, New Orleans, Louisiana; Wallace, McHarg, Roberts, and Todd, *Central Area New Orleans Growth Management Program: Technical Report Containing the Proposed CBD Community Improvement Plan and Program, 1974 to the Year 2000* (New Orleans, LA: Bureau of Governmental Research, 1975).

33 Lester Kabacoff was another of the preeminent developers of this first-wave growth coalition. The New York City native was responsible for later development of Riverwalk, a festival marketplace styled after Boston's Faneuil Hall. His son, Pres, has become one of the biggest developers in New Orleans both pre- and post-Katrina.

34 Report: Clarence Barney, "Community Economic Development," Box B21, Folder Economic Development 1978, Ernest N. Morial Collection, New Orleans Public Library, New Orleans, LA.

35 James R. Bobo, *The New Orleans Economy: Pro Bono Publico?* (New Orleans, LA: Division of Business and Economic Research, College of Business Administration, University of New Orleans, 1975), 26.

36 "Moon Landrieu on Bridge, Blacks, Past, Future, Unigov, JFK, Water . . . ," *Times-Picayune*, May 5, 1975, 10.

37 "Reviews Mixed for Landrieu," *Times-Picayune*, August 26, 1979, 34; see also "Two Blight Areas Need $180 Million, 15 Years," *Times-Picayune*, September 29, 1972, 8; "Residents Say Central City Project Ineffective," *Times-Picayune*, June 7, 1973.

38 "Reviews Mixed for Landrieu."

39 Michael Peter Smith and Marlene Keller, "Managed Growth and the Politics of Uneven Development in New Orleans," in *Restructuring the City: The Political Economy of Urban Redevelopment* (London: Longman Group, 1986), 129.

40 Bobo, *The New Orleans Economy*, 51.

41 For a debate on how this has occurred in post–Katrina New Orleans, see Cedric Johnson, "Gentrifying New Orleans: Thoughts on Race and the Movement of Capital," *Souls* 17:3 (October 2015), 175–200.

42 "Mid-City Demons Hear Hopefuls," *Times-Picayune*, October 26, 1973, 43.

43 Germany, *New Orleans After the Promises*, 267.

44 "Black Politics 15: Landrieu a Popular Champion or a Product of Percentages?" *New Orleans States Item*, March 2, 1973; see also Peter Eisenger, *Black Employment in City Government, 1973–1980* (New York: Rowman & Littlefield, 1986).

45 Daniel C. Thompson, "Black Leadership in New Orleans," 1977, Folder Leadership in New Orleans, Box 123, Moon Landrieu Collection, Loyola University, New Orleans, LA; see also Philip Shabecoff, "Thousands on Public Payrolls Face Layoff," *New York Times*, October 1, 1979.

46 Bobo, *New Orleans Economy*.

47 Germany, *New Orleans After the Promises*, 268.

48 "DiRosa Led in White Precincts," *Times-Picayune*, October 5, 1977, 2; "Blacks Win and Lose Some," *Times-Picayune*, February 24, 1978, 19; Hirsch, "Simply a Matter of Black and White," 304; Monte Piliawsky, "The Impact of Black Mayors on the

Black Community: The Case of New Orleans' Ernest Morial," *Review of Black Political Economy* 13:4 (1985), 5–23.

49 "Landrieu, Morial Urge Development of N.O. Resources," *Times-Picayune*, May 28, 1978, 28.

50 Inaugural Address, Ernest N. Morial, May 1, 1978, Box J6, Folder Mayor's Policy Statements, Ernest N. Morial Mayoral Papers, City Archives of New Orleans, New Orleans Public Library, New Orleans, LA (hereafter ENMM Papers).

51 Alongside these issues, the city had suffered from its failure to pass progressive tax measures. Morial would follow in Landrieu's footsteps and attempt to steer a municipal earnings bill through the city council, evading the ban on the tax by classifying it as an "employment privilege fee." The bill proposed a 1% tax on all income earned within the municipality but maintained a $5,200 exemption so that working-class residents would not pay out most of their income. Yet, after a series of progressive tax measures repeatedly failed to muster votes in the council, Morial resorted to passing an increase on the city's sales tax. At the time it was passed, the increase to 9% made it the highest city sales tax in the country. See Sal Anzelmo to all city attorneys, October 16, 1984; Box B21, Folder Earnings Tax, ENMM Papers.

52 New Orleans Comprehensive Economic Development Strategy, Box J62, Folder New Orleans Comprehensive Economic Development Strategy, ENMM Papers.

53 "A Black Calvin Coolidge?" *Wall Street Journal*, May 1, 1979; "Urban Politics, Poor Must Pay," *Black Enterprise* 11 (October 1980), 22.

54 Biographical Information—Dutch Morial, Box 2, Folder Dutch Morial, John Pecoul Papers, Amistad Research Center, Tulane University, New Orleans, LA.

55 Memo, Alma Young to Anthony Mumphrey, February 7, 1979, Box J6, Folder Mayor's Policy Statements, ENMM Papers.

56 The commitment to development could not have been more obvious in the campaign contributions to Morial's 1982 election bid. It was no surprise to those who had watched the mayor operate that Joseph Canizaro made the largest donations. The list of supporters donating big dollars to the incumbent mayor read like a virtual who's who in the real estate and tourism world, including support from Lester Kabacoff, Owen Brennan, Edward J. DeBartolo, Laurence Eustis of Canal Mortgages, and Bill Hess of the Stern fortune. "Morial Spends Three Times Faucheux Total," *Times-Picayune*, January 8, 1982, 17. For his letters to leaders of the real estate world, see Ernest Morial to Chris Bellone, Box B17, Folder Tourist and Convention Commission, ENMM Papers. For a glimpse into the personal friendships of Morial with developers, see Memo, Ernest Morial to Lester Kabacoff, March 13, 1979, Box B22, Folder Exhibition Hall, 1979–1986, ENMM Papers.

57 Speech, Ernest N. Morial to the Propeller Club, January 9, 1980, Box J6, Folder Mayor's Policy Statements, ENMM Papers.

58 Press Release, Office of Economic Development, n.d., Box B6, Folder Megalink Concept, ENMM Papers.

59 "City Seeks Funds," *Times-Picayune*, March 16, 1979, 1.

60 Morial Administration Fact Sheet: Economic Strategy 1981, Box 4, Folder Fact Sheet, John Pecoul Papers, Amistad Research Center, Tulane University, New Orleans, LA.

61 "City Oks Millions in Bonds," *Times-Picayune*, July 28, 1979, 2; "Morial's Statement to Council Hearing on Land Swap," *Times-Picayune*, October 29, 1982, 28.

62 Morial would utilize connections with private-sector developers in a number of ways to solidify influence in various realms of development. While historians have praised the mayor's willingness to eschew prior patronage arrangements, his rejection of Landrieu's arrangements did not mean the mayor was not committed to a system of exchanging appointments for loyalty. In fact, he extended positions of authority and influence to many of his developer friends in exchange for their commitment to his particular vision of the city politic. Thus, Canizaro held influential seats on the French Market Commission and the Tourism Board and Jerome Glazer was appointed as the commissioner of the Aviation Board, a position that was used to give the mayor broad say in matters concerning the airport. Indicative of these arrangements, Morial once chided his staff for not running appointments by him, saying, "No patronage positions or contracts should be committed without first discussing the situation with me . . . all things being equal we should endeavor to select persons who will be friendly and loyal to the administration." See memo, Ernest Morial to Reynard Rochon and Tony Mumphrey, June 24, 1980, Box A8, Folder Correspondence January–September 1980, ENMM Papers.

63 The swap was so controversial that the mayor and council had to testify as part of a grand jury investigation of the deal. See "DeBartolo Land Swap Had Beginnings in '80," *Times-Picayune*, October 5, 1984, 4; see also "Lessons of Poydras Square," *Times-Picayune*, October 31, 1982, 33; "Morial's Statement to Council Hearing on Land Swap," *Times-Picayune*, October 29, 1982, 28.

64 "Morial's Statement to Council Hearing on Land Swap."

65 See John T. Metzger, "The Failed Promise of a Festival Marketplace: South Street Seaport in Lower Manhattan," *Planning Perspectives* 16 (2001), 44.

66 "Morial's First-term Grade," *Times-Picayune*, May 2, 1982, 33; Piliawsky, "The Impact of Black Mayors," 13.

67 Report, Ernest N. Morial, "Report to the City Council on Federal Budget Reduction Proposals, March 26, 1981," Box L5, Folder Federal Budget Cuts, ENMM Papers; Piliawsky, "The Impact of Black Mayors," 7.

68 In 1975, University of New Orleans urbanist James Bobo published a scathing indictment of the city's economic development strategy. He focused attention on the issue of subemployment, arguing that in a service-sector economy, official unemployment numbers did not account for those who were employed seasonally or on a temporary basis. In working-class black areas, Bobo contended, the unemployment and subemployment rate was near 40%. Bobo, *The New Orleans Economy*.

69 "Urban Politics, Poor Must Pay," 22.

70 Allan Katz, "N.O.'s Black Underclass," *Times-Picayune*, February 7, 1982, 33.

71 Ibid.

72 Austin Penny to Reynard Rochon, February 21, 1983, Box A8, Folder Correspondence January–February 1981, ENMM Papers.

73 "City Minority Business Program Sputters," *Times-Picayune*, June 30, 1985, 1; "Morial: Minorities Will Have to Learn the Ropes of Capitalism," *Times-Picayune*, November 8, 1981, 33.

74 Inaugural Address, Ernest N. Morial, May 1, 1978, Box J6, Folder Mayor's Policy Statements, ENMM Papers.

75 For his part, Jackson offered: "The black community is moving from civil rights to silver rights, from aid to trade. The last frontier for blacks is the private sector. We previously believed the key for us was the creation of jobs. We have come to see that the real key in the private sector is development opportunities . . . Cut us in or cut it [the fair] out." See "Jackson Warns of '84 Fair Rights Fight," *Times-Picayune*, July 8, 1982, 11.

76 Ibid.

77 Ed Tunstall, "Mayor—'World's Fair Will Benefit City," *Times-Picayune*, August 15, 1982.

78 John D. Arena, *Driven from New Orleans: How Nonprofits Betray Public Housing and Promote Privatization* (Minneapolis: University of Minnesota Press, 2013), 133.

79 While Morial has been depicted time and time again as operating above the fray of corrupt New Orleans city politics, it should be noted that after the minority set-asides were announced, it was revealed that Marc Morial, Dutch's son and future mayor of New Orleans, had won a huge contract to supply caps for the fair. See "No Politics in Fair Caps, Spurney Says," *Times-Picayune*, July 21, 1983, 15; "Minority Goals Met, World's Fair Officials Say," *Times-Picayune*, July 7, 1983, 27. See also Hirsch, "Simply a Matter of Black and White," 262–320.

80 "Morial's First-Term Grade," *Times-Picayune*, May 2, 1982, 23.

81 "Morial: Minorities Will Have to Learn Ropes of Capitalism," *Times-Picayune*, November 8, 1981, 33; see also Piliawsky, "The Impact of Black Mayors," 5–23.

82 This, of course, is the core of Daniel Patrick Moynihan's argument in *The Negro Family: A Call for National Action*. Touré Reed, "Why Moynihan Was Not So Misunderstood at the Time: The Mythological Prescience of the Moynihan Report and the Problem of Institutional Structuralism," *Nonsite* 17 (September 2015), https://nonsite.org/article/why-moynihan-was-not-so-misunderstood-at-the-time, argues that by framing the issue of black poverty as an issue of institutional racism, Moynihan abandoned a broader economic structuralist argument that accounted for economic transformations, namely automation and deindustrialization, and thus turned his back on seeking solutions that could address economic inequalities.

83 Jane S. Brooks and Alma H. Young, "Revitalizing the Central Business District in the Face of Decline: The Case of New Orleans 1973–1993," *Town Planning Review* 64:3 (1993), 264.

84 "Get Up Early, Hunt for Job, Mayor Says," *Times-Picayune*, August 9, 1983, 18; see also Piliawsky, "The Impact of Black Mayors," 23.

85 Piliawsky, "The Impact of Black Mayors," 20.

86 Allan Katz, "Ten Years after 'Pro Bono Publico,'" *Times-Picayune*, June 16, 1985, 27.

87 Ibid.

88 See Christine C. Cook and Mickey Lauria, "Urban Regeneration and Public Housing in New Orleans," *Urban Affairs Review* 30:4 (1995), 538–57.

89 In an interview, Canizaro confessed that he had actually voted for Barthelemy's opponent, William Jefferson, at the behest of Morial. "Dutch was my mayor at the time. Dutch had been a great help to me, I think he was a great mayor and I would have done whatever he asked," the developer recounted. From the city's largest developer, this statement dissuaded any claim that Morial had been antagonistic to development in any way. "Canizaro's Development Eye," *Times-Picayune*, May 18, 1986, 27.

90 Susan S. Fainstein and Norman Fainstein, "Regime Strategies, Communal Resistance and Economic Forces," in *Restructuring the City: The Political Economy of Urban Redevelopment*, ed. Susan S. Fainstein and Norman Fainstein (London: Longman, 1986), 246.

91 Quoted in Jamie Peck, "Liberating the City: Between New York and New Orleans," *Urban Geography* 27:8 (2006), 696.

92 The irony here is that the school workforce had been a mainstay of black middle-class stability. See Adrienne Dixson, "Whose Choice? A Critical Race Perspective on Charter Schools," in *The Neoliberal Deluge: Hurricane Katrina, Late Capitalism and the Remaking of New Orleans*, ed. Cedric Johnson (Minneapolis: University of Minnesota Press, 2011), 130; Campbell Robertson, "Louisiana Illegally Fired 7,500 Teachers, Judge Says," *New York Times*, June 21, 2012.

93 Bill Quigley, "New Orleans Katrina Pain Index at 10: Who Was Left Behind," *Huffington Post*, July 20, 2015, http://www.huffingtonpost.com/bill-quigley/new-orleans-katrina-pain_b_7831870.html.

5

The Color of War

Race, Neoliberalism, and Punishment in
Late Twentieth-Century Los Angeles

DONNA MURCH

To many observers, Los Angeles has long represented a failed urbanism, an unplanned collection of disjointed and alienated suburbs in search of a city. According to one popular historian, it embodies a dystopic vision of an urban future devoid of public space and governed by militarized and market-driven logic. Indeed, the spatial turn in the social sciences treated Los Angeles not only as a place, but as a concept that epitomized the unfolding of a new set of processes that forged the contemporary neoliberal metropolis. At the same time, its position at the apex of the Sun Belt in postwar America has set L.A. apart from the decaying urban cores of the Rust Belt and generated a gravity of its own. Los Angeles is an immensely wealthy metropolitan region with the United States' largest manufacturing sector that spans five counties: Los Angeles, Orange, Ventura, Riverside, and San Bernardino. Urban planning scholar Edward Soja argued that its propulsive and uneven growth epitomized the working of twentieth-century capitalism itself. In 1989, he described the city as "the capital of capital" a place where "it all comes together."[1]

In revisiting the city, nearly thirty years after its notoriety as a failed experiment in unchecked growth, real estate investment, defense production, and extractive industry, it is clear that Los Angeles now has the dubious distinction of being the United States' largest urban site of mass incarceration. If one includes the full carceral archipelago of jails, detention centers, and holding facilities, the city of Los Angeles houses more prisoners than any city on the planet. Along with its surrounding counties and other embattled municipalities of Southern California, L.A. has also pioneered new instruments for police militarization, anti-drug campaigns, youth criminalization, and anti-gang prosecution that influenced and anticipated developments in other parts of the country. Arguably, in the decades since the Watts rebellion of 1965, the city has waged continuous domestic warfare on its poorest and most vulnerable citizens who are overwhelmingly composed of black and brown youth.[2]

The city's overlapping war(s) on drugs and gangs offers us a window onto the convergence between the United States' punishment regime and neoliberal social policy at the end of the twentieth century. One of the most surprising developments in recent scholarship is how separate these two research clusters remain. Although popular histories such as Mike Davis's *City of Quartz* understood neoliberalism and racial punishment as inseparable, the academic literature that has emerged over the past decade has often viewed these realms as separate and distinct.[3] Social science scholarship has largely emphasized a top-down global movement toward trade liberalization, pro-market governance, deunionization, privatization, and social welfare retrenchment, while historical analysis of the American carceral state has focused on domestic racial politics in the United States; comparisons between the post–civil rights America's embrace of mass incarceration with convict leasing following Reconstruction; debates about the New Right versus bipartisan support for law and order; the utility of punishment campaigns for increasing state power; and the criminalization of youth in response to mass social movements of the 1960s and 1970s.[4]

One of the reasons for the separation of writings on race and neoliberalism has to do with the historical nature of the liberal state itself in which the perennial problem of conceptually integrating race and class continues to haunt the historiography of twentieth-century liberalism. When examined from the point of view of black people, the economic liberalism of the Roosevelt era reflects a bifurcated, unequal, and often punishing approach to social welfare in which African Americans face exclusion, means testing, and social control. While these policies have been well documented by a number of scholars, few of the people writing mournfully about the retreat of the redistributive state in the mid-1970s have fully reckoned with liberalism's cloven, uneven nature that heightened economic disparities between black and white citizens.[5]

More recently a new group of historians and social scientists, led by Elizabeth Kai Hinton, Naomi Murakwa, and Heather Thompson, have created a counter-historiography that locates the origins of the modern carceral state in liberal programs themselves, most importantly the simultaneous emergence of the War on Poverty and the War on Crime during Lyndon Johnson's Great Society.[6] In the context of the continual assaults on the American welfare state over the last fifty years, it is understandable that its virtues are celebrated in order to highlight the destructive effects of subsequent retrenchment. But drawing a definitive line between liberalism and neoliberalism blurs and erases the racially discriminatory policies of the New Deal order. In other words, if African Americans are treated as integral to our national history, the disjuncture between liberalism and neoliberalism looks much less clear.[7]

Nevertheless, as this chapter will show, a great deal more historical research remains to be done in other arenas, especially exploring the intersections between racial capitalism, political economy, and incentive structures of neoliberal-era law enforcement. The timing of American mass incarceration's takeoff in the mid-1970s in the midst of a global capitalist crisis is, of course, significant,[8] as is the coterminous development of new state extractive capacities like expanded powers of asset forfeiture in the Racketeering Influenced and Corrupt Organizations (RICO) Act passed under the Nixon administration in 1970 that later became powerful tools for raising law enforcement revenue at the public's expense.[9] Under Ronald Reagan's Crime Control Act of 1984 and the Comprehensive Drug Abuse Act of 1986, municipal police departments received large amounts of state and federal funds from narcotics seizures. Additionally, the LAPD was allowed to confiscate 90% of property and cash from drug cases, thereby providing immense incentives to pursue this type of police work.[10] Finally, if my own research on Los Angeles is any indicator, the related difficulties faced by activists and reformers trying to oppose such lavishly funded "wars" on drugs, gangs, and crime in Southern California raises a number of compelling questions about structural impediments to organized resistance in post–New Deal America.

Before proceeding, a few words about the use of the term neoliberalism. As this term has many different meanings and remains highly contested, I am primarily using it to signify the domestic United States in the period after the oil shocks and stagflation that coincides roughly with the presidencies of Jimmy Carter, Ronald Reagan, and their successors. Neoliberalism references both a time period during which we see a steady retreat from many of the redistributive policies of the New Deal as well as a conceptual frame that emphasizes rising social inequality and the application of market principles and metrics to multiple forms of human agency and public goods.[11] A crucial and less discussed aspect of the neoliberal turn is how its punitive components utilize the increased state capacity of the New Deal to launch more expansive forms of criminalization in policing, surveillance, and correctional control.[12] It is, of course, also striking that the ascent of mass incarceration in the United States coincides with a global retreat from the redistributive welfare state. However, tracing the particular history and trajectory is difficult, because so many of the practices that we associate with the neoliberal punishment originate in earlier eras.[13]

Drawing on Los Angeles's racialized punishment campaigns against gangs and drugs in the late twentieth century, this chapter reflects on the advantages (and disadvantages) of integrating neoliberal analysis with new research on the carceral state. Exploring the punitive aspects of governance in L.A. demonstrates both the importance of the securitization state to the neoliberal turn in the United States and the centrality of racial ideology to its existence. Perhaps most important, Southern California's "carceral city" reveals the difficulty in mobilizing organized resistance among black Angelinos who suffered the worst effects of criminalization. Instead, in the 1980s and 1990s, we see a heightening of class fractures within the African American community and a capitulation of significant portions of the "black leadership class" to punishment regimes that ultimately proved harmful to large numbers of their constituents. Similarly, grassroots activists like Michael Zinzun and the Coalition Against Police Abuse found themselves too often superseded by a neoliberal-era nonprofit organizing model, which lacked an independent funding structure as well as left analysis that animated significant portions of the black freedom struggle in the postwar period.

Los Angeles's War(s) on Drugs and Gangs

In late twentieth-century Los Angeles, punishment campaigns against drugs and gangs rationalized a new martial infrastructure. The carceral effects of increased criminalization can hardly be overstated. From 1977, the California Department of Corrections (CDC) prison population rose from 19,623 to 162,000 in the year 2000, with more than 40% drawn from Los Angeles and 70% from Southern California more broadly. By 1990, drug offenses comprised 34.2% of new admissions to California prisons and 25% of detainees in Los Angeles County jail, which contained the world's largest urban prison population.[14] By the new millennium, the combined totals of African Americans and Latinx people made up more than 64% of the total population of the CDC.[15] Moreover, black people represented only 6.7% of California's general population, but made up 31% of the state's prisoners.[16]

Major components of the Los Angeles Police Department (LAPD), Los Angeles Sheriff's Department (LASD), and the California Highway Patrol's (CHP) militarized infrastructure could be traced to law enforcement's hostile response to the civil unrest of the postwar years, nearly a decade before what many scholars consider the start of neoliberal policies. In the aftermath of the Watts Rebellion in which law enforcement arrested more than 4,000 people, the LAPD deployed military grade hardware and elite tactical units to tamp down perceived social disorder. Under the leadership of chiefs William Parker (1950–1966), Tom Reddin (1967–1969), and Edward M. Davis (1969–1978), the LAPD developed signature policing strategies that became essential to the city's brutal prosecution of the wars on drugs and gangs two decades later. The department founded the Strategic Weapons Assault Team (SWAT) with a compact force of former military veterans in 1967. Subsequently, the LAPD deployed SWAT for the first time against the Southern California Black Panther Party's (SCBPP) office on 41st and Central Avenue in 1969. The commando force used a tank on loan from the National Guard and won Department of Justice authorization to obtain a grenade launcher.[17]

During the 1970s, education and surveillance programs within the Los Angeles Unified School district accompanied the LAPD's militarization. In 1974, the department dispatched undercover police into schools to pose as students. A decade later, Chief Davis's successor, Daryl F. Gates (1978–1992), expanded this partnership with the Board of Education by starting the Drug Abuse Resistance Education Program (DARE), which became a national anti-drug campaign reaching 1.5 million students by 1988.[18]

SWAT, DARE, and a succession of high-profile programs and command units combined a militarized ethos with a marketing flair that represented the LAPD as a powerful occupying force in the city. With funding from the Law Enforcement Assistance Administration (LEAA), the department created the Total Resources Against Southeast Hoodlums (TRASH) five years later. Under community protest, it was later renamed Community Resources Against Street Hoodlums (CRASH) and went on to become the city's most notorious anti-gang unit in the 1980s, with the LASD's Operation Safe Streets (OSS) and District Attorney's Hardcore Drug Unit soon following in their wake. As this list of martial alphabet agencies implies, starting with the invention of SWAT, Los Angeles helped lead the national march toward police militarization.[19]

One of the most striking elements about law enforcement's domestic warfare model was how it drew on imagery from the United States' imperial battlefields abroad. In 1979, Chief Daryl Gates offered to deploy LAPD SWAT to Iran to help President Jimmy Carter liberate American hostages. The police chief's proposal clearly sought to heighten the LAPD's national and international visibility, but it also demonstrated the shocking conflation of the Armed Services with domestic police. Similarly, during a massive police sweep in 1988, the District Attorney's Hardcore Drug Unit described its "war" on local gangs by proclaiming, "This is Vietnam here."[20] Los Angeles law enforcement's invocation of racial warfare was far from unique. The rhetoric and hardline anti-crime stance of the Reagan administration drew frequently on racialized war metaphors, which justified state-building in an era of fiscal conservatism. "For all our science and sophistication, for all our justified pride in intellectual accomplishment, we must never forget the jungle is always there, waiting to take us over," declared Ronald Reagan in a presidential address announcing new federal initiatives against drug trafficking and organized crime. "Only our deep moral values and strong social institutions can hold back that jungle and restrain the darker impulses of human nature."[21]

In addition to personnel restructuring that channeled more manpower and funding toward elite command units, LAPD's militarization also represented a purging of social service components from policing, focusing instead on crime and territorial control. Geographic dispersion of the city and the establishment of the LAPD Air Support Division

(ASD) in 1974, which became the largest "airborne municipal law enforcement system in the world," contributed to tactical surveillance and
distance from city residents.[22] While William Parker's vision of profes-
sionalization in the postwar years laid the foundation for this approach
in the 1950s and 1960s, under the auspices of the Reagan era's intensified
wars on crime, drugs, and gangs, the martial imperative grew stronger
and received large increases in funding and direct support from municipal, state, and federal governments.[23]

Los Angeles's high-profile war on drugs reflected the larger policies
and strategic aims of Reagan's national punishment campaign, including
saturation policing, eradication of youth gangs, asset forfeiture, federal-
ization of drug charges, and strict enforcement of mandatory minimum
sentencing. At the street level, the use of massive police sweeps with
spectacular displays of overwhelming force embodied the city's militarized vision of law enforcement, as did Chief Daryl Gates's repeated calls
to arms. Testifying on the one-year anniversary of the Bush administration's War on Drugs, the LAPD police chief told the Senate Judiciary
Committee, "The casual drug user ought to be taken out and shot."[24]

Behind his bombastic rhetoric lay a larger neoliberal truth. In an
era of drastic reduction of social services and deindustrialization, mass
incarceration fueled by anti-drug and anti-gang campaigns became de
facto urban social policy for the residents of impoverished communities
like South Central and Pico Union. The prescription for widespread job-
lessness and the illicit economies that accompanied urban divestment
was simply to remove a significant percentage of the population from
the streets through prison warehousing. Strikingly, in 1980, *prior* to the
advent of the alleged "crack epidemic" and Reagan's declaration of a new
war on drugs, Chief Gates argued that the rate of 0.1% incarceration
of California's population (26,000) was insufficient. In order to achieve
greater public safety, he advocated that 2–3% of California's residents
should be locked up.[25]

In Los Angeles much of the carceral infrastructure for the city's war
on drugs relied on geographically targeted gang sweeps together with
anti-gang legislation and prosecution tools. The conflation of drug
crimes with street gang membership created a comprehensive net for
the criminalization of nonwhite youth.[26] Drawing on a repertoire of historical "demonologies" with their own prosecutorial regimes, the LAPD

alternately viewed black and Latinx gangs through the lens of organized crime or of terrorism.[27] The slippage from street gangs, to drug trafficking, organized crime, and terrorism represented the defining principle of the Reagan/Bush era war on drugs. Its solution was total suppression and use of RICO-style conspiracy prosecutions to remove as many alleged gang members from the streets as possible.[28]

Between 1984 and 1988, California passed more than eighty separate anti-gang measures and developed powerful new legal tools, including the civil gang injunction and gang enhancements in sentencing. In December 1987, Los Angeles city attorney and future mayor, James Hahn, pioneered the injunction's use against the Playboy Gangster Crips from West Los Angeles.[29] Gang injunctions permanently prohibited members from engaging in specified behaviors in a designated geographic area. The prosecuting agency sued a gang as an "unincorporated association," in order to allow for the continual addition of new names. Injunctions' civil nature also meant the state was not required to provide a public defender.

Defining the war on drugs as a war on gangs justified the criminalization of everyday life in black and brown Los Angeles. Modes of dress, movement, color of shoelaces, hand gestures, and mere association became defined as prosecutable offenses. Gang injunctions worked in tandem with municipal, state, and federal databases. In 1985, the LASD created its own computerized list, the Gang Reporting Evaluation and Tracking system (GREAT). Seven years later, the federal General Accounting Office revealed that the LASD listed 47% of all African American men in L.A. County between the ages of twenty-one and twenty-four as gang members. Racially targeted policing combined with the denial of legal representation made it virtually impossible for youth to have their names removed. In this sense, anti-gang injunctions also contained a brutal class component; their success hinged on their targets' inability to hire lawyers.[30]

While anti-gang injunctions and databases provided mechanisms for surveillance, control, and the admission of large numbers of minority youth into "the system" for minor offenses, gang enhancement legislation ultimately had the most damaging effects for mass incarceration. In 1988, the California legislature passed the Street Terrorism and Prevention Act (STEP), which mandated that persons convicted of crimes who have been designated as gang members face additional charges and sentencing. In the initial 1988 law, prosecutors could "enhance" gang members' convictions from one to five years of additional time in state prison per offense.[31] Subsequently, California's Proposition 21 amended the STEP Act in 2000 by increasing gang enhancements to sixteen months to five years for nonviolent offenses, and to 10, 15, 20, and 25 years to life for violent offenses. Moreover, in first-degree murder cases with special circumstances, Prop 21 mandated the death penalty or life imprisonment without the possibility of parole. The dense layering of STEP and its subsequent revisions, including added prison time for gun charges and for crimes committed within 1,000 yards of a school, meant that it was not uncommon for very young offenders to receive multiple consecutive life sentences.[32]

The repressive legal regime in Los Angeles worked in tandem with law enforcement's spectacular shows of force, mass arrests, and saturation policing. After the murder of the suburban resident Karen Toshima, the LAPD proclaimed 1988 the "Year of the Gang Enforcement." "This is war," declared Chief Daryl Gates. "We want to get the message out to the cowards out there . . . that we're going to come and get them." With this battle cry, the department sent more than 1,000 officers into South Los Angeles in conjunction with the task force "Operation Hammer."[33] On Saturday, April 9, 1988, the police set up an impromptu holding facility in the parking lot of the Los Angeles Coliseum and proceeded to arrest more than 1,400 people, including more African American youth than in any other single incident since the Watts rebellions in 1965.[34] Over the course of the next six months, law enforcement jailed more than 18,000 people, declaring more than half of the arrests as "gang related." The price not only in human but financial terms was considerable; journalists estimated that "Operation Hammer" cost up to $150,000 per day.[35] Significantly, the prosecutors charged only a handful of people with actual crimes.

So, the question is, how does this story of racial punishment and domestic warfare fit within a broader history of neoliberalism's advance? The answer is not as neat as we might wish. The intense militarization of policing combined with the expansion of the incarceration state are crucial aspects of what we think of as the neoliberal era. Nevertheless, tracing a precise tale of origins is complex because, as we see, racialized policing, criminalization, and assertion of territorial control extends far back in time. Indeed, as the work of Kelly Lytle Hernandez, Sally Hadden, Richard Slotkin, and many others shows, these processes extend well into pre-statehood California and even colonial-era American settlement.[36] Racial criminalization and punishment is a *longue durée* story in US history, and the last fifty years are arguably a change in degree rather than kind.

Neoliberalism, Race, and Punishment

Nevertheless, the sheer scale in the numbers of people incarcerated and the proliferation of municipal, state, and federal agencies devoted to fighting the modern wars on drugs, gangs, and crime does matter. Despite problems of periodization and continuity with previous historical eras, when both late twentieth-century Los Angeles and the broader United States are assessed in hindsight, one of the first and most striking elements is the reallocation of municipal and federal resources from "a social state to a penal state" (to draw on one of Loïc Wacquant's earlier formulations).[37] This policy shift took two major forms: a diversion in federal financing from provision to punishment and the expanded "privatization of costs" through asset forfeiture. In order to really understand the interconnections between neoliberalism and punishment, we need more city-, county-, and state-level studies examining government officials' financial incentives for supporting the punitive turn as a way to capture federal dollars as the US government diverted revenue from entitlement spending to anti-crime funding agencies like the LEAA. Similarly, more detailed historical study of asset forfeiture, public private partnerships, and other revenue-generating activities of law enforcement is also sorely needed.[38]

In this regard, the case study of Los Angeles is instructive. Historically, Los Angeles had a comparatively small municipal infrastructure like other western cities in the United States that contrasted with the better-developed urban bureaucracies of Eastern Seaboard and midwestern cities.[39] This lack of capacity was further exacerbated by the oil shocks and tax revolts of the late 1970s. Los Angeles Mayor Tom Bradley relied on federal grants to pay for up to 75% of the city's social welfare expenditures. However, when the Reagan administration cut federal monies to American cities, service delivery plummeted, while federal funding for law enforcement increased significantly. This reallocation of resources was aided by the expanded use of civil forfeiture in which persons accused (not convicted) of drug crimes could have their personal property seized, including cash, cars, boats, and even homes. Between 1984 and 1990, this "privatization" of police funding netted the LAPD a return of $20,746,935.21. Indeed, they took in so much money that there was uncertainty about exactly how to spend it.[40]

As discussed earlier, another challenge for bringing together neoliberal analysis with historical studies of race and the carceral state is the difficulty of periodization and continuity with earlier eras. As the work of Khalil Muhammad and others have shown, the criminalization of African Americans is an enduring thread of US history that precedes, includes, and postdates the New Deal social welfare state.[41] Therefore, the emergence of racially disparate mass incarceration and the punishment campaigns in the early 1970s taps into previous social cleavages and accelerates these dynamics rather than inaugurating them. Criminalization and expansion of the carceral state cannot be attributed exclusively to larger neoliberal structures of governance or rationality and their negative effects on the poor, as some have argued.[42] In the case of the LAPD, anti-black bias and the targeting of leftists and other radical activists under the reign of William Parker, Chief Daryl Gates's mentor, profoundly influenced subsequent policing practices in the war on drugs, gangs, and so-called street terrorists.[43]

This is not to say that larger neoliberal currents did not have important effects on black and brown communities. In addition to the technological advances and new matrices of criminalization in the 1980s and 1990s that led to mass tracking, surveillance, and prosecution of youth of color, another striking aspect of the neoliberal era is the difficulty activists faced while trying to mobilize systematic opposition to these repressive measures. Legal scholar Dorothy Roberts developed an important formulation to try to explain why African American women advocates she interviewed from the contemporary foster care system simultaneously embraced more punitive controls on foster parents and greater financial subsidy. "I came to realize that this apparent paradox reflects the consequences of neoliberal social reforms," noted Roberts. "As these neighborhoods are stripped of social programs in the government's shift to market solutions for poverty, residents must increasingly rely on more institutions to meet their needs."[44]

The history of black Los Angeles in the 1980s and 1990s offers some compelling insights into why populations most affected by punishment campaigns have found it so difficult to launch sustained and effective opposition against carceral policies until very recently. There are multiple reasons for this. In the case of Los Angeles, one of the most important elements is the support of a highly visible "black leadership class" for law and order policies. In its formative years, Los Angeles's war on gangs and drugs took place under a black mayor and former police captain, Thomas Bradley, who was elected by a multi-racial coalition that brought together black voters form South L.A. with the historic liberal power base on the West side.[45] The contradictions of the Bradley administration have a great deal to tell us, not only about elite embrace of punishment in the age of mass incarceration, but about the fate of African American elected officials in the period after the long black freedom struggle.[46] The Bradley administration sought to simultaneously reform the police while expanding the number of officers and promoting law and order politics. Despite the historic enmity between Mayor Bradley and police chief Daryl Gates, the mayor used comparable language when he routinely referred to gang members as "urban terrorists."[47]

The sense of social crisis created by widespread unemployment, capital abandonment, and failure to provide adequate public health and social welfare support to impoverished communities during the crack cocaine era was crucial background to black elite support for carceral policies.[48] During the 1980s, much of the discourse from black politicians and the press centered on the "crisis" of crack cocaine addiction and sale rather than on the repressive apparatus of the war(s) on drugs, gangs, and crime. In Los Angeles, at the epicenter of the crack economy, the scale of panic engendered can hardly be overestimated. In 1989, Congresswoman Maxine Waters declared, "The most urgent problem facing ghettoized African Americans today is the lethal infestation of drugs in our communities."[49] Although the solutions that Waters sought emphasized social welfare and public health for troubled neighborhoods reeling from Reagan-era divestment, unwittingly the lens of crisis strengthened law enforcement's justification for the war on drugs and gangs, and provided it with a thin humanitarian veil.

African American class politics in the era of neoliberalism proved integral to community approaches to the drug wars.[50] Historically, black Angelenos had the largest intra-racial income gap nationally, and economic disparity shaped how different strata understood the war on drugs. In the early 1980s, white-led middle-class reformist organizations sponsored popular marches that called attention to the plight of neighborhoods in South Central and East Los Angeles. In July 1985, shortly after the ACLU won an injunction against the use of the LAPD's battering ram on residents' homes, nearly 10,000 residents gathered on the downtown campus of St. Mary's College for an anti-crime rally. The Southern California Organizing Committee (SCOC) and East Los Angeles's United Neighborhoods Organization (UNO) co-sponsored the protest. Formed in 1982 by a network of churches, SCOC's demands revealed a mixture of law and order politics with maternalist advocacy for social welfare and youth programs.

Given historical fights for adequate policing and higher rates of violent crime in South Los Angeles—African Americans were six times more likely to be killed by homicide than whites—their concerns were not surprising. Nevertheless, the hallmarks of militarized law enforcement remained unmistakable in their punitive vision of reform. SCOC and UNO advocated establishing "combat zone" teams drawn from multiple law enforcement agencies to target "gangs" and "drug traffickers" in high crime areas; higher taxes on liquor to pay for more police; increases in federal drug agents in Los Angeles; and perhaps most important, building a black and brown coalition to force local officials to provide more police protection. "We come here to make a choice today," argued Father Luis Olivares of La Placita Catholic Church, "We can fight those who stuff drugs into our children, or we can just sit on our butts and wish that it weren't so."[51]

In the context of massive cuts to American cities under the Reagan administration, carceral solutions to the problems of impoverished communities had much greater efficacy than redistributive liberalism. Rather than approaching the problem from the standpoint of public health or structural inequality (deindustrialization, outsourcing, capital flight, etc.), these early reformers looked to the problems and contradictions within impoverished neighborhoods. Christian churches, in particular, played an important role in advocating for more punitive, self-help approaches. Exploring how welfare retrenchment, militarized law enforcement, and its crisis-driven rationale fostered an increasingly conservative grassroots "politics of personal responsibility" is an under-studied theme not only in the history of Los Angeles, but throughout black America in the neoliberal era.

While more research is needed into these new areas of historical inquiry, African American elite responses to the wars on drugs, gangs, and crime cannot be understood in isolation from the rest of late twentieth-century American governance. It is clear that black politicians reflected rather than drove the punitive turn in criminal justice.[52] Presidents Ronald Reagan, George Herbert Walker Bush, and William Jefferson Clinton all deployed bombastic rhetoric against Aid to Families with Dependent Children (AFDC) recipients, drug users, sellers, and other vulnerable segments of the urban poor to justify new instruments of mass criminalization and the cutting of social welfare programs. In the last decades of the twentieth century, multiple levels of government and the mainstream press effectively co-opted much of the anger and disorientation created by social crisis inside impoverished neighborhoods into an anti-crime framework that blamed the alleged "pathological culture" of black men, women, and children for the problems of poverty and urban divestment. The welfare queen and the super-predator played a pivotal role not only as tropes of color-blind racism, but also as powerful ideological retinue for discrediting the redistributive welfare state.[53] As Clarence Lang has argued, the mythic underclass "became the key social category that legitimized neoliberal policy in the United States. . . . [It] was the literal bête noir that elected officials, social scientists, campaign strategists, and media . . . used to mobilize a popular consensus against the liberal social welfare policies of the New Deal and Great Society, including those benefiting the comfortable white middle classes."[54]

While it is clear that major sectors of local black elites and home-owners supported Los Angeles's punishment campaigns, ranging from Thomas Bradley's administration to rank-and-file participants in SCOC, the responses of the majority of low-income residents in South and East Los Angeles remain much harder to discern through traditional historical sources. As historians document resistance to the carceral state and the war on drugs, exploring how social service retrenchment, neoliberal restructuring, and pro-market governance influenced African American and Latinx modes of protest is crucial background. In contrast to the era of the Great Society and the long black freedom movement, by the early 1990s, not-for-profits and community development corporations competed with grassroots social movement groups as the legitimate medium for organized dissent.[55] Future California State Assembly Speaker and Congresswoman Karen Bass's Community Coalition For Substance Abuse, Prevention and Treatment (abbreviated Community Coalition or CC) offers a compelling example of a larger structural shift in political modalities of protest in this period.

In 1990, Bass sponsored an inaugural conference "Crack: Crisis in the African American Community" to help launch the Community Coalition. The new organization countered the rationale for militarized law enforcement by redefining crack and addiction more broadly as a public "health crisis." Having worked as a physician's assistant at the Los Angeles County–USC Hospital emergency room, Bass had witnessed firsthand the devastating effects of addiction. "I just really became obsessed with how the drug problem, specifically the crack epidemic, was impacting the community," she later explained.[56]

From its inception, the Community Coalition saw itself as working inside the parameters of the "community partnerships" model supported by the Bush era Department of Health and Human Services (DHHS). Rather than a grassroots social movement organization, Community Coalition was a nonprofit that initially sought funding from the Office of Substance Abuse Prevention and private foundations. In the realm of public policy, early participants in the Coalition discussed mandatory school counseling, drug/gang diversion programs, and use of "forfeiture-seizure" monies to finance drug treatment.[57] Bass subsequently became involved in local gang prevention efforts by serving on the Los Angeles City Council's ad hoc Committee on Gangs, Youth and Violence, which sponsored the L.A. Bridges After-School Gang Prevention Program.[58]

"Our mission, essentially, is to address the drug and alcohol problems of the community," Bass explained. "We don't do that by providing direct services such as treatment or counseling, but we do that by organizing and empowering community residents to change the environment that creates drug and alcohol problems in the first place."[59] In contrast to the state-sponsored war on drugs, Community Coalition redirected the public's focus from illicit drugs like heroine and crack cocaine to the licit commodities of alcohol and tobacco saturating South Los Angeles.[60] The group did not directly confront the most punitive aspects of carceral drug policy, including anti-gang injunctions and asset forfeiture, whose monies it hoped to reallocate to fund drug treatment. Instead, the Coalition's most sustained activism centered on preventing the re-opening of liquor stores after the Los Angeles rebellion of 1992.[61]

Modeling their efforts on homeowner associations, the Community Coalition sought to organize neighborhood residents to clean up the streets in South L.A. By eliminating the environment that fostered crime and addiction, including liquor stores, transient hotels, open-air sex and drug markets, CC sought to rebuild community and transform the "hopelessness and despair" of South Central Los Angeles.[62] While the Community Coalition played an important role in promoting public health approaches to the perceived drug crisis in the city, the organization also reflected the shifting political terrain of the 1980s and 1990s. The case of Community Coalition is particularly striking because Karen Bass herself had long-standing ties to black left organizations and study circles. By many accounts, she represented one of the more caring and progressive black politicians in Los Angeles. Nevertheless, the Coalition's modern temperance approach and related focus on environmental- and behavior-based solutions to the crack crisis and its companion punishment campaigns highlighted the narrowing constraints within which reform efforts operated in late twentieth-century Los Angeles.

In contrast to postwar black radical activism, by the late twentieth century, nonprofits had increasingly displaced independent, subscriber-based organizations. While 501(c)(3)s should not be categorically condemned, a diverse array of scholars and activists have criticized the ways in which nonprofits diverted the attention of grassroots organizing from political mobilization to the more mundane problems of qualifying for external funding to pay for staff and facilities. Often the transformation from a grassroots participatory style of organizing to more elite, post-collegiate personnel, who have little commonality with the low-income populations they often purported to represent, created important tensions and contradictions. Drawing inspiration from a wide-ranging interdisciplinary scholarship on the centrality of Non-Governmental Organizations (NGOs) to neoliberal restructuring globally, more scholarship is emerging on nonprofits as the NGO's domestic analogue in the

United States. Researchers emphasize, for example, how the nonprofit model has helped to divert "public monies into private hands" through foundation tax exemptions, while simultaneously allowing business interests to revitalize their public image through corporate philanthropy. As home to the Broad, Annenberg, and Milken Family Foundations and dozens of other peer institutions, Los Angeles is one of the major centers of what scholar Dylan Rodriguez has provocatively termed "the non-for-profit industrial complex." While the case of Community Coalition offers some intriguing hints, more research is needed into how the late twentieth-century shift in protest politics affected radical organizing against racialized punishment campaigns.[63]

Michael Zinzun and the Coalition Against Police Abuse

The most enduring voice against police violence in Los Angeles was former Black Panther Michael Zinzun and the Coalition Against Police Abuse (CAPA). Founded in 1976, CAPA drew on the anti-capitalist and anti-statist tendencies of the Black Panther Party, while seeking to build a multi-racial organization without a fixed system of hierarchy. Its motto, "We will work with you not for you," reflected a preference for egalitarian decentralized styles of organizing.[64] Starting out with a handful of participants in the late 1970s, CAPA compiled documentation of police abuse and murders in the Los Angeles area using statistics, photographs, media clippings, and interviews. When the LAPD, under pressure from the Coalition and other police accountability groups, released a list of its employees of color, Zinzun noted that thirteen of CAPA's past and present members, including his own secretary, were on the police department's payroll. In 1981, with the ACLU's assistance, CAPA filed a successful lawsuit against the Los Angeles Police Commission charging that the LAPD's Public Disorder Intelligence Division (PDID) had violated their civil liberties. On the eve of the Los Angeles drug war, CAPA and its fellow plaintiffs won a $1.8 million settlement that ultimately led to the disbanding of the PDID.[65] Unfortunately, this victory proved short-lived when the Anti-Terrorist Division (ATD) replaced its predecessor. And in 1984, after attempting to intervene in the assault of another man, Michael Zinzun was beaten so badly by Pasadena police that he lost sight in one eye.[66]

Despite these setbacks, CAPA and its small circle of activists continued to teach community members how to document police abuses, utilize media attention, and wage legal campaigns during the height of the Los Angeles militarized drug war. While the Coalition created an intergenerational channel for organizing, it never succeeded in building a large base in South Central Los Angeles. However, in the early 1990s, CAPA gained greater visibility in the aftermath of the Rodney King beatings. As a bridge between an older generation of black power radicals and younger Angelenos, CAPA's most important role was as a clearinghouse for new activist formations. The Coalition worked so closely with the organizers of the Community in Support of the Gang Truce (CSGT) that they shared offices.[67]

After the 1992 rebellion in Los Angeles, CAPA's criticisms of state violence, police militarization, and mass incarceration gained greater visibility. At the height of the city's militarized war on drugs and gangs, CAPA's small cadre of activists taught community members how to document police abuses, utilize media, and wage legal campaigns. Michael Zinzun's successful lawsuits against the LAPD and Pasadena police, penetrating analysis, and nurturance of younger activists helped forge an intergenerational channel for radical activism. Nevertheless, the group really struggled during the 1980s to attract a broader base and often found itself overshadowed by more mainstream, punitive efforts. In the early 1990s, however, CAPA gained greater visibility as the carceral effects of a decade-long war on black and brown youth became visible in the vast increase in the number of youths of color who were incarcerated. From 1982 to 1995, the numbers of African Americans in the CDC increased three and a half-fold from 12,470 to 42,296, while Latinx incarceration grew more than fivefold from 9,006 to 46,080.[68]

The history of the Coalition Against Police Abuse offers an intriguing example of how we might differentiate black poor and working-class "drug war politics" from their neoliberal counterparts. In the early 1990s, a palpable shift became visible as a variety of African American-led organizations proposed alternate frameworks to the city's punishment campaigns against drugs and gangs. The cumulative effects of mass criminalization, mandatory minimum sentencing, disparate crack prosecution, and the expansive municipal, state, and federal apparatus created to criminalize drug use, distribution, and alleged gang participation resulted in an explosion of the jail and prison population. As residents watched this happen, a commitment to developing less punitive approaches emerged. Redefining the crack crisis in terms of public health, structural economic decline, and as a product of Reagan-era anti-communist foreign policy became powerful tools for mobilizing anti–drug war sentiment in L.A.'s African American community.

Zinzun's organization offered a sharp contrast to Community Coalition and corporatist neighborhood advocacy of organizations like SCOC and UNO, who have subsequently emerged as supporters of school charterization. Together with Mothers Reclaim Our Children (ROC), CAPA and its network of grassroots radicals embodied an earlier protest ethos in which poor and working-class populations of color, who suffered the worst effects of L.A.'s militarized drug wars, began mobilizing against gang suppression and mass incarceration. Far to the left of black elected officials, the local clergy and nonprofit organizers, CAPA, and Mothers ROC highlight a number of compelling issues for studying the difference between corporate and foundation funded groups and more grassroots efforts to oppose the programs and policies of carceral state expansion, all of whom were forced to reckon with neoliberal incentives and constraints.[69]

* * *

In studying Los Angeles's punishment campaigns against drugs and gangs in the neoliberal era, what is most striking is the scale of resources deployed against some of the most vulnerable populations in the city, who are simultaneously marginalized by and central to late twentieth-century governance. Given the scale of the penal infrastructure in Los Angeles and its development of new forms of militarized policing, the city is an integral part of the larger national history of mass incarceration. As future scholarship seeks to bridge histories of the carceral state with the growing historical literature on neoliberalism, more research is needed into how racial capitalism and extraction have informed neoliberal modes of governance. The private contracting of drug abstinence programs, the development of "offender funded justice" after the LA Rebellions of 1992, and perhaps most important, the obstacles faced by individual activists and organizations attempting to mobilize populations of color against the overlapping war(s) on drugs and gangs, are all crucial themes for future inquiry. Equally important is the tracing of class fractures inside the black and brown communities in the decades after the civil rights movement. Finally, drawing on the new scholarship on liberal law and order politics, more research into electoral politics of the war on drugs at the municipal and state levels is needed.[70] There is still so much that we do not know. To broach these new arenas of knowledge, it is necessary to bring together the insights from historical carceral studies with the broader political and economic cross-currents of late twentieth-century America. Perhaps integrating these two realms will allow us to better grasp not only racial punishment's shift in degree and scale, but why it has proved so impervious to resistance in Los Angeles and other cities across the country.

NOTES

I would like to thank Heather Thompson, Julilly Kohler-Hausman, Thomas Sugrue, and Andrew Diamond for suggestions and insights that have informed this chapter in significant ways. Portions of this chapter are taken from an earlier version: Donna Murch, "Crack in Los Angles: Crisis, Militarization, and Black Response to the Late Twentieth-Century War on Drugs," *Journal of American History* 102:1 (June 2015), 162–73.

1   Mike Davis, *City of Quartz: Excavating the Future in Los Angeles* (New York: Verso, 1990); Edward Soja, *Postmodern Geographies: The Reassertion of Space in Critical Social Theory* (New York: Verso, 1989).

2   Max Felker-Kantor, *Policing Los Angeles: Race, Resistance, and the Rise of the LAPD* (Chapel Hill, NC: University of North Carolina Press, 2018); Davis, *City of Quartz*.

3   On neoliberalism: Daniel Stedman Jones, *Masters of the Universe: Hayek, Friedman and the Birth of Neoliberal Politics* (Princeton, NJ: Princeton University Press, 2012); Angus Burgin, *The Great Persuasion: Reinventing Free Markets Since the Great Depression* (Cambridge, MA: Harvard University Press, 2012); David Harvey, *A Brief History of Neoliberalism* (New York: Oxford University Press, 2005); Loïc Wacquant, *Punishing the Poor: The Neoliberal Government of Social Insecurity* (Durham, NC: Duke University Press, 2009); Wendy Brown, *Undoing the Demos: Neoliberalism's Stealth Revolution* (New York: Zone, 2015); Naomi Klein, *The Shock Doctrine and Disaster Capitalism* (New York: Picador, 2008). For accounts that shed light on the contours of neoliberalization in the Sunbelt,, see Kirkpatrick Sale, *Powershift: The Rise of the Southern Rim and Its Challenge to the Eastern Establishment (New York: Random House, 1975)*; Andrew Needham, *Powerlines: Phoenix and the Making of the Modern Southwest* (Princeton, NJ: Princeton University Press, 2014); Elizabeth Tandy Shermer, *Sunbelt Capitalism: Phoenix and the Transformation of American Politics* (Philadelphia: University of Pennsylvania Press, 2013); Michelle Nickerson

and Darren Dochuk, *Sunbelt Rising: The Politics of Space, Place, and Region* (Philadelphia: University of Pennsylvania Press, 2013).

4 Michelle Alexander, *The New Jim Crow: Mass Incarceration in the Age of Colorblindness* (New York: New Press, 2012); Amy E. Lerman and Vesla M. Weaver, *Arresting Citizenship: The Democratic Consequences of American Crime Control* (Chicago: University of Chicago Press, 2014); Kathleen J. Frydl, *The Drug Wars in America, 1940–1973* (New York: Cambridge University Press, 2013); Naomi Murakawa, *The First Civil Right: How Liberals Built Prison America* (New York: Oxford University Press, 2014); Heather Thompson, Kelly Lytle-Hernandez, and Khalil Muhammad, "Introduction: Constructing the Carceral State," *Journal of American History* 102:1 (June 2015), 18–24; Heather Thompson and Donna Murch, "Urban America and the Carceral State," special section of the *Journal of Urban History* 41:5 (September 2015).

5 George Lipsitz, *The Possessive Investment in Whiteness: How White People Profit from Identity Politics* (Philadelphia: Temple University Press, 1998).

6 Murakawa, *The First Civil Right*; Elizabeth Hinton, *From the War on Poverty to the War on Crime: The Making of Mass Incarceration in America* (Cambridge, MA: Harvard University Press, 2016).

7 Frances Fox Piven, *Regulating the Poor: The Functions of Public Welfare* (New York: Vintage, 1993); Ira Katznelson, *When Affirmative Action Was White* (New York: W.W. Norton, 2011); Linda Gordon, *Pitied But Not Entitled: Single Women and the History of Welfare* (New York: Free Press, 1994); Annelise Orleck, *Storming Caesar's Palace: How Black Mothers Fought Their Own War on Poverty* (Boston: Beacon Press, 2006); Jefferson Cowie and Nick Salvatore, "The Long Exception: Rethinking the Place of the New Deal in American History," *International Labor and Working-Class History* 74 (Fall 2008), 3–32.

8 Ruth Wilson Gilmore, *Golden Gulag: Prisons, Surplus, Crisis and Opposition in Globalizing California* (Los Angeles: University of California Press, 2007); Gilmore's book pioneered a structuralist analysis of the economic interests supporting the punitive turn in California, but much more historical research needs to be done to uncover the specific historical actors and entities.

9 Radley Balko, *Rise of the Warrior Cop: The Militarization of America's Armed Forces* (New York: Public Affairs, 2013), 140–41.

10 Max Felker-Kantor, "Managing Marginalization from Watts to Rodney King: The Struggle over Policing and Social Control in Los Angeles, 1965–1992" (PhD diss., University of Southern California, 2014), 378–79.

11 Wendy Brown interviewed in Timothy Shenk, "Booked #3: What Exactly Is Neoliberalism?" *Dissent*, April 2, 2015, https://www.dissentmagazine.org/blog/booked-3-what-exactly-is-neoliberalism-wendy-brown-undoing-the-demos; Wendy Brown, *Undoing the Demos: Neoliberalism's Stealth Revolution* (New York: Zone, 2015).

12 More study and reflection are needed to consider how expanded state capacity in the New Deal forward intersects with Michel Foucault's interpretation of neolib-

eralism as a "reprogramming of liberalism"; Shenk, "Booked #3"; Brown, *Undoing the Demos*.

13 Nancy MacLean, "Southern Dominance in Borrowed Language: The Regional Origins of Neoliberalism," in *New Landscapes of Inequality: Neoliberalism and the Erosion of Democracy in America*, ed. Jane L. Collins, Micaela di Leonardo, and Brett Williams (Santa Fe, NM: School for Advanced Research Press, 2008).

14 Gilmore, *Golden Gulag*, 108; Joe Domanick, *To Protect and to Serve: The LAPD's Century of War in the City of Dreams* (Los Angeles: Figueroa Press, 2003), 322; John C. Quicker, Yvonne Nunley Galeai, and Akil Batani-Khalfani, "Bootstrap or Noose: Drugs in South Central Los Angeles," unpublished paper in author's possession; Soja, *Postmodern Geographies*, 193.

15 Michael Tonry, *Malign Neglect: Race, Crime and Punishment in America* (New York: Oxford University Press, 1995); Marc Mauer and Ryan S. King, *A 25-Year Quagmire: The War on Drugs and Its Impact on American Society* (Washington, DC: The Sentencing Project, Research and Advocacy for Reform, 2007); see also n. 6.

16 Gilmore, *Golden Gulag*, 108, 110–11, 185.

17 Domanick, *To Protect and to Serve*, 11–12, 207–8. Daryl Gates, *Chief: My Life in the L.A.P.D.* (New York: Bantam, 1992), 105–23, 131–39, 355. For official institutional histories of SWAT within the Los Angeles Police Department (LAPD), see "S.W.A.T.," *Official Site of the Los Angeles Police Department*, http://www.lapdonline.org/inside_the_lapd/content_basic_view/848; "History of S.W.A.T.," ibid., http://www.lapdonline.org/metropolitan_division/content_basic_view/849; and "History of the Metro Division," ibid., http://www.lapdonline.org/metropolitan_division/content_basic_view/6359.

18 Gates, *Chief*, 266–68.

19 Felker-Kantor, "Managing Marginalization from Watts to Rodney King," 141, 368, 372, 377; Gates, *Chief*, 292.

20 Davis, *City of Quartz*, 268. Article dates are misquoted in footnotes; for correct article citations, see *Los Angeles Times (hereafter LAT)*, April 3, 1988 and April 6, 1988; Donna Murch, "The Many Meanings of Watts: Black Power, 'Wattstax,' and the Carceral State," *OAH Magazine of History* 26:1 (January 2012), 37–40.

21 Balko, *Rise of the Warrior Cop*, 145; Ronald Reagan, "Remarks Announcing Federal Initiatives Against Drug Trafficking and Organized Crime," October 14, 1982, available at http://www.presidency.ucsb.edu/ws/index.php?pid=43127.

22 Domanick, *To Protect and to Serve*; Eric Malnic, "Sky Patrol Arm of the Law Goes to New Heights," *LAT*, April 3, 1988; "History of the Air Support Division," Official Site of the Los Angeles Police Department, http://www.lapdonline.org/air_support_division/content_basic_view/1179.

23 Felker-Kantor, "Managing Marginalization from Watts to Rodney King," 421.

24 Gates, *Chief*, 287; Ronald J. Ostrow, "Casual Drug Users Should Be Shot, Gates Says," *LAT*, September 16, 1990.

25 Felker-Kantor, "Managing Marginalization from Watts to Rodney King," 409–10.

26 Domanick, *To Protect and to Serve*, 328–29.

27 Quicker et al., "Bootstrap or Noose," 30; Francisco Delgado, "The Drugs Connection: Cocaine Is Big Business on Southland's Shady Sidewalks," *Long Beach Press Telegram*, December 16, 1986; Felker-Kantor, "Managing Marginalization from Watts to Rodney King," 369, 409, 412.

28 Felker-Kantor, "Managing Marginalization from Watts to Rodney King," 378; Domanick, *To Protect and to Serve*; Dan Baum, *Smoke and Mirrors: The War on Drugs and the Politics of Failure* (New York: Back Bay Books, 1996), 141–42; Balko, *Rise of the Warrior Cop*, 140–141.

29 Mike Davis, "Los Angeles: Civil Liberties between the Hammer and the Rock," *New Left Review*, I/170 (July–August 1988), 44; Beth Caldwell, "Criminalizing Day-to-Day Life: A Socio-Legal Critique of Gang Injunctions," *American Journal of Criminal Law* 37:3 (2010), 245; Nina Siegel, "Ganging Up on Civil Liberties," *Progressive* 61 (October 1997), 28–31.

30 Felker-Kantor, "Managing Marginalization from Watts to Rodney King," 381–83; Siegel, "Ganging Up on Civil Liberties"; Caldwell, "Criminalizing Day-to-Day Life," 241–90.

31 Gilmore, *Golden Gulag*, 108.

32 Additional revisions to STEP were issued in 2007 and 2013; Sara Lynn Hofwegen, "Unjust and Ineffective: A Critical Look at California's Step Act," *Southern California Interdisciplinary Law Journal* 18 (2009), 679–701. Informal conversation with gang expert Alex Alonso, May 8, 2014; First District Appellate Project, http://wiki.fdap.org/main_page/gangs.

33 Baum, *Smoke and Mirrors*, 250.

34 Gates, *Chief*; Davis, *City of Quartz*, 37; Felker-Kantor, "Managing Marginalization from Watts to Rodney King," 401.

35 Robert Welkos, "700 Seized in Gang Sweeps," *LAT*, September 19, 1988. Quicker et al., "Bootstrap or Noose," 16.

36 Kelly Lytle Hernandez, "Hobos in Heaven: Race, Incarceration, and the Rise of Los Angeles, 1880–1910," *Pacific Historical Review* 83:3 (August 2014), 410–47; Sally Hadden, *Slave Patrols: Law and Violence in Virginia and the Carolinas* (Cambridge, MA: Harvard University Press, 2003); Richard Slotkin, "Narratives of Negro Crime in New England, 1675–1800," *American Quarterly* 25:1 (1973), 3–31; Leslie C. Patrick Stamp, "The Numbers That Are Not New: African Americans in the Country's First Prison, 1790–1835," *Pennsylvania Magazine of History and Biography* 119 (1995), 95–128.

37 Loïc Wacquant, *Prisons of Poverty* (Minneapolis: University of Minnesota Press, 1999).

38 In the contemporary moment, the recent report from the Department of Justice on the city of Ferguson in St. Louis County is a fascinating look at the ways in which criminalization of black populations was used to fund significant portions of the municipalities budget. More historical research is needed to trace the origins and duration of these practices throughout the United States; https://www.

justice.gov/sites/default/files/opa/press-releases/attachments/2015/03/04/fergu-son_police_department_report.pdf. For the Ferguson report in context, see Colin Gordon, *Citizen Brown: Race, Democracy, and Inequality in the St. Louis Suburbs* (Chicago: University of Chicago Press, 2019).

39 Amy Bridges, *Morning Glories: Municipal Reform in the Southwest* (Princeton, NJ: Princeton University Press, 1997).

40 Felker-Kantor, "Managing Marginalization from Watts to Rodney King," 379; Domanick, *To Protect and to Serve.*

41 Khalil Muhammad, *The Condemnation of Blackness: Race, Crime, and the Making of Modern America* (Cambridge, MA: Harvard University Press, 2010); Lytle Hernandez, "Hobos in Heaven; Slotkin, "Narratives of Negro Crime in New England."

42 Wacquant, *Punishing the Poor.*

43 Muhammad, *The Condemnation of Blackness*; Wacquant, *Punishing the Poor.*

44 Dorothy Roberts, "The Racial Geography of State Child Protection," in *New Landscapes of Inequality: Neoliberalism and the Erosion of Democracy in America*, ed. Jane L. Collins, Micaela di Leonardo, and Brett Williams (Santa Fe, NM: School for Advanced Research Press, 2008).

45 Raphael J. Sonenshein, *Politics in Black and White: Race and Power in Los Angeles* (Princeton, NJ: Princeton University Press, 1993).

46 See Keeanga-Yamahtta Taylor, *From #BlackLivesMatter to Black Liberation* (Chicago: Haymarket Press, 2016), especially chapter 3, which has made an important contribution to this discussion; Clarence Lang, *Colin Powell and Condoleezza Rice, Foreign Policy, Race and the New American Century* (New York: Praeger, 2006).

47 Felker-Kantor, "Managing Marginalization from Watts to Rodney King," 355. There is currently a vibrant debate about the racial politics of law and order campaigns among social scientists. For competing views see Vesla M. Weaver, "Frontlash: Race and the Development of Punitive Crime Policy," *Studies in American Political Development* 21 (Fall 2007), 230–65; Michael Javen Fortner, "The Carceral State and the Crucible of Black Politics: An Urban History of the Rockefeller Drug Laws," *Studies in American Political Development* 27 (April 2013), 14–35; and Michael Javen Fortner, "The 'Silent Majority' in Black and White: Invisibility and Imprecision in the Historiography of Mass Incarceration," *Journal of Urban History* 40:2 (March 2014), 252–82.

48 For a more extended discussion of crisis as essential background to black elite support for the wars on drugs and gangs, see Murch, "Crack in Los Angeles." For more general scholarship on the importance of crisis to conservative policy shifts, see also Stuart Hall et al., *Policing the Crisis: Mugging, the State, and Law and Order* (London: Palgrave, 1978); and Naomi Klein, *The Shock Doctrine and Disaster Capitalism* (New York: Picador, 2008).

49 Maxine Waters, "Drugs, Democrats and Priorities," *The Nation*, July 24/31, 1989, 141.

50 In an earlier draft, I used the "post-civil rights" era to refer to this period. These two different conceptualizations of the late twentieth century need to be more

carefully engaged and integrated. Loïc Wacquant makes this slippage in *Punishing the Poor* but does not adequately address its meaning theoretically in relationship to neoliberalism.

51 Felker-Kantor, "Managing Marginalization from Watts to Rodney King," 357–58, 365, 389–96; Darnell Hunt, *Black Los Angeles: American Dreams and Racial Realities* (New York: New York University Press, 2010); Edward J. Boyer, "Dual Goal Told at Rally: Strike at Crime, Win Olympic Funds," *LAT*, July 15, 1985.

52 For a contrary point of view, see Michael Javen Fortner, *Black Silent Majority: The Rockefeller Drug Laws and the Politics of Punishment* (Cambridge, MA: Harvard University Press, 2015); Donna Murch, "Who's to Blame for Mass Incarceration?" *Boston Review*, October 16, 2015.

53 For new research in this vein, see Rosemary Ndubuizu, "Where Shall the Monsters Live? Black Women and the Politics of Urban Disposability," dissertation in progress, Rutgers University.

54 Clarence Lang, *Black America in the Shadow of the Sixties: Notes on the Civil Rights Movement, Neoliberalism, and Politics* (Ann Arbor: University of Michigan Press, 2015).

55 Felker-Kantor, "Managing Marginalization from Watts to Rodney King," 397, 388.

56 Karen Bass, "Alcohol's Relationship to Urban Violence: When Free Enterprise Threatens Community Welfare," *Black-Korean Encounter: Toward Understanding and Alliance*, ed. Eui-Young Yu (Los Angeles: Institute for Asian America and Pacific, 1994) 5, 6, 70–72. Angela Hill, "California Lawmaker Works to Improve Her Community," *The Crisis*, March/April 2005, 8.

57 Application for Crack Cocaine Conference by Karen Bass, Fall 1989, Liberty Hill Foundation Records, Box 35, Folder 6, Southern California Library.

58 Hill, "California Lawmaker Works to Improve Her Community," 8.

59 Bass, "Alcohol's Relationship to Urban Violence," 6.

60 For a *longue durée* history of African Americans and temperance, please see Denise A. Herd, "Contesting Culture: Alcohol Related Identity Movements in Contemporary African American Communities," *Contemporary Drug Problems* 20 (Winter 1993), 739–58.

61 Kyeyoung Park, "The Morality of a Commodity: A Case of 'Rebuilding L.A. without Liquor Stores," *Amerasia Journal* 21:3 (Winter 1995/1996), 1–24.

62 Application for Crack Cocaine Conference by Karen Bass, Fall 1989.

63 Dylan Rodriguez, "The Political Logic of the Non-Profit Industrial Complex," in *The Revolution Will Not Be Funded: Beyond the Not for Profit Industrial Complex*, ed. Incite! Women of Color Against Violence (Cambridge, MA: South End Press, 2007), 21–40. For a broader literature on the emergence of neoliberalism and civil society, please see Linsey McGoey, "The Philanthropy Hustle," *Jacobin* 19 (Fall 2015); Linsey McGoey, *No Such Thing as a Free Gift: The Gates Foundation and the Price of Philanthropy* (New York: Verso, 2015); Jane L. Collins, Micaela di Leonardo, and Brett Williams, *New Landscapes of Inequality: Neoliberalism and the Erosion of Democracy in America* (Santa Fe, NM: School for Advanced Research

Press, 2008); Stephen Rathgeb Smith and Michael Lipsky, *Nonprofits for Hire: The Welfare State in the Age of Contracting* (Cambridge, MA: Harvard University Press, 1998); John Arena, *Driven from New Orleans: How Nonprofits Betray Public Housing and Promote Privatization* (Minneapolis: University of Minnesota Press, 2012; Joan Roelofs, *Foundations and Public Policy: The Mask of Pluralism* (Albany: State University of New York Press, 2003).

64 Mary Pauline Roche, "Unfinished Business: The Production of Resistance to State Violence in London and Derry" (PhD diss., University of Southern California, 2004), 154; Joao H. Costa Vargas, *Catching Hell in the City of Angels: Life and Meanings of Blackness in South Central Los Angeles* (Minneapolis: University of Minnesota Press, 2006), 109–40.

65 Vargas, *Catching Hell in the City of Angels*, 119–21.

66 Gates, *Chief*, 230; Vargas, *Catching Hell in the City of Angels*, 122.

67 Vargas, *Catching Hell in the City of Angels*, 186–87.

68 On the increases in numbers of African Americans and Latinos in the California Department of Corrections, see Gilmore, *Golden Gulag*, 111, table 4.

69 Ibid., 181–240.

70 Hinton, *From the War on Poverty to the War on Crime*; Murakawa, *The First Civil Right*; Felker-Kantor, *Policing Los Angeles*.

6

Is Gentrification the Result of Neoliberalism?

The Cultural Making of the Real Estate Market in Boston's South End, 1965–2005

SYLVIE TISSOT

Everything seems to point to neoliberalism as the explanation for the phenomenon of gentrification. Neoliberalism is purportedly a determining factor in gentrification, which—according to some—even "brings about" or "reveals" neoliberalism. Gentrification in this view is not just a consequence of neoliberalism, but also its translation or symbol. In his work on "neoliberal gentrification," geographer Jason Hackworth describes this process as "a revealing window into much broader processes like neoliberalism."[1] In fact, how can one not draw a link between the rapid transformation of dilapidated downtown (inner-city) neighborhoods and market forces, specifically the real estate market? Isn't the exclusion of the poorest inhabitants, displaced by an increase in rents, the result of a shift in priorities among public authorities from the right to affordable housing to the attractiveness and competitiveness of cities?

The multitude of words certainly adds a dose of confusion to a debate that mixes political and social scientific considerations, as is often the case with this subject.[2] Are we speaking about "neoliberalism" as a doctrine that does not limit itself, along the lines of liberalism in the European sense, to advocating for a rule by markets to the detriment of government intervention, but instead imposes a market-based rationale in all spheres of social life, using government intervention whenever necessary to incentivize private development? Does neoliberalization benefit public policies and institutions? However vaguely defined, the concept has seeped into the world of urban studies. Wyly and Hammel, and Smith discuss a "neoliberal urbanism"—with gentrification as one of its key characteristics.[3] More recently, Hackworth identifies the "neo-

liberal city," not characterized merely by a governance subject to market logic, but by a growing dualization between the commercialization
of public spaces through privatization and the simultaneous control—
especially by the police—of these spaces, phenomena to which gentrification is said to contribute directly.[4]

Rather than characterizing the state of contemporary cities in this
manner—at the risk of homogenizing and creating a fictive binary between the "old" and the "new"—the discussion of neoliberalism and
gentrification would benefit from greater historical and sociological precision. This is complicated by the fact that the current debate about neoliberalism and gentrification has also called into question the relevance
of a standard model, developed primarily by Neil Smith. Smith insists
on the role of supply created by the return of economic investors to city
centers, establishing a close connection between the two phenomena.
In one of his major articles, Smith, a neo-Marxist geographer, proposed
a three-step chronology that emphasizes the 1990s as a turning point.
According to Smith, the first wave of gentrification consisted of artists
and other marginal figures in the 1950s–1970s; from the end of the 1970s
to the end of the 1980s, this phenomenon extended to other neighborhoods due to the intervention of real estate developers. Gentrification
then became generalized in the mid-1990s. Planned by government authorities who worked hand in hand with investors, it began to reach
non-central neighborhoods.[5]

Through a case study of Boston and its South End neighborhood, this
chapter demonstrates the links, on one hand, between the city's integration into globalized capitalism and the neoliberalization of its urban
policies, and, on the other, the transformation of a gentrified neighborhood. Building on the work of Zukin and Mele, I extend this line of
analysis to studying how "gentrified property" was created through the
means of its own representation.[6]

To market the underdeveloped South End and thus accelerate the
transformation of its real estate market, it was first necessary to construct
a South End made up of "artists." Neoliberalism only partially explains
this story. A socio-historic analysis of the actors involved reveals the decisive role played by South End residents themselves, who mobilized as
part of continuous, collective local mobilization between the late 1960s
and the late 1980s. In this period, newcomers to the South End sought

to increase the value of their neighborhood by distancing themselves from the stigma of its working-class, immigrant, black, and Hispanic character. In this sense, the "city" was already "revanchist," to use Neil Smith's term.[7] Moreover, the South End's new residents did not merely create a demand for gentrified housing, as upholders of the "cultural" approach to gentrification would have it.[8] It is true that their residential trajectory expressed new values that broke with traditional, middle-class suburban life. Yet, they also produced the city themselves, by creating a market with a new supply of housing and renovated "brownstones," and a new demand that generated and spread a "taste for the Victorian." The key actor in this phase of the neighborhood's history was the South End Historical Society, created in 1966, which played a role similar to civic organizations in other cities during this period. An analysis of the South End Historical Society and the later development of the South End as an "artists' enclave" will lead us to question Smith's three-step chronology and the weight he assigns to the last step.

The Social and Cultural Construction of a New Real Estate Market (1966–1990)

For Neil Smith, the gentrification spread by neoliberalism occurs in three phases. The last phase, that of its diffusion, stands in opposition to the first one, which is of a more "spontaneous" nature, and which involves "marginal" actors.[9] In his view, artists, intellectuals—people with a generally anti-establishment stance—unwittingly spur a gentrification process that then extends to other neighborhoods, even before being directly cultivated by private investors and public authorities. The case of Boston allows us to question this narrative and, thus, underline more complex links between gentrification and neoliberalism. A gentrifying market in city centers had already been developing long before neoliberalism began to leave its mark on politics. This was the result of new forms of investment in older urban neighborhoods, and primarily the mobilization of residents in the 1960s and 1970s, a process that was at once political, cultural, and of course economic. How did their local mobilizations contribute to the process of neoliberalization?

The gentrification of the South End must be analyzed in the context of postwar urban policy. Beginning in the 1950s, Boston had taken advantage of federal urban renewal funds to demolish and rebuild large parts of the city's downtown and surrounding, older, mostly working-class neighborhoods. The process resulted in large-scale displacement and spurred the outward movement of residents.[10] But urban renewal had the unanticipated consequence of sparking protests and resistance, which came to a head in the 1960s. In particular, anti-establishment activists resisted new urban renewal projects, fought to preserve their neighborhoods, and gained influence in city politics. In parts of the city slated for demolition, African American, Latinx, and white activists as well as counterculturally oriented residents and even conservative homeowners opposed the government in fighting the destruction of their neighborhood. The resistance to urban renewal was energized by 1960s antiwar, civil rights, and black power protests. In 1967, a group of activists, led by African American leader Mel King, formed the Community Assembly for a Unified South End (CAUSE) to demand greater investment in the community's development and citizen participation in the development process. Protests in the South End took on particular urgency after Martin Luther King's assassination on April 4, 1968. The working-class neighborhoods of the South End and Roxbury exploded in riots. A few weeks later, on April 26, 1968, African American and Puerto Rican protesters organized a march to demand the construction of affordable, public housing.

Protests changed the city's balance of power. In May 1969, the city's urban development agency (the Boston Redevelopment Authority) decided to suspend demolition and relocation operations, and to pledge a new commitment to "resident participation," that called for "democratically" oriented development, in part to diffuse protests. The shift in power relations also grew out of postwar efforts to reform Boston's political machine. Kevin White, who was elected mayor in 1968, sought to forge a new alliance that brought together "downtown business elites, ambitious political leaders seeking to modernize urban politics, middle class, good government reform groups, the professional city planners to whom they turned for advice, a powerful new stratum of public administrators, and private development interests, including developers, lenders, builders and the construction trade."[11] These actors became involved in the renewal of inner-city areas traditionally neglected by a city hall that had long redistributed public resources and services toward its bastions of political supporters, especially in South Boston and Dorchester, working-class, largely Irish American neighborhoods.

In the late 1960s, the South End attracted the attention of developers and at the same time attracted younger, upwardly mobile, mostly newcomers. Crucial to the process was the construction of the massive Prudential Tower in 1964. Built at the edge between the Back Bay and the South End, this tower was seen as a symbol of the old, dilapidated city's transformation into a "New Boston." It also had the effect of "extending downtown a mile to the south," meaning toward the South End.[12] Therefore, the beginnings of gentrification in the South End, as in many neighborhoods in other US cities, lacked the "spontaneous" nature that has been assigned to them by scholars like Smith. The South End's transformation was instead fundamentally connected to city politics.

The South End's new educated, upwardly mobile residents formed a particularly vocal and active community. And as the city launched the construction of social housing, it would also seek out and select interlocutors who supported its renewal efforts, especially the South End's newcomers, who were more receptive than radicals to White's modern, socially engaged style. In Boston, as in Brooklyn, City Hall approached young white professionals to get around the traditional networks of the "machine."[13] Gradually over the course of the next decades, this local elite would come to rally around the catchword "diversity," which it both flaunted and carefully controlled.

By the end of the 1960s, the South End's population of newcomers grew polarized. Some would join the ranks of local activist organizations committed to expanding affordable housing. Others would enter the more conservative South End Historical Society. This latter group would play a very particular role that illustrates the complex ways in which the supply and demand for gentrified housing was created. The Historical Society, created and nurtured by a number of real estate agents, would turn the South End's Victorian housing into a new, much sought-after asset, far from the moneymaking operations of the downtown business district or the residential suburbs, where big developers were hard at work. At the same time, it helped create a new trend that began to draw a growing number of suburban families. My analysis of the South End Historical Society will illustrate my argument about the social construction of neoliberalism.

Beginning in 1966, when the Historical Society was founded, a whole project of redefinition, and beyond that a symbolic takeover of the history of the South End, was undertaken by way of the promotion of Victorian architecture. Residents-turned-real-estate-agents fashioned a new image of the neighborhood, erasing the destitution of working-class lodgings and foregrounding the beauty of high ceilings and crown molding. The promotion of brownstones from the 1960s onward in the United States (and, beyond that, the rediscovery of the charms of the old center cities in Europe) was at once a cultural, political and, especially, an economic project.

The South End Historical Society organized lectures and visits to historic homes, published brochures, and prepared historical building inventories, all with the aim of promoting a form of housing, a style of architecture and interior design, whose value at once was summed up and also augmented by the designation imported from the Old Continent: "Victorian." This enterprise in cultural revaluation paid off in 1983 with the official recognition of the South End as a Historical District, which banned the demolition and exterior modification of historically designated structures. This material preservation went hand in hand with efforts to transform the neighborhood by transforming its image.

This cultural undertaking was directly political. In many neighborhoods like the South End, residents strongly mobilized against demolition. The mayor elected in 1968 campaigned on his intention to put in place a "modern" municipal government, inclined to tackle social and racial problems on the basis of knowledge and professional expertise. He worked to integrate the desires of the residents by favoring a strong base in working-class neighborhoods as well as more extensive municipal consultation with residents. Significant federal grants were available for implementing the plan to renew the South End, passed in 1965, using the tool of eminent domain expropriation that allowed the municipal authority to access significant financing. Neighborhood associations, churches, social centers, and activists' groups, all battling to influence the future of the South End, formed an extremely active milieu, fueled by the Civil Rights Movement and the mobilization against the Vietnam War. A generation of radical black activists emerged in the second half of the 1960s. The Historical Society, situated at the most conservative end of the political spectrum in the South End, emerged as the most powerful institution of the white property owners. Housing was at the center of the struggles.

Between 1960 and 1970, the South End began to change. A gay culture already existed around the bars of the city center in the interwar period. In the decades following World War II, gay and lesbian citizens became more present and active in neighborhood associations, including in the Historical Society, although not "out of the closet" as the Society organized its activities on the basis of explicitly heterosexual norms. In this "pre-Stonewall" period, socioeconomic changes were more striking and visible. From 1960 to 1970, the neighborhood's median annual income rose from $4,542 to $6,122. But the percentage of African American residents in the neighborhood remained constant (39%), the Hispanic population rose from 1% to 7%, and the Chinese population also grew, from 2% to 13%; meanwhile the white population declined as the poorest residents left the area. The future of the South End remained uncertain, especially as urban renewal plans called for the construction of new or renovated housing for low- or middle-income households. The Historical Society and the real estate agents leading it sought to stop urban renewal, because they were concerned that the construction of affordable, publicly subsidized housing—especially for Hispanic or black residents—would slow the growth of real estate prices in the neighborhood.

More radical activists challenged the Historical Society by taking control of the municipal government's citizen participation requirements to involve local residents in the urban renewal process. Activists blockaded one of the Historical Society's first tours of the neighborhood and a few years later, greeted participants in the Historical Society's 1974 annual ball with chants of "Stop the Victorian Criminals" and "South End Historical Society is an Upper-Class."[14]

For the Historical Society, what was at stake was not only cumulating financial profits but also establishing the legitimacy of the South End's "new residents." The official history it promoted in its publications contrasted the Victorian splendor of the South End in the nineteenth century with the neighborhood's subsequent "decline," and then celebrated its "urban Renaissance." This version of the past relegated poor and immigrant populations to symbolic invisibility in favor of a new figure of reform: the urban "pioneer."

The Historical Society's trumping of architectural elements rests on a close and glorifying association between a space and a social elite. While "Victorian splendor" was explicitly attributed to the bourgeoisie of the second half of the nineteenth century, its decline was implicitly attributed to the poor populations who came after them. The description of architectural interiors in the Historical Society's brochures emphasized the separation between the space occupied by the owners and that used by the servants. By insisting on the family's life unfolding in the various rooms of the house, this vision of the past rendered invisible many of the South End's residents past and present—immigrants and the working class, not to mention prostitutes, the homeless, and the barflies who occupied public spaces and appeared to flout family values.

The interest in an "objectively" precious heritage served as a very effective form of social distancing. The adjectives used to describe the houses, especially the interior or exterior ornamentation, evoke a dialectic between the delicate and the vulgar, and between elegance and bad taste. The brochures boasted of "elegant rows of red brick," the "charming Victorian houses and the residential squares," and the "sophisticated parquet flooring from the Edwardian period." Emphasis was given to the "complexity of the ornamentation" and "the attention to remarkable details." A series of singular nouns—"splendor," "beauty," "glory"—accompanied by qualifiers such as "nineteenth century" and of course "Victorian" began to attribute the same "spirit" or "character" to objects, buildings, and populations. The recurrent use of the adjective "Victorian" evoked, all at once, a continent (Europe), a monarchic regime, and the economic power of an Empire in full expansion, as well as a Queen whose name and long reign (1837–1901) invoked an image of the invincibility of aristocratic power. This ignored the social transformations that the United States underwent, namely the formation of an urban proletariat and the growth of its power (symbolized by the growth of trade unions and, starting in the 1870s, the first strikes) as well as the arrival of immigrants that began to characterize the South End's history as of the 1880s.[15]

The discredited image of the neighborhood's immigrant and African American populations helped justify the end of active social housing policies in the 1970s; furthermore, as these populations were subject to intense symbolic depreciation, the brownstone gained a new reputation:

no longer the furnished home for migrant families, it became the elegant habitat of adventurous white families, branded as urban "pioneers."

The battle for the South End was not solely symbolic: At the same time that it celebrated the Victorian past and the glory of its brownstones, members of the Historical Society launched a battle against the construction of public housing through the same processes deployed against the municipal agency. And it challenged the proposed construction of a homeless shelter, in the name of environmental protection laws but also in defense of historical heritage.

In 1974, the Boston Redevelopment Authority announced that it would no longer prioritize the construction of new public housing, in part because of significant cuts in federal urban spending. At the same time, the reduction in the number of housing units accessible to the most destitute, and the growing control of the logic of the marketplace, cannot be understood solely as the consequences of neoliberalism's unrelenting progress.

The Historical Society greatly contributed to the social construction of a real estate market, which in the following decades fed the accelerating process of gentrification of the neighborhood. The promotion of a new taste for Victorian architecture made it possible for a new "demand" to emerge. That became the decisive economic effect of the cultural activities led by the Historical Society. The novice real estate agents who moved into the South End in the 1960s and 1970s opposed the destruction of older buildings, which would have brought in a market of actors more powerful than themselves. Unable to raise the asking price, instead they sought to manipulate the demand. The path they chose to increase migration to the city center was not to wait for the renovation of buildings, the improvement of infrastructure, and the demographic transformation to raise the value of the neighborhood. Rather, it was a matter of "contribut[ing] to the changing of the image of the South End among those outsiders who still think of it as a colossal skid row," as the minutes of the Historical Society explained in April 1967. Once created, this image needed to be promoted, and most of all it was necessary to socialize potential buyers to this perspective. The neighborhood tours organized by the Historical Society came precisely to persuade middle and upper classes, then living in the suburbs, to the superior charms (and eventually, the superior value) the crown molding, staircases, and wrought iron could have, compared with the uniformity of their detached homes and the ennui that prevailed in the suburbs. These tours shaped a new taste and at the same time helped this new demand meet an equally new supply created by the real estate agents. They represented a source of financing, with the added perk of including the homes currently for sale. To quote one of the three individuals who each founded real estate agencies that presided over the South End real estate market until the 1980s, and who launched the tour, "The Historical Society, they would help us. If I have a house on the market, it would be on the tour. So we got good publicity that way."

The Fabrication of Widespread Gentrification (1990–2008)

In Boston, as in many other US cities, the beginning of the 1990s marked a turning point in the history of urban public policy. In what are known as "entrepreneurial cities," mayors began to prioritize commercial development over redistributive policies.[16] As support for large-scale public developments (like those undertaken by Robert Moses in New York or Ed Logue in New Haven and Boston) declined in an era of anti-statism and fiscal restraint, city governments encouraged real estate developers to invest in poor and working-class neighborhoods, particularly in neighborhoods in or near downtowns. The process of gentrification accelerated in post-industrial cities like Boston, where high-tech, finance, health care, and high-end retail employment took the place of a long-declining manufacturing sector. Hoping to market the city and increase its tax base, Boston, like many older central cities, tried to attract young professionals and sought to develop the retail and cultural amenities that would attract them.

At the same time, Boston struggled to maintain its infrastructure, social welfare obligations, and housing amidst heavy cutbacks in federal spending. From the 1970s through the early 1990s the city had made efforts to meet the needs of its low-income residents. Raymond Flynn, mayor from 1984 to 1993, had championed the construction of mixed-income, publicly supported housing at a moment when state and federal support for the poor was waning. Under his successor, Ed Menino, that came to an end.

The consequences were particularly stark in the South End. A once-grand row house neighborhood, bordering Boston's downtown office and shopping district, the South End had just barely been spared the urban renewal process of the postwar period. Beginning in the 1960s, City Hall had implemented a "concerted" urban renewal process in the South End, which it then considered one of Boston's "slums," by acquiring a number of lots in the neighborhood. These lots were initially used for building public housing complexes, and later, mixed-income housing.

Thirty years later, they were sold to private developers for market-rate redevelopment. The process of gentrification intensified throughout the neighborhood. It began in the "historic" part closest to downtown and expanded into an entirely different area, the dilapidated industrial zone to the southwest along Washington Street, where affordable real estate, long overlooked by both urban renewers and gentrifiers, began to whet developer appetites. By 2004, an estimated 1,571 new or renovated housing units had been completed in the South End, and three acres of commercial areas were developed.[17]

The issue of the right to housing for the most underprivileged did not disappear completely during the period of heightened gentrification. But, by the 1990s, the public sector no longer provided housing for low-income residents in the South End. Rather than constructing public housing or renovating existing buildings for low-income occupancy, the city turned to "private initiatives to finance a regulatory share of affordable housing."[18] Those programs were small in scale because of the sharp increase in South End real estate prices. Gentrification accelerated as major financial institutions, corporate investors, and large, consolidated real estate firms replaced small brokers and do-it-yourself or artisanal redevelopers who had bought, renovated, and resold properties in the neighborhood since the 1960s.[19]

The trajectory of gentrification in the South End is embodied in the career of the owner of a real estate agency that, in the 1970s, began buying and renovating properties between the Back Bay, a traditionally well-to-do neighborhood in the heart of the city, and the South End. In the 1980s, anticipating future development possibilities, he acquired several dozen buildings, especially in the decaying former industrial areas along Washington Street, where he tried (unsuccessfully) to evict artists who were living there illegally. Those industrial buildings were still distant from the core of the gentrified South End. Local gentrifiers described it as an area where "people" (meaning themselves) would "never go."[20] Washington Street and its environs constituted a symbolic boundary, marked by architectural rupture, with its dilapidated industrial structures, as well as a large housing project, the equally imposing cathedral, and the city's gigantic public hospital. Numerous decrepit buildings there housed a particularly poor population, artists squatted in a former shoe factory, and a homeless shelter was not far away. A symbolic effort was necessary to turn these urban spaces into sellable assets. Labeling the area as a colony of artists was one of the developer's key tactics, as was the case in changing neighborhoods in other cities. The evolution of the Lower East Side in Manhattan, to name one nationally prominent example, made clear the commercial advantages of labeling a neighborhood as an artists' enclave.

Artists were barely active or visible during the first decades of the South End's gentrification, and they developed only the slightest connections with gentrifiers. But the developer sought allies among artists to transform the area's reputation. In 2000, he launched a huge publicity campaign "to rechristen a blighted area of the South End in hopes of transforming it into a trendy arts district, renaming it SoWa (for South of Washington)," a branding tactic borrowed from New York's famed South of Houston (Soho), which had risen from a grimy post-industrial area to an artists' colony to one of the most expensive commercial and residential areas in the country. He flew SoWa flags from his buildings, published a SoWa newsletter, established a shuttle to the subway with "SoWa Express" emblazoned on the side. He also spent $250,000 a year to set up a private security patrol.[21] In the early 2000s, he created studios inside a former textile mill and offered them to artists. His company's website described SoWa as "a lively commercial district serving artists, residences and creative business" that sought to rival Newbury Street, the chic artery that runs through the Back Bay. By 2004, twenty galleries were clustered in SoWa, twelve of which had been open for less than two years.

To market the area as "artistic," SoWa's developers sponsored "open studios" held on the first Friday of every month, and "SoWa Walks," which lasted for an entire weekend once a year. These events drew large crowds of well-to-do residents from the South End and the rest of the city. The "First Fridays" were described as "a giant, arty block party, attracting hundreds of visitors who sip wine, view art, and then pop over to the Red Fez or Cafe Umbra for dinner."[22] Restaurants in renovated buildings served as another marketing tool.[23] Real estate ads, like one in the *Boston Courant* (July 12, 2008), combined descriptions of new housing units with the area's cultural amenities: "Spacious loft with built out bedroom area in boutique building in the rapidly emerging SOWA district."[24]

This SoWa urban development effort had another side. The new label explicitly distanced the new development from the sociodemographic reality of Washington Avenue. The sales director of the real estate firm unabashedly expressed his desire to chase out all "undesirables." When asked about the homeless shelter located next door, he said: "We're in the business of turning the lights on. You create a reason for people to come here, like the galleries or the restaurants. Then you have people walking around. For lack of a more interesting metaphor, when you turn the lights on, the roaches scatter."[25] The "neoliberal city" that seemed to permeate this part of the South End through a process of gentrification had an undeniably repressive side to it, which has already been noted in considerations of gentrification as a form of "colonization" or "neoliberal urban development."[26] However, neoliberal policies were not the only factor in this process of constructing a sellable asset by ridding it of any negative connotations, meaning, or association with the population occupying the lowest rungs of the urban ladder, namely the homeless, the poor, African Americans, and Latinx residents. In reality, the city and its residents had conducted this process of erasure long before the 1990s.

South End newcomers participated in the neoliberalization of urban spaces, but for motivations that are not simply economic. Following Thompson's analysis of the making of class,[27] I analyzed gentrification in the South End as the result of the formation of a new social group, whom I called "good neighbors." These good neighbors did not suddenly endorse neoliberal values. Rather, they built their legitimacy on a mix of economic interests, political commitments, and moral values, thus succeeding in appropriating an urban space. In the 1990s, diversity became a core reference, even a "credo," among gentrifiers, who thus professed a distinct attitude of progressivism while at the same time diluting the racial question and the socioeconomic inequalities among the multitude of categories that make up diversity: low-income residents, African Americans, Hispanics, and gays. If the taste for "diversity" proved perfectly compatible with economic interests, it also shaped moral attitudes, produced gay-friendliness, and generated philanthropic activities. In other words, it was not only a façade masking profit-oriented forces.

Part of the social as well as economic process I describe was the reframing of the South End as an emblem of a new cosmopolitan Boston that had transcended its contentious, working-class past. In the 1990s, Boston's city government aggressively recruited companies and high-level executives, with hopes of creating a cosmopolitan, international city. To do this, they had to disassociate Boston from its reputation as a provincial, racist backwater, whose reputation was sealed by the city's violent white protests against school desegregation in the 1970s.

The city also launched improvements in the city's infrastructure and in its neighborhood commercial districts to appeal to new cosmopolitan interests. In 1987, the city demolished the noisy elevated subway line that cut through the South End. Neighbors supported these efforts to improve their quality of life. In 1995, members of the neighborhood association on Washington Street staged a protest at city hall against the delays in the implementation of the bus line that replaced this elevated subway. In 1997, a South End working group set up a semi-public organization called Washington Gateway, to take advantage of federal financing to rehabilitate arteries running through older neighborhoods and promote commercial development. The Washington Gateway would contribute to the emergence of the artistic "SoWa," but through the continuing erasure of signs of the area's industrial, working-class, and African American past—a process that had been under way in the South End since the 1970s. In 1975, several neighborhood associations, influential members of the South End Historical Society, and several large property owners waged a big campaign after the Pine Street Inn homeless shelter moved to the South End. Enraged residents began to mobilize, and in compensation for the increased presence of homeless people, they demanded that city hall consider their request concerning bars, twenty-eight of which would be shut down in all.

In place of the "nuisance bars" came new establishments that catered to gentrifiers. "We lost the worst of liquor licenses. Now we have the best," I was told by a real estate developer active in this campaign. The replacement of one set of restaurants and bars with another was not a simple question of supply and demand; it required mobilization. In other words, in the hospitality as well as in the real estate sector, the balance of supply and demand was socially engineered. The opening of new bars and upscale housing was initially made possible by closing working-class bars and through the progressive disappearance of populations considered to be subverting the public space. The second step—creating the "best" commercial supply after having shed the "worst," to use the developer's expression—began with the renovation of Washington Street, which gave a new commercial face to the South End, lifting it to the rungs of the neighborhoods described glowingly in guidebooks and the "nightlife" pages in newspapers for the quality of its restaurants. Most of the subsidies granted by Washington Gateway were awarded to businesses. An old Lebanese restaurant received $14,000 for renovations so that it could welcome a wealthier clientele. One café received subsidized rent and a city tax credit upon opening. Along Washington Street, seven new restaurants, a bar (called Bank), and a café replaced older establishments. The businesses were not chosen at random. Development grants favored cafés, chic restaurants, home decoration and furniture stores, and pet stores at the expense of cheap hair salons and pawnshops. Dark liquor stores selling cheap booze were transformed into upscale stores, which mostly sold wine, displayed in spacious interiors, lit by large glass windows. The appearance of commercial façades was always a powerful social marker. Using community development grants, businesses renovated their storefronts to attract newcomers to the South End. They removed window bars, metal shutters, and plexiglass, and replaced them with large expanses of glass. Transparency was reassuring to new residents arriving in an unknown space, a contrast to the bars and stores that lacked openings onto the street, whose darkness and impenetrability undoubtedly reinforced the impression that they were only for the population already living there. The South End's new restaurants were thus called on to expunge Boston's provincial and outdated image and give it a more international aspect. "No Chowdah Here," proclaimed one 2006 article appearing in the *New York Times*, which celebrated Boston's renaissance, though certainly with some circumspection and a dose of irony and condescension. "Boston, while still not quite an avatar of cool, is showing plenty of new signs, for better or worse, of hipness." So, in the South End there was to be no more chowder—the soup so typical of New England—but a Venezuelan restaurant where the wine-loving journalist could taste "malbec from Argentina [and] carmenères from Chile."[28]

In the 2000s, Washington Gateway supported another local initiative: the renovation of Peters Park, a rundown public space next to Washington Street that had long attracted homeless people. South End homeowners mobilized to raise a large sum of money to support the effort. More than simply maintain the park, the goal was to create a space for a certain population: dog owners, especially wealthier ones, owners of purebreds with expensive tastes for the neighborhood's new dog food bakeries or pet grooming salons. The presence of dog owners in this new park proved that the creation of a new social enclave, however small, served primarily to erase the park's bad reputation, replacing the homeless with well-groomed pets.[29] The aforementioned developer provided generous financing for the park. He also let out space to Washington Gateway free of charge and participated in its fund-raisers. Generally speaking, given the decisive support one needed to get from Washington Gateway to enter this market, developers were actively invited to finance the organization, under the pretense of helping the "community." Nevertheless, aside from the joint initiatives taken by city hall and the developers that were so characteristic of the neoliberalism of the 1990s, the development of the real estate market was also influenced by the role played by a local elite with clear economic interests, whose mobilization was, however, rooted in a very different history, that of the struggles of the 1960s.

Conclusion

As Pierre Bourdieu demonstrated for the single-family home market, economic phenomena, including upgrading of urban spaces, are based on and generated by social forces.[30] In other words, the economy does not function according to the frameworks of the prevailing neoclassical theory. Yet, the distancing from economicism claimed by social scientists questions economists as well as geographers. The analysis of the field and of the agents who produce the supply and demand for an economic asset challenges the neo-Marxist approach in geography. Scholars such as Smith and Harvey have been extremely instrumental in shedding a critical perspective on gentrification. As they demonstrated, financial deregulation and the neoliberalization of public policies, especially at the municipal level, encouraged the growing influence of the real estate market in gentrified city centers in the 1990s, mainly in North America. However, the historical scrutiny of the actors who produced this market reveals a more complex logic. Rather than using a three-step analysis that put too much emphasis on the 1990s neoliberal policies, neo-Marxist geographers fail to see that the history of gentrification is part and parcel of the history of the 1960s conflicts, the upheaval of the social and racial order in the United States, and the resulting cultural redefinition of the dominant groups' values. The younger generation that moved to neighborhoods like the South End in Boston, Brooklyn in New York, and numerous other cities in the United States and Europe tried to break away from this order of things. Their migration to these "diverse" spaces embodied this rupture, but it collided against very real difficulties tied to a residential downgrading and an unprecedented proximity to poor, African American, and Latinx populations. These strong tensions would give rise to a particular management of these spaces, one that expressed a progressive championing of "diversity," but that was initially focused in the 1960s and '70s on certain needs, namely the assertion of the authority of these "pioneers" and the halting of the construction of social housing. This was the work of the Historical Society in the larger context we described. In its effort to promote the architectural heritage of the brownstones, it turned them into a new real estate asset. It paved the way for the accelerating gentrification of the following decades and the victory of economic interests over public regulations.

NOTES

1 Jason Hackworth, *The Neoliberal City: Governance, Ideology and Development in American Urbanism* (Ithaca, NY: Cornell University Press, 2007).

2 Tom Slater, "The Eviction of Critical Perspectives from Gentrification Research," *International Journal of Urban and Regional Research* 30:4 (2006), 737–57.

3 Elvin K. Wyly and Daniel J. Hammel, "Mapping Neo-Liberal American Urbanism," in *Gentrification in a Global Context: The New Urban Colonialism*, ed. Rowland Atkinson and Gary Bridge (New York: Routledge, 2005), 18–38; Neil Smith, "New Globalism, New Urbanism: Gentrification as Global Urban Strategy," *Antipode* 34:3 (2002), 427–50.

4 Hackworth, *Neoliberal City*.

5 Smith, "New Globalism, New Urbanism."

6 Sharon Zukin, *Loft Living: Culture and Capital in Urban Change* (Baltimore, MD: Johns Hopkins University Press, 1989); Christopher Mele, *Selling the Lower East Side: Culture, Real Estate, and Resistance in New York City* (Minneapolis: University of Minnesota Press, 2000).

7 Neil Smith, *The New Urban Frontier: Gentrification and the Revanchist City* (New York: Routledge, 1996).

8 David Ley, *The New Middle Class and the Remaking of the Central City* (Oxford: Oxford University Press, 1996).

9 Smith, *New Urban Frontier*; Damaris Rose, "Rethinking Gentrification: Beyond the Uneven Development of Marxist Urban Theory," *Environment and Planning D: Society and Space* 2:1 (1984), 47–74.

10 John H. Mollenkopf, *The Contested City* (Princeton, NJ: Princeton University Press, 1983); Thomas H. O'Connor, *Building a New Boston: Politics and Urban Renewal. 1950–1970* (Boston: Northeastern University Press, 1993).

11 Langley Keyes, *The Rehabilitation Planning Game: A Study in the Diversity of Neighborhoods* (Cambridge, MA: MIT Press, 1969).

12 J. Anthony Lukas, *Common Ground: A Turbulent Decade in the Lives of Three American Families* (New York: Knopf, 1985), 68.

13 Suleiman Osman, *The Invention of Brownstone Brooklyn: Gentrification and the Search for Authenticity in Postwar New York* (New York: Oxford University Press, 2011).

14 Lukas, *Common Ground*, 264.

15 1968 and 1977 tour brochures.

16 Dennis R. Judd and Paul Kantor, *The Politics of Urban America: A Reader* (Boston: Allyn and Bacon, 1998), 8.

17 Karl Seidman, *Revitalizing Commerce for American Cities: A Practitioner's Guide to Urban Main Street Programs* (Washington, DC: Fannie Mae Foundation, 2004), 87.

18 Marie-Hélène Bacqué, ed., *Projet urbain en quartier ancien. La Goutte d'Or, South End* (Paris: PUCA, 2005).

19 Mele states: "Prior to the 1980s, landlords operating in the East Village were primarily petty capitalists, rarely holding more than a few buildings and viewing their property as a supplemental source of income. As the costs (purchase price and tax costs) of entry into the neighborhood land market skyrocketed in the early 1980s, the form of ownership shifted heavily to mid-sized firms and corporations capable of paying exorbitant property costs. Small-scale or single 'mom and pop' owners began to drop out and brokerage firms, property management corporations and individuals with extensive property holdings within the neighborhood and in similar neighborhoods, such as Harlem, began to purchase and develop properties." Mele, *Selling the Lower East Side*, 244.

20 Unlike all of the South End, where whites made up half the population, the population of the district along the Washington Gateway was 31% white, 39% black, 20% Asian, and 16% Hispanic. Data from Seidman, *Revitalizing Commerce*, 82.

21 *Boston Globe*, September 5, 2005.

22 *Boston Globe*, December 9, 2003.

23 Richard Lloyd, *Neo-Bohemia: Art and Commerce in the Post-Industrial City* (New York: Routledge, 2006).

24 *Boston Courant*, July 12, 2008.

25 *Boston Globe*, June 3, 2007.

26 Atkinson and Bridge, *Gentrification in a Global Context*; Wyly and Hammel, "Mapping Neoliberal American Urbanism."

27 E. P. Thompson, *The Making of the English Working Class* (New York: Pantheon, 1964).

28 Rick Friedman, "36 Hours in the South End of Boston: Row Houses on Union Park in Boston's South End," *New York Times*, June 30, 2006.

29 Sylvie Tissot, "Of Dogs and Men: The Making of Spatial Boundaries in a Gentrifying Neighborhood," *City and Community* 10:3 (2011), 265–84; Sylvie Tissot, *Good Neighbors: Gentrifying Diversity in Boston's South End* (New York: Verso, 2011).

30 Pierre Bourdieu, *The Social Structures of the Economy* (Malden, MA: Polity Press, 2005).

7

Race, Participation, and Institutional Transformation in the Neoliberal City

Black Politics in Cleveland, 1965–2010

MICHAEL MCQUARRIE

Understanding race and participation in the United States requires understanding the variety of forms participation can take, the institutional locations in which they take place, and their trajectory. Secondarily, it is necessary to objectify this changing landscape in order to avoid facile conclusions that current arrangements are "more of the same," are the product of a hegemonic "neoliberalism," or indicate a transition to a "post-racial society." The goal is not to claim things are bad or good, it is to understand the shifting landscape of possibility in contemporary society. I will focus on this landscape as it pertains to black Americans. This might seem overly particular. After all, immigrant politics and the politics around other forms of racial and ethnic stigma are certainly important and, in some cases, clearly becoming more important. All could teach us much about minority politics in a democracy. I am interested in black Americans for a few reasons. The political and institutional struggles over participation and the terms of participation by black Americans have historically been heated and distinctly productive (in the Foucauldian sense) of political practices. Moreover, given the historical stigmatization and marginalization rooted in hereditary race slavery, black inclusion is a limit case for the democratic possibilities of the US polity.

In order to examine the shifting landscape of participation for black Americans, I will turn to a single city, Cleveland, Ohio. This focus enables me to take a fine-grained approach which reveals the relational and path-dependent nature of political practices and technologies of participation. Unfortunately, the story that emerges is not a positive one. Black voices are being marginalized in the public sphere, even in majority black cities like Cleveland. The effects of this marginalization will be increasing racial inequality and a further homogenization of urban space, culture, and politics. This homogenization will not be overtly exclusionary, but will privilege lifestyles, forms of consumption, and dispositions that are not equitably distributed across the socio-racial diversity of the city. At the same time, the mechanisms, technologies, practices, and discourses around black participation in politics have changed. The institutional means for sustaining alternative and critical black voices, at least until the emergence of the Black Lives Matter movement (though it remains to be seen how Black Lives Matter will become institutionalized), have been in decline; meaning that the organization of possibility and constraint for urban black political participation has changed. Most basically, between the 1970s and today the institutional supports for sustaining a distinctively black political voice in urban politics have been whittled away.

The Institutional Infrastructure of Inclusion

I approach the problem of race and democracy in the neoliberal city through an institutional and organizational lens. Institutions—the rules, laws, and norms that govern politics—and organizations—the typical settings for participation—together constitute the terrain on which politics takes place.[1] The goal here is to show how the morphology of this organizational and institutional landscape has changed for black Americans and how it has enabled and disabled different *technologies of participation*.[2] Treating participatory practices as *technologies* is a necessary step to break with tacit assumptions about the essential qualities of participation and the common tropes about participation that often result (for example, that it is inherently democratizing). At the same time, focusing on this infrastructure of politics moves beyond questions of the strategies and choices made by leaders, parties, or movements. The political ground has shifted beneath our feet, but tacitly rather than overtly. As a consequence, the re-marginalization of black politics has occurred without much political debate or discussion about the transformation.

By "technology" I mean a bundle, or "mangle,"[3] of practices, metrics, discourses, and actors. "Technologies of participation" refers to arrangements of practices, metrics, discourses, and actors that facilitate particular types of representation or the construction of particular types of political subjects. From this perspective, political participation should be thought of, not as a practice with essential characteristics, but as a practice that derives its significance from how it is situated relative to other practices, actors, and meanings. In the case of African Americans in Cleveland, my case here, this is an essential point to make because while they have been welcome as participants in political and civic life since inclusion was won in the 1960s, the meaning, significance, and possibilities of such participation have radically changed such that inclusion now facilitates marginalization rather than serving as a barrier to it.

The inclusion of African Americans has not unfolded equally across different fields and institutional arenas. However, politics has often been understood as one of the bright spots in the landscape of possibility and constraint for African Americans. The United States had a black president, Barack Obama, from 2009 through 2016, who directly benefited from previous struggles which won a huge expansion in access to the political system. Given that racial exclusion in politics had relied on various unsavory mechanisms—from literacy tests to violent repression—the sudden and significant opening up of voting and elected offices to black Americans in the 1960s is a significant achievement and one that should not be ignored.

Exclusion and marginalization can operate through mechanisms other than legal exclusion and violence, and when they do so it is not simply a matter of norms and customs but of formal rules enforced by bureaucracies. It is certainly true that the organization of policing and criminal justice in the United States serves to marginalize black Americans in the service of neoliberal authority.[4] But while such developments are disastrous enough to sustain the argument that black people are now subject to a new Jim Crow regime,[5] they distract us from more insidious and subtle practices of marginalization that operate through inclusion rather than exclusion, while also masking current trends toward decarceralization.[6] Institutional and organizational practices often put the lie to written rules. Frontstage purposes and goals are often undermined backstage, whether through conscious manipulation or more subtle processes of goal displacement and socialization. These practices can harden into authoritative practices and discourses that have the secondary effect of marginalization. This can be enabled by overt racism, but also by tacit racism or simple indifference. The contemporary landscape of urban political participation for African Americans in cities like Cleveland is shaped by these more subtle institutional and discursive processes which alter the meaning of black political participation. The implication of this is that our scholarly gaze has been distracted by the overt state repression entailed in the criminalization of African Americans and that this has distracted us from the more subtle transformation that has reduced the space of possibility for black political voices in urban politics.

On the other hand, there has long been a critical discourse about the nature of black political incorporation. Incorporation has often been evaluated relative to the aspirations and promise of the Civil Rights era. This has produced a sizable literature on political incorporation and de-radicalization through inclusion.[7] This observation is not wrong. However, its meaning has shifted radically as the politics of the welfare state and the New Deal coalition have been rolled back and neoliberal institutions have been rolled out.[8] The mechanisms of incorporation (government funding of neighborhood organizations, minority contracts, public worker bargaining rights, symbolic recognition) have mostly been dismantled.[9] The result is that many black neighborhoods are deprived of resources that they won in the wake of the Civil Rights Movement. Given the forms of extreme marginality that have emerged in cities since the 1980s, our appreciation of these mechanisms of incorporation must shift. In fact, the politics of incorporation won resources for black communities that had been deprived of them. Dismantling the basic exchange of symbolic recognition and material resources for quiescence is a setback that has had extreme symbolic and material consequences for African Americans, including their criminalization. By itself, these effects are not necessarily decisive in constituting a modern black precariat, but it is probably more accurate to understand these changes as a layer which, when placed on top of various other layers of marginalization, can produce levels of extreme social and political marginalization. To appreciate this it is necessary to step back from evaluating the trajectory of black politics based on the standard of racial equality, not because such a goal isn't worth aspiring to, but because it causes us to misunderstand and underestimate the political consequences of urban neoliberalism for African Americans.

It is also worth noting that, while there are extreme material and symbolic consequences for ending the exchange of quiescence for inclusion, it is also probably true that this exchange ended before the authority of liberal solutions to racial marginality could be brought into question and alternative ideas about racial inclusion could be considered. The combination of marginality and a collapsing consensus around liberal solutions to race is what makes Black Lives Matter possible, along with the reactionary challenge to the civil rights settlement.

Given that marginality and exclusion are not necessarily constituted by overtly exclusionary political projects, a focus on practices and institutions is necessary to grapple with contemporary forms of political participation. Treating African American political participation as a space of possibility that is defined by a prevailing set of institutional arrangements and organizational vehicles enables a break with both the democratizing narrative and the assumption that political institutions are inherently racist. The fact is that the neoliberal city has facilitated some forms of African American political inclusion while marginalizing or undermining others. So what, finally, does the landscape of political participation look like for African Americans in the neoliberal city?

Race, Politics, and the Neoliberal City

I want to begin by suggesting an analogy. William Julius Wilson and Loïc Wacquant have been very articulate about discussing the changing landscape of socioeconomic inclusion and mobility for African Americans in the period from the early 1970s to the mid-1990s, a period that we usually think of as the era in which the "neoliberal city" was "rolled out" in institutional terms.[10] Wilson and, later, Wacquant both did this using studies of the South Side of Chicago. In order to make a tendential argument, they relied on the extraordinarily detailed Chicago School ethnography of Bronzeville on Chicago's South Side, *Black Metropolis*, conducted by St. Clair Drake and Horace R. Cayton.[11] Drake and Cayton described a community that was deeply troubled by the weight of racial stigma and institutional exclusion. However, as a community, the South Side nonetheless functioned quite well. Exclusion had resulted in the formation of a vibrant and economically diverse community that depended heavily on money from union jobs which, in turn, enabled small businesses and professional practices. Doctors lived near factory workers, store owners, domestics, and schoolteachers. South Side residents were marginalized, but that marginalization did not mean destitution. Mutual self-reliance was made necessary by exclusion, but such self-reliance also sustained a community that was becoming more affluent and more politically confident.

Contrast that with the 1990s, when the South Side supplanted the South Bronx as the nation's avatar of urban poverty. Wilson convincingly described the processes that led to the emergence of a black underclass on Chicago's South Side. On one hand, the Civil Rights Movement had made it possible for affluent African Americans to leave the South Side for the suburbs, depriving the people and organizations that remained of economic resources and social capital. At the same time, the collapse of American manufacturing during the 1973 crisis began a long process of economic transformation that deprived African Americans of their main avenue for social mobility: union jobs in manufacturing.[12] The South Side became an organizational desert, leaving few institutions for community to develop around. Criminal activity and, most important, drugs, began to occupy this vacuum, further undermining community solidarity. This occurred as one of the most important providers of resources, the state, shifted to a policy paradigm of social disinvestment—a process that got rolling in earnest during Ronald Reagan's presidency. The result was again a form of community autarky, but with few of the positive trappings evident in Drake and Cayton's ethnography.

The people who remained on the South Side were those who did not have the resources to leave. Concentrated poverty sustained a "culture of poverty" which ensured that the social and institutional exclusion that was emerging on the South Side would become self-sustaining. Today, some research suggests, merely having a South Side address will produce social stigma and an uphill climb in the labor market.[13] The marginality of the people who remain in urban ghettos like the South Side sustains new and extreme forms of racial stigma which, in turn, is a justification for the criminalization of poor people of color. Economic and governing institutions exacerbate exclusion and marginalization even as legal and representative institutions become more inclusive.

The story is, of course, ironic. At the very moment African Americans start winning legal victories that secure access to important institutions for enabling social and geographic mobility, the meaning and significance of those victories are undermined in political economic terms. This is not true for all African Americans, of course. Many are able to leave and move to other neighborhoods, where they can live comfortable, affluent lifestyles. But for those left behind, conditions are extreme. The end result, according to Wacquant, is a new form of urban "advanced marginality" based on the combination of class and racial exclusion. When we take into consideration the criminalization of poor blacks, environmental injustice, the abandonment of spatial Keynesianism in favor of concentrating state investment in growth poles, and the dumping of undesirable residents and institutions (jails, halfway houses, public housing, etc.) in these neighborhoods, it is possible to sustain the argument that this is not a product of neglect. It is actually an important component of governance in the neoliberal city.

There are problems with the narrative laid out by Wilson and Wacquant. Thinking about their claims as a narrative, it draws too much from the contrast with Drake and Cayton's account of Bronzeville and not enough on changes in the institutional and policy environment. More important, the narrative (even for Wacquant's book, which was published in 2008) is most powerful because it ends in the mid-1990s. If we carry the narrative forward to the foreclosure crisis, it is clear that the circumstances of blacks (and to a lesser extent people of color generally) in the neoliberal city is not simply a matter of systematic social exclusion and criminalization. Indeed, Wacquant's account of neoliberalism is misleading to the extent that it focuses on exclusion and criminalization. In states such as New York, carceralization was at its peak in the mid- and late 1990s. Wacquant's account is not of an emerging carceral archipelago, but of one reaching its limit.[14] Neoliberal discourse and the logic of neoliberal institutions is not simply to exclude those who do not have the "capital" necessary to contribute to the economy. The disciplining of those who are not appropriate neoliberal citizens only makes sense if we are aware of what they are being disciplined for. In the absence of understanding this other side of the coin, the picture that emerges is simply a new advanced, urban, and northern version of Jim

Crow. Such a conclusion radically underestimates the complexity and sophistication of institutions of urban governance in the neoliberal era.

Another issue that must be clarified before proceeding is what "black politics" refers to. Speaking of African Americans as a "corporate racial subject"[15] or as a unitary constituency with common interests is often, though not always, misleading. African Americans overwhelmingly voted for Barack Obama in 2008, indicating more commonality of interest on the issue of presidential candidates in 2008 than any other demographic group. However, such unity is rare. In politics and institutions African Americans are, like everyone else, divided by class, status, regional differences, education, religion, and gender. One important shift that occurred with the dismantling of Jim Crow was that black politics began to fragment. All could be united against legal and political exclusion (albeit with heated differences about tactics), but once the issue turned to other forms of exclusion, even at the height of the Civil Rights Movement, that unity fractured.

Wilson's account suggests one of the main lines of fragmentation: class. This is a basic division the significance of which is noted by many scholars.[16] More important, it means that reading the relative inclusion of African Americans from some deduced "group interest" is, at best, problematic.[17] Unity, to the extent it is established, is established politically, in the public sphere, in social movements, and through political engagement. Such moments occur, but when they do, they should be understood as a political achievement, not as some simple expression of interest.[18] This is necessary to understand the fragmentation of black politics in the neoliberal era and it motivates an analysis that focuses on opportunities and constraints. At the very least, awareness of this directs analytical attention to the disorganization of the institutions and organizations that had sustained black politics, rather than simply focusing on repression.

With these caveats in mind, I want to extend Wilson and Wacquant's ironic account of the marginalization of the urban black poor to politics. In the political arena too, African Americans had to confront new rules of the game which disadvantaged them very shortly after they used the old rules to become established. The result was, in many ways, a hollow victory. African Americans secured access to representative politics and municipal governments at almost the exact moment that those institutions began to decline in significance. The result is not simply a new form of repression. Rather, it is a more sophisticated mode of governance that utilizes inclusion and participation to reinforce the authority of urban agendas that poorly serve African Americans (and many other minorities).

A related dynamic that underpins the shifting status of African Americans in politics is the always troubling dilemma for democratic polities, which is the relationship between minorities and the interests of the whole. The importance of particularity is not consistent across time. The trajectory and content of black participation is related to the relative status of the particular versus the civic in urban politics. The 1960s until the 1980s were a time when the authority of "community" in urban politics was at a high point and the civic was understood to be, in part, rooted in the ability of communities to be healthy and self-determining.[19] Such a configuration of this relationship arguably served African Americans well. Unfortunately, the neoliberal era has witnessed a rolling back of that discourse in favor of the universalist discourse of market value.

The rest of this chapter will be taken up with explaining these dynamics. I will begin with the racial revolution in municipal politics between 1965 and 1985 and then turn to the various ways that revolution has been rendered less significant than it originally appeared to be. I will do this by focusing on several of the key arenas in which Cleveland's black population engages with politics and the technologies of participation that prevails in them. I will then situate them in a narrative of neoliberal institutional transformation. By the end of the chapter I hope to have illustrated how urban political authority in the neoliberal city simultaneously rests on some forms of black political participation while, at the same time, being unresponsive to many African American constituencies and their needs.

The Racial Transformation of Urban Politics: Revolution or Incorporation?

The politics of growth has not served African Americans well. However, prior to the Civil Rights Movement the pursuit of value-free development as the primary function and goal of municipal politics was relatively easy because the costs of growth could simply be concentrated on a stigmatized and largely disenfranchised African American population.[20] Cleveland, for example, eventually subjected a quarter of its total territory to urban renewal, highway building, and slum clearance—a huge percentage by national standards. The largely black Central neighborhood was nearly razed in its entirety in the name of slum clearance, the creation of a new university, and the provision of new public housing—an effort from which the neighborhood has never recovered. However, by the early 1960s this simple if brutal way of managing growth was unraveling.

In Cleveland, African Americans began mobilizing in 1963 over school construction issues.[21] Residents of the largely African American East Side of Cleveland were sending their children to severely overcrowded schools even though new school construction was proceeding apace on the city's West Side. Community organizers began staging protests which persisted and expanded in scope. By 1965, the African American neighborhoods of Hough and Central were mobilized and began applying their newfound power to the electoral arena. Before that could happen, however, the Hough "riot"—it was more of a police riot—exploded out of an altercation in front of a nightclub.

The combination of community organizing and the Hough riots made it clear that the costs of growth were not going to continue to be borne by African Americans. At the same time, the city's business and cultural elites were being thwarted by white politicians representing the city's Eastern European and Catholic neighborhoods and voters. When the young African American lawyer and politician, Carl Stokes, decided to run for mayor, he found that he had the support of the city's corporate and philanthropic community. Stokes was elected the first African American mayor of a large American city in 1965 (after being the first African American Democrat elected to the Ohio House of Representatives).

Of course, part of the assumption behind this support was that Stokes could keep a lid on the city's black neighborhoods and provide legitimacy to a development agenda focused on downtown. This is the basic dilemma of black urban politicians: how to balance support for elite development agendas with serving black constituencies.[22] However, unlike the situation with Maynard Jackson a few years later in Atlanta,[23] the city's business and philanthropic community also funneled resources into Hough and Central in order to support Stokes's agenda. The emerging coalition between growth-oriented elites and Stokes was thwarted in municipal government by ward-heeling councilors (both white and black). However, Cleveland had always been a pioneer in community philanthropy, and elites were comfortable using private action and means to pursue their goals. The city's philanthropies and business leaders set up a private fund, Cleveland NOW!, worth $177 million, administered by the Cleveland Foundation (still the third-largest community foundation in the United States), in order to direct money into the East Side via the new community-based nonprofit organizations like Hough Partners in Progress, a community development corporation (CDC). Unlike what Stone and Reed describe in Atlanta, the tensions between black reformers and the city's elite were, for a time, subordinated to their shared hostility to clientelist ward heelers who were opposed to downtown development and to sharing ward resources with African Americans.

A second riot, this time in the Glenville neighborhood in 1968, closed the door on cooperation between growth-oriented elites and African American reformers. Not only had Stokes failed to keep a lid on the East Side, but the black nationalist gunman who was responsible had actually received funding from Cleveland NOW. But trouble was already brewing in the coalition. On one hand, Stokes and his administration quickly became familiar with the myriad ways that African Americans were poorly served by the institutions of municipal governance and they worked hard, though mostly unsuccessfully, to deal with them. Stokes threatened to sue the local committee on government over unequal representation.[24] Stokes also attempted to establish a rival Democratic Party organization that would not be under the control of the white and clientelist local Party apparatus and, therefore, would provide a more reliable source of support to African American reformers. Finally, the idea that African Americans were a unitary political voice fell apart in Stokes's second term. Stokes secured resources for a rapid expansion of public housing. However, he was also suspicious of concentrated poverty. Residents of white suburbs made it clear that under no circumstances would they take new public housing. Stokes turned to the new black suburban communities that emerged in the wake of the Civil Rights Movement and housing desegregation. The result was determined public resistance. Even Stokes could not establish a corporate black political identity in Cleveland.

Stokes's legacy for black politics in Cleveland is complicated. The city has absolutely had more controversial mayors since, so he isn't really understood as a failed mayor. His mayoralty inspired many people to become involved in the city's politics, even non-local successful academics like Norman Krumholz, the developer of the principles of "equity planning," who moved from his job as a professor at Wisconsin to be Stokes's planning director. The symbolic significance of Stokes should not be underestimated even though he failed to realize many of his reformist goals. The result was that a generation of ambitious African Americans could enter city government as reformers. There had already been ward heelers. George Forbes, an African American, was elected to City Council before Stokes was mayor and he would go on to be president of the City Council for many years. However, he was resolutely opposed to reformist black politicians. Nonetheless, throughout the 1970s he would be challenged by black reformers like Lonnie Burten who, in turn, was an inspiration for Cleveland's current mayor, Frank Jackson—the third African American mayor of Cleveland (all elected to multiple terms).[25]

The reformist impulse has largely died out among the city's black politicians. However, Stokes did open up municipal politics to African Americans and helped institutionalize city government as a pathway for social mobility for the city's African American residents. With the legalization of public sector unions and the passage of anti-discrimination laws governing public sector employment, African Americans could move into government and expect to earn a middle-class living. On a broader scale, this was all further sustained by lucrative federal policies, including the Community Action Program (CAP) and later the Community Development Block Grant (CDBG) and Urban Development Action Grants, which transferred significant money into the municipal coffers, enabling a general expansion in the size of municipal government. Policies like CDBG and CAP actually privileged poor neighborhoods like those on the East Side of Cleveland, ensuring that the city's black population would be able to make use of these funds and programs.

If we think about this from the perspective of political participation, these institutional changes opened up many new avenues for African Americans to participate in the civic and political life of the city beyond the more traditional venues of church and industrial union. African Americans were major players in urban politics, through representative politics, municipal unions, churches, and minority small business associations. In terms of the representative structure, the apparatus of participation included activities like voting and ward clubs. Stokes failed to institutionalize black reformist politics in Cleveland, though he certainly tried, but his efforts did much to secure access to politics and government for African Americans. Yet the main question remained open. How would the city manage the tension between an elite-driven agenda of growth while granting access to African Americans?

The Community Revolution in Urban Politics

Until the 1960s, urban neighborhoods were primarily relevant as objects of academic and charitable interventions. Neighborhood organizations like settlement houses had been around for decades, along with all manner of associations and churches, but notably, settlement houses only rarely claimed to represent the neighborhoods in which they operated. This began to change in the 1960s. Community emerged as a more general rallying cry for decentralizing governance, securing neighborhood self-determination, and authentically expressing popular desires. These struggles often pitted African American communities against school bureaucracies, teachers' unions, police departments, banks, slumlords, elected politicians, and government bureaucracies. In Brownsville, New York, African American parents fought with teachers over "community control" of schools. In Oakland, California, Black Panthers sought economic autarky for African American neighborhoods. In Cleveland, civil rights organizers sought equity at the neighborhood scale for school construction spending. Initially, it appeared that the fight for community self-determination and equity in the distribution of resources was a matter of racial justice and equity because, a few exceptions aside, it was often African Americans making the claim. But by the 1970s the movement for neighborhood control had spilled out of African American neighborhoods to encompass the rest of the city and, in many cases, even the suburbs. A wave of community organizing and neighborhood mobilization crested in the 1970s, a wave that the political scientist Harry Boyte referred to as the "Backyard Revolution."[26]

It would be a mistake to view the nationwide efforts to establish the legitimacy of community in politics as simply an authentic expression of popular aspirations and understandings. A variety of elite actors were also working to constitute community as a legitimate category of distinction. Most obviously, politicians attempted to surf the wave of neighborhood mobilization by claiming to represent neighborhoods against growth-oriented elites.[27] In the early 1960s, the Ford Foundation began experimenting with policies that would encourage neighborhood bootstrapping to overcome poverty. A few years later, the Johnson administration launched the Community Action Program, which mandated that the distribution of federal resources to communities be controlled by members of the community itself, not municipal politicians or bureaucrats. This, in turn, encouraged a wave of organization-building around the country to create vehicles that could capture and spend federal funds. In the 1970s, community organizing networks secured stricter reporting requirements for banks in order to combat redlining and, shortly thereafter, secured the passage of the Community Reinvestment Act (1977), which subordinated banks' ability to allocate capital to the right of communities to utilize their deposits. The Carter administration organized a "Neighborhood Summit" to further respond to neighborhood mobilizations.

The black political revolution in Cleveland may have secured unprecedented levels of access for African Americans in government, but it did not solve the problem of racial tensions in the city. And while it secured a degree of access for the black "community," the voice of the city's neighborhoods was still poorly reflected in the polity. This changed in the 1970s and, at the same time, further institutionalized avenues of African American participation in the city.

One of the most volatile issues was neighborhood transition. As whites moved to the suburbs and African Americans were no longer legally confined to the East Side, they began moving into housing in white working-class neighborhoods. The neighborhood of Buckeye was one example. Wedged between black Glenville and the wealthy suburb of Shaker Heights, it was home to the city's Hungarian community but began experiencing racial transition in the late 1960s and early 1970s.

A fortuitous collaboration between the Catholic Archdiocese and a young community organizer named Tom Gannon yielded the creation of the Buckeye-Woodland Community Congress (BWCC). Originally, the goal was to build a network of organizations that would bring Buckeye's street clubs, nationality groups, churches, and businesses under one umbrella. With the hiring of Gannon, the goal became developing a political citizenry that would be internally diverse and externally united. Gannon and the early leaders of the organization recognized that the neighborhood's problems were more heavily determined by the political and economic leadership of the city, not new African American residents.

The Commission on Catholic Community Action (CCCA) and the BWCC were sitting on a powder keg. For the first time since the organizing around schools in Hough in the early 1960s, Cleveland's neighborhoods mobilized and quickly formed twelve "community congresses" under the national banner of Chicago-based National People's Action (NPA). However, unlike in the 1960s, they did so under the symbol of a black hand shaking a white hand. Indeed, racial animosity found little room for expression in the neighborhood politics of CCCA. Veterans of the movement often assert that the difference was not that they suddenly had no racial animosity, but it just took a back seat to what they were trying to accomplish together. Recalling this aspect of the Congresses, a BWCC leader's thoughts are indicative: "I'm not saying people weren't prejudiced, but they managed to put it in their back pockets long enough to deal with the issues that assaulted all of us."[28] What had been a black issue, marginalization in the context of growth politics, had become a neighborhood issue. Unlike what occurred in many other cities, Cleveland's communities were de-racializing neighborhood problems.

Discursively and dramaturgically, the Congresses made the case that they were more authentic representatives of communities than elected politicians and, therefore, they were the true source of political authority. It was the participatory and organizational construction of the People in the Congresses that gave them the right to hold politicians, bureaucrats, and corporate leaders accountable. In the case of the Congresses, participation became a tool for constituting the "People," imagined as neighborhood residents (both black and white) and challenging urban elites and governors.

The movement was contentious and challenged both the city's populist mayor, Dennis Kucinich, and local growth-oriented elites. Ultimately, this resulted in the destruction of the community congresses. They depended on the support of the archdiocese and local philanthropies, both of which withdrew their support after a hit (protest), in 1982, on the chairman of the SOHIO corporation. Moreover, the split divided the Congresses internally and the division was in some ways about race. The ostensible issue was about whether the protest was tactically sound. For many organizers and the Congresses from African American neighborhoods it generally was, even if it had a bad result. Congresses in transitional and white neighborhoods were more ambivalent. Either way, the event effectively killed community organizing in Cleveland. At the time, area philanthropies wrote letters to the congresses which stated that they were no longer funding organizing but would instead focus on bricks-and-mortar development. The relative absence of resources, both symbolic and material, for community organizing lasted until 2002.

At the same time, consensus had developed around the idea that communities should be able to make decisions for themselves on issues of concern for them, but especially with regard to neighborhood development issues. The resistance by elites was to the idea that the Congresses were appropriate representatives of the community. The emerging consensus was evident in an explosion in the population of community development corporations, the rapid growth in policy tools and funding, and the devolution of governance functions onto nonprofit community-based organizations. The combination of civil rights, black incorporation, and the Congresses, as well as new policy tools like CAP and CDBG, had produced a community revolution in the institutions of the city. Community had become an authoritative scale for governance. This inevitably meant that African Americans would have more say in what happened in their neighborhoods and that they would have access to the organizations that made those decisions, whether they were ward clubs, nonprofit boards and employment, street clubs, or churches. At the same time, the fact that race was subordinated in the movement that did the most to secure these changes has probably had lasting effects.

The legitimacy of the idea that the city's black communities and population were members of the polity had been institutionalized, and this was evident in funding flows, political access, and the prominence of African Americans in the political and civic life of the city.

Neoliberalism, Race, and Participation in Cleveland since 1982

The 1960s and 1970s saw widespread neighborhood and political protest against the exclusive focus on value-free development advocated by urban growth coalitions. The fact that African Americans were now serious players in urban politics (though not on equal terms) contributed greatly to this transformation. So did an explosion in neighborhood and community organizing that frequently bridged racial lines. The result was an emergent populist and progressive position in American urban politics exemplified by politicians like Cleveland's Carl Stokes and Dennis Kucinich.[29] On the other hand, the reformist impulse launched by Stokes had largely petered out by the mid-1980s with the collapse of the city's "backyard revolution."[30]

What this period did establish was the authority of the community scale in the city's governance. Given that African Americans have highly concentrated residential patterns, and rarely represent a majority of voters outside of those communities, this was a significant development. The scale of governance was, throughout the 1970s and 1980s, being shifted downward which, in turn, expanded opportunities for African Americans. But the content of community and participation was, at the same time, very much contested. Black reformist politics and neighborhood-based community organizing both failed to institutionalize their participatory approaches to politics.

This set of opportunities and constraints was further defined by the state of the city as a whole. The 1970s had not been kind to Cleveland. American manufacturing was no longer competitive internationally. The city was hit especially hard by unemployment and outmigration which produced knock-on crises in neighborhoods and housing. The city finally went bankrupt in 1979 after surviving an earlier capital strike during the Kucinich administration (1977–79).

Facing decline, the agenda was one of restarting growth. Local government did not have the resources to do much about this, being bankrupt, but the city still received substantial federal funds via mechanisms like Community Development Block Grants (CDBG) and Urban Development Action Grants (UDAG). At the same time, philanthropic and private resources were mobilized by growth-oriented elites to once again make the city attractive for private investment and mobile capital. The city, it was increasingly understood, needed to make itself competitive again. However, unlike before the neighborhoods revolted, this had to be done alongside neighborhood investment. The political consensus was one of physical redevelopment. Of course, most resources were to be concentrated downtown and around University Circle, as they always had, but with elites now feeling the need to be deferential to neighborhoods, both Kucinich's successor, George Voinovich (1980–1989), and local philanthropies committed resources to neighborhood physical redevelopment. This shift was further facilitated by new policy tools, like the Low-Income Housing Tax Credit (LIHTC) and the growing acceptance of neighborhood redevelopment using nonprofit community development corporations (CDCs), advocated for most visibly on the national scale by the Ford Foundation. Indeed, Cleveland was a pioneer in developing and institutionalizing a national model for nonprofit housing development.[31]

Alongside this, however, two other developments were unfolding. The first was the federal government's withdrawal from developing and funding urban policy. To the extent that new policies were developed, like LIHTC, they relied heavily on private providers and private funding. Local governments were becoming facilitators of private action rather than strategic actors.[32] This shift curbed what had been a rapid expansion of municipal unions and strangled a government funding stream that was relatively accessible to African Americans (accessing private capital would remain a problem until the 1990s). The institutional settings that African Americans won access to in the 1960s were the same ones that were experiencing declining resources and authority in the 1980s.

The second important development was the reorganization of growth-oriented elites in order to better realize their goals in Cleveland. As I noted above, the city's business and civic leadership had historically made great use of organized philanthropy and nonprofit organizations to realize their goals. However, their civic authority had taken a beating in the struggle with Kucinich and with congresses. They developed a reputation, during the 1970s, of insisting on using federal money for white elephant projects that would enhance the value of their real estate investments rather than actually help a struggling city. Pursuing the politics of growth, though considerably easier with Voinovich in office, was more difficult given the reputation of the city's business community, the institutionalization of black access to the polity, and the rescaling of governance to the community scale.

In response, local business leaders partnered with the management consulting firm McKinsey to create a strategic business organization, Cleveland Tomorrow, which has since become a model of urban business leadership globally. The organization would represent the city's CEOs (notably not small businessmen) who would pay substantial dues. That money would be partnered with philanthropic money to fund start-up organizations that would facilitate an agenda of economic growth through the capture of private capital.[33] Cleveland Tomorrow initially set up a number of organizations designed to ensure the competitiveness of Cleveland's manufacturing firms. But Cleveland Tomorrow also pursued concessionary contracts from unions and the introduction of lean production techniques.[34] Cleveland Tomorrow notably supported neighborhood physical redevelopment, but also lobbied actively for securing government money to provide incentives for downtown development. Tax abatements became a key component of Cleveland's physical development strategy, effectively undermining the city's school system. The purpose behind all of this was simple: Make Cleveland more competitive for private capital. The city was losing investment and losing people. The only way to change that would be to enhance the city's competitiveness for mobile people and mobile capital. In order to achieve this, Cleveland was becoming a "partnership city" in which interorganizational and cross-sectoral cooperation was the preferred mode of action.[35]

This approach is typical of urban growth strategies, though the level of sophistication and the complexity of interorganizational ties were being ramped up considerably. What is particular to the neoliberal era is that these developments occur in a moment when federal spatial Keynesianism is in decline and legal citizenship carries with it a shrinking claim on governmental resources. More broadly, what was becoming institutionalized was the idea that markets are the arbiter of social worth.[36] This did not bode well for the majority black population in a shrinking city. So, for example, it is one thing to invest in order to attract the residents who yield the highest returns in terms of real estate values (suburban white professionals, the "creative class") in a context when government channels resources to those who aren't privileged in the private market-place. It is something else entirely when the most "profitable" populations are benefiting from an increasing share of public investment.

Of course, given the political history of Cleveland between 1960 and 1982, and the role of African Americans in it, there was a lot of reason to fear that this strategy would incite new mobilizations. Indeed, this fear was probably one of the motivations for the rescaling of governance to the community scale. Yet even at the height of the foreclosure crisis, when the effects of an investment-driven policy culture finally became fully apparent, the city's neighborhoods never mobilized as they had in the 1960s and 1970s. Given that African Americans had won greater access to the polity and that they were probably not well served by the economic and community development strategies of the city, the puzzle is clear. What happened to black reformist politics and neighborhood mobilizations?

The most important factor was the reemergence of a general policy consensus in favor of growth via competitiveness.[37] Decline is a particularly intractable problem for cities, and starting in the 1970s, cities like Cleveland did not have many policy tools to draw on in order to deal with their situation. This imperative, combined with the demise of the progressive option in the city's politics, meant that policy choices and the allocation of resources were increasingly defined in terms of return on investment rather than social need. Even policies that were explicitly designed to help the poor became imbued with this thinking. Take the low-income housing tax credit as an example. It has been heavily used as a tool for redevelopment in Cleveland.[38] LIHTC is structured as a bond for purchase by private investors, which means that for projects to attract investors they must demonstrate that they will be able to produce a return.[39] It also increasingly came to prevail in urban finance with tools like tax-increment financing, which justifies projects in terms of anticipated future return rather than their ability to receive allocational support from city government.[40] This shift was also evident in the phil-anthropic arena, a particularly important one in Cleveland, with programmatic evaluation increasingly being tied to measurable outcomes and "best practices." More important, in 1968, legislation was passed that would allow "program-related investments" to count toward the requirement that philanthropies distribute 5% of their assets in giving every year (enabling a shift to loans—which get a return—from grants).

The issue wasn't just the content of available policy. The organization of governance was shifting. The strategic role of municipal governments was in decline as the resources available to them diminished. Realizing strategic goals in the city did not just increasingly require that resources be gathered through public-private partnerships, rather, this practice of governance increasingly required a politics of consensus. For example, politicians needed to point to successes in order to be elected, but visible successes now required cooperation with a host of individuals and organizations over which politicians had little control: banks, philanthropies, intermediary organizations, and investors. So the issue was not simply that an emerging policy consensus around competitiveness was emerging, it was that action in the city increasingly required consensus because of the emerging institutional form of urban governance. In some ways, this emerging model of governance was very old: consensus around value-free development and technocratic implementation of it; but in other ways it was radically new, namely, the absence of centralized authority over policy formation and implementation meant that this new model technocracy was "hyper-relational," networked, civic, and consensual.

In terms of the way this affected the political inclusion of African Americans, there are a few points to make. First and most important, the value of different investments was being defined in terms of return on investment, which meant that policy effectiveness was measured in terms of the quantity of new physical redevelopment and the resulting increase in area median real estate values. The authority of these measurements was institutionalized in area philanthropies, municipal government, and community-based organizations. The primary work of CDCs on the East Side was about using a palette of policy tools to leverage increases in real estate values.

The challenges on the East Side were far greater than on the West Side. The root of the problem was that real estate values are, despite their presentation as transparent markers of worth, highly racialized.[41] These dynamics are explicitly reflected in real estate values in Cleveland, which show a sharp disparity between majority white and majority black neighborhoods despite the fact that the overall context of value is low. What this means in practical terms is that redevelopment strategies in Cleveland, even community-based ones in African American neighborhoods, favored the reorganization of space in order to appeal to white suburbanites, or, barring that, affluent blacks. The needs of the existing population were devalued in policy terms.[42] Moreover, the idea that black communities might be able to constitute an alternative vision of what their neighborhoods might be like has become increasingly problematic despite increased access for African Americans.

This is not to say that African American voices were excluded—far from it. The policy paradigm of competitiveness was not contrary to inclusiveness. The paradigm of consensus and inclusion has never been seriously challenged in Cleveland. CBOs in black neighborhoods are almost uniformly led by African Americans. Black wards are uniformly led by African American politicians. Philanthropies and intermediaries are conscientious about distributing resources equally between the East Side and the West Side. African Americans are a growing presence even in organizations that had been long used as tools of elite influence, such as the Cleveland Foundation. This inclusion serves many roles. Critics are quick to say that such inclusion legitimates policies that serve African Americans poorly.[43] It is certainly true that inclusion serves as a useful performance of policy consensus, but this is useful to both black leaders and white leaders. There is also a concept of drawing from "local knowledge" and leveraging "local resources" in the development of programmatic interventions. The idea is that African Americans must be included in order to be able to access such knowledge. However, these dynamics do confront African American politicians and community leaders with a choice. Either support the politics of competitiveness and hope to draw on those resources as a way of serving constituents or criticize it and lose access.

Participation by African Americans has not only not been discouraged, since 2002 it has been actively encouraged. Funding for "consensus organizing" has been provided by local foundations to reenergize participation in community-based organizations. Town hall meetings for the discussion of strategic policy have also increased in frequency. But it is not participation that is designed for creating a community position on strategic objectives and appropriate policy. Residents are frequently asked for input on design issues (the width of porch overhangs or whether to use street parking or driveways) and are often organized into street clubs, the purpose of which is to unify the community around the defense of real estate values (collecting money for street lights, ensuring the provision of services, organizing welcome wagons for new homeowners, enforcing community norms around mowing grass). But street clubs are often key points of contact between city officials and community residents. They provide access, but of a particular type.

On one hand, it is clear that those who support the agenda of growth via competitiveness are sincere in their support. The fact is, there are resources to draw upon and those resources organize commitments and interests. There are examples of this paradigm having a positive impact on the East Side. What is surprising is that many of the most zealous advocates for this model of community development come from the East Side. Regardless, it is certainly true that whether or not a policy paradigm of growth via competitiveness serves blacks equally as well as it serves whites, it is now a common style and approach to politics in black neighborhoods and cities,[44] though it is probably a politics of African American affluence.

On the other hand, Cleveland's East Side has also produced an alternative style of politics that is most resistant to this neoliberal and entrepreneurial policy paradigm. Clientelist politics, or the politics of the ward heeler, is not uncommon in US cities, but grows most lavishly in cities like Cleveland with ward-based council systems. Central to the logic of modern clientelism is what Nicole Marwell calls "triadic exchange."[45] Triadic exchange operates when elected officials distribute resources such as government contracts to community-based nonprofits who then distribute them in the form of jobs, preferential service access, and other forms of assistance. To work most effectively, CBOs organized around the logic of triadic exchange must generate some adherence to the organization, which can be translated into votes, in a reciprocal exchange for services and jobs. The key difference between triadic exchange and old-fashioned patronage is the use of a nonprofit organization as a buffer between the elected official and the voter, which is essentially all that is required to shift the relationship from the realm of the illegal to the realm of the legal.

Triadic exchange, and clientelism more generally, have persisted because of an accommodation in 1980 between the then president-of-council George Forbes and newly elected mayor George Voinovich. City council members would receive a large portion of the Community Development Block Grant (CDBG) funds that come into the city to distribute in their wards. In 2008, this allocation amounted to around $550,000 per year, though the CDBG program has been radically cut since then. This money is the core of triadic exchange because in many wards it is mostly spent on operating support for CDCs. If the councilperson is only supporting one CDC, this usually amounts to about $150,000 per year. This money, along with other sources of free cash flow (for example from developers' fees), enables the persistence and reproduction of clientelism despite the dominance of performance- and market-based metrics.

The importance of clientelism is distinct in African American wards. Given that real estate values are the measure of competitiveness and that real estate value is heavily racialized, the technocratic paradigm of competitiveness does not serve black communities particularly well. Clientelism, however, does. It is not entirely unreasonable for the modern clientelist politician in Cleveland to say that without them, black communities would receive an even smaller share of government resources than they already do. Triadic exchange is justified, not unreasonably, as a matter of social justice and the rectification of past injustices to African Americans. Given the absence of a reformist position and the prevalence of economic value as an arbiter of resource allocation, clientelist politicians have a legitimate argument to make. On the other hand, the lack of transparency, the lack of professional standards, the likelihood that resources will be distributed for reasons other than the public good, and the rent-seeking of clientelist politicians and their allies are all infuriating to technocratically inclined politicians, philanthropies, intermediaries, academics, and good-government progressives. We must keep this in mind—after all, clientelism does deliver resources to underserved communities on terms other than investment return.

Clientelist arrangements also provide alternative avenues for participation and connection to city government. Clientelism rests heavily on relationships rather than professional or technocratic expertise. Clientelist politicians often invite participation as a way of building networks which, it is hoped for the politician's sake, translate into votes and contributions. The ward club is the most basic venue for this, but the network also connects social service agencies, community development corporations, small business associations, and churches (community organizers sometimes lament the very close relations between pastors and politicians on Cleveland's East Side). These settings do enable inclusion and participation, but not usually in ways that are designed to produce new leaders. In general, the authority of the councilor is unquestioned. But at the same time, these arrangements do enable the articulation of a position that is at odds with that of growth-oriented elites and is perhaps the only institutional location that both has an established position in the polity and argues for a redistributive and egalitarian allocation of resources. Unlike in the case of technocratic managers, clientelist politicians are oriented to existing residents, rather than future ones who might increase area real estate values.

The hostility to clientelist politicians and their organizational allies in Cleveland is palpable. Clientelist politicians are always "corrupt" and sometimes "Maoist" (in the personality-cult sense). Institutional reforms are frequently meant to make triadic exchange more difficult. Indeed, with declining resources available for triadic exchange, one politician I spent considerable time with had turned to halfway houses as a source of labor and favors that could be exchanged for votes—a choice that also flew in the face of a common position of black politicians against inequality in the distribution of services for undesirables like ex-cons. Funding for organizations is frequently tied to governance requirements and fiscal reporting that is difficult for unprofessionalized clientelist organizations. Violations are often illegal and clientelist politicians often spend time in jail.

The clientelist position in Cleveland's politics had the merit of sustaining a discourse about citizenship and worth that was contrary to the prevailing neoliberal ones. For this reason, the demise of the clientelist position matters. While clientelist politicians had managed to resist the hostility of the alliance in favor of securing growth for decades, three things changed starting in 2000. First, growth-oriented elites became much more sophisticated about their assault on the clientelist position. They established criteria for governance and management in distributing funding through both public and private grant-making. Second, with ward clubs filling the bench of possible politicians in many wards, local foundations took it upon themselves to train future "leaders" of the city by inculcating technocratic standards and dispositions with regard to governance and policy, and offering ongoing support to budding politicians as they launched their political careers. Third, and most important, has been the shrinking pie of available CDBG dollars. Obama's retrenchment compromise budget severely cut CDBG allocations. The other problem is that the amount (like a lot of government funding) is tied to population, and Cleveland's population has been shrinking precipitously. This is so worrying that Cleveland politicians and bureaucrats frequently float the idea of merging with East Cleveland, one of the few municipalities in Ohio that is actually poorer and more troubled than Cleveland.

The attack on clientelism in Cleveland is merely one part of a broader rolling back of the authority of "community" in institutions of governance. Market-based conceptions of value and the use of investment returns as criteria for demonstrating effectiveness are ostensibly universal criteria and this, in turn, is part of their authority. It is well-established that such metrics do not serve African Americans as a group particularly well. But this logic has also underpinned a broader institutional transformation which has been particularly destructive for African Americans. On the one hand, retrenchment has resulted in an increased reliance on private action to meet the strategic needs of the city. This shift is both enabled and enables fiscal retrenchment in the public sector and the declining relevance of the public sector in general, the very sector that had been opened up by black reformist politics in the 1960s. On the other, municipal government in Cleveland is again being rescaled. Ideas of community self-determination and geographic equity in terms of resource allocation have been subordinated to the logic of competition which favors the concentration of resources in regional growth poles. The effect in a city like Cleveland is to subordinate the particularistic needs and demands of East Side, which carry considerable weight in Cleveland politics, to the needs of civic competitiveness, which privileges neighborhoods and communities that are already "competitive," meaning affluent and white. The appropriate scale of governance for pursuing this strategy is the region, not the community. In 2009, Cleveland joined a growing list of cities that have reorganized themselves for regional rather than city government (Indianapolis, Pittsburgh, and Louisville, among others). In each city, some African American politicians and leaders have argued that this rescaling is a veiled effort to silence minority voices in the city.

Conclusion

The neoliberal city has not been kind to black neighborhoods. Neoliberal institutional transformations and the decline of public sector spending and authority have enabled multiple layers of marginalization to operate. At the same time, this is not because of formal political exclusion. Indeed, while some states have worked to put up new barriers to black participation in politics, Cleveland has remained open and even supportive of black participation. The city continues to elect African American mayors, even as institutional change and discursive definitions of the civic sacred and profane make it increasingly difficult for such mayors to act on behalf of their main source of votes.[46] Participation continues to be possible and even encouraged, but only on the specific terms that have solidified in the context of neoliberal institutional transformation. So then, what are these institutional transformations?

First and most important has been the decline of the public sector and its authority, public sector spending, and the various organizations that depend on such spending. The public sector was the beachhead for racial inclusion in Cleveland as it was in many American cities. While the public sector continues to play an important managerial role in Cleveland's governance, its strategic role has been minimized in comparison to the 1970s. Stokes, after all, secured support from the city's business interests because of their conviction that they needed legitimate allies at the head of city government. Today the array of philanthropies, strategic business organizations, and nonprofit intermediaries has made it much less imperative to have strong allies in city government. Securing political inclusion was a victory that should not be underestimated, but it was not the strategic victory it originally appeared to be. Furthermore, the assault on clientelism, which is an element of this attack on public sector authority and resources, has undermined the only institutional alternative to market competitiveness as a paradigm for policy interventions.

Second, while the idea of a corporate black political subject has made little sense, a key issue is whether African Americans have the civic infrastructure necessary to construct and temper collective subjectivity at all. Pieces of that institutional infrastructure still exist in community centers, ward clubs, street clubs, rump unions, and churches. But the fact is that this infrastructure has thinned and become less healthy. Just as important, the prevailing practices in many of these organizations are specifically designed to subvert the constitution of collective subjectivities. Technologies of participation on Cleveland's East Side engage with citizens as asset owners or stakeholders who have opinions to be valued and welcomed in open and civil participatory contexts. However, the authority of the idea that all actionable issues are subject to consensus among stakeholders both short-circuits the agonistic politics that had served blacks so well in the 1960s and 1970s and marginalizes particularistic concerns and topics in civic and political discussion. Indeed, while particularistic claims were authoritative in the city's politics following the community revolution in governance in the 1960s and 1970s, since then they are increasingly treated as anti-civic and illegitimate, as a parasitic tax on the civic whole which undermines civic competitiveness.

Third, the institutionalization of a market-based conception of value as the arbiter of the public good and effective policy has a marginalizing effect on African Americans. While individual African Americans can certainly meet these criteria, the stigma associated with blacks and black neighborhoods is often constructed as the opposite of what the market values and, indeed, this bias goes back to the very first real estate appraisal tools.[47] Markets value productivity, entrepreneurialism, and efficiency. Blacks are often culturally understood to be characterized by the opposite qualities of self-indulgence, laziness, and reliance on public support, making them a burden on the city. Market value is universal, the needs and claims of African Americans are often particular. Because those needs cannot be (and often are not intended to be) justified in civic terms, if they are acknowledged and granted, they amount to a burden on the civic whole. Particularism, in neoliberal terms, is desirable to the extent it contributes to civic competitiveness. Hipster neighborhoods, immigrant restaurants, and the insights to be derived from different cultural worldviews are all useful and should be encouraged. But African American claims are often couched in terms of equity, redistribution, and social justice. There are exceptions. Harlem, the French Quarter, and Beale Street have all become theme parks of African American culture and, indeed, one of Cleveland's clientelist politicians worked, unsuccessfully, to do the same thing in Hough. But actually addressing the layered modes of marginalization in black neighborhoods requires more powerful interventions. The marginalization of such particularistic claims in neoliberal discourse makes such interventions discursively impossible even if they were economically and politically viable.

Fourth, contemporary trends in the institutional configuration of urban governance are marginalizing African American voices and the needs of black communities. There are three distinct components of this, none of which rest on the exclusion of blacks. First, governance is now based on intersectoral cooperation among actors that are more or less equals. Such arrangements privilege the politics of consensus rather than the politics of agonistic mobilizations. In the 1970s, Cleveland's neighborhoods mobilized across racial lines in order to force concessions from institutions of power in Cleveland. Today, winning a victory in city hall is, at best, a limited victory. For anything to happen, given contemporary policy and fiscal environments, requires the active participation of multiple constituencies, including philanthropies, strategic business organizations, and government. Securing such broad-based support produces a politics of the lowest common denominator, which has generally been growth through competitiveness. Particularistic claims are troublesome from this perspective and so, predictably, the community revolution in urban governance of the 1970s has been rolled back while new institutions of regional government have been rolled out, including a county council (established in 2009). Regionalism moves government away from the networks and institutions that sustain the politics of geographic propinquity which has served African Americans well.

This narrative overemphasizes declining possibilities for African Americans in the neoliberal city. The foreclosure crisis was a watershed moment in Cleveland's politics. After twenty-five years in which the boosterish discourse of competitiveness had prevailed despite its growing disconnection from reality, the foreclosure crisis finally forced the city's political, philanthropic, and business elites to confront reality. Cleveland was not going to be saved by a sudden influx of people and money. No companies were going to suddenly decide that Cleveland was better for business than San Jose. The foreclosure crisis was so destructive in Cleveland that even the most deluded civic leaders had to acknowledge that decline had to be confronted and dealt with using the resources that were locally available. The Cleveland Foundation decided to incubate new businesses rather than attract and retain old ones. Most visibly, the Cleveland Foundation started and supports a laundry cooperative that serves the medical institutions around University Circle but that mostly employs African American East Side residents. Similarly, the crisis launched the community organizing group, East Side Organizing Project, from its purgatory in a church attic to national prominence, suggesting that the agonistic politics of the Congresses might not be dead after all.

But the narrative generally holds. African Americans continue to have access to the political and civic life of the city. In fact, in some ways black participation is more welcome than it has ever been. At the same time, the technologies of participation available to African Americans have been shrinking in their diversity. In the 1970s, blacks had a palette of participatory practices to choose from and multiple modes of engagement available to them. By 2007, that diversity was gone. More important, what remained was openness, but only on terms that subverted the legitimacy, and perhaps the possibility, of a distinctively black politics. The neoliberal city includes while delegitimating particularity. Cleveland's civic life suggests both the ways in which governance is becoming more sophisticated while, at the same time, constraining the possibilities for black politics in US cities. In such a context, repression is not functionally necessary to ensure the persistence of white privilege in city politics.

NOTES

1 Michael McQuarrie and Nicole Marwell, "The Missing Organizational Dimension in Urban Politics," *City and Community* 8:3 (2009), 247–68.

2 Caroline Lee, Michael McQuarrie, and Edward Walker, eds., *Democratizing Inequalities: Dilemmas of the New Public Participation* (New York: NYU Press, 2015); Michael McQuarrie, "No Contest: Participatory Technologies and the Transformation of Urban Authority," *Public Culture* 25:1 (2013), 143–75.

3 Andrew Pickering, *The Mangle of Practice: Time, Agency, and Science* (Chicago: University of Chicago Press, 1995).

4 Loïc Wacquant, *Punishing the Poor: The Neoliberal Government of Social Insecurity* (Durham, NC: Duke University Press, 2009).

5 Michelle Alexander, *The New Jim Crow* (New York: New Press, 2012).

6 Lee, McQuarrie, and Walker, *Democratizing Inequalities*; McQuarrie, "No Contest."

7 See, for example, Adolf Reed, *Stirrings in the Jug: Black Politics in the Post-Segregation Era* (Minneapolis: University of Minnesota Press, 1999); Phillip J. Thompson, *Double Trouble: Black Mayors, Black Communities, and the Call for a Deep Democracy* (Oxford: Oxford University Press, 2006).

8 Neil Brenner and Nik Theodore, *Spaces of Neoliberalism: Urban Restructuring in North America and Western Europe* (Oxford: Blackwell, 2002).

9 Steven Gregory, *Black Corona: Race and the Politics of Place in an Urban Community* (Princeton, NJ: Princeton University Press, 1998); John Krinsky, *The Urban Politics of Workfare: New York City's Welfare Reforms and the Dimensions of Welfare Policy Making* (Chicago: University of Chicago Press, 2007).

10 William Julius Wilson, *The Truly Disadvantaged: The Inner City, the Underclass, and Public Policy* (Chicago: University of Chicago Press, 1987); William Julius Wilson, *When Work Disappears: The World of the New Urban Poor* (New York: Vintage, 1996); Loïc Wacquant, *Urban Outcasts: A Comparative Sociology of Advanced Marginality* (Cambridge: Polity, 2008); Brenner and Theodore, *Spaces of Neoliberalism*.

11 St. Clair Drake and Horace R. Cayton, *Black Metropolis: A Study of Negro Life in a Northern City* (Chicago: University of Chicago Press, 2015 [1945]).

12 Thomas J. Sugrue, *The Origins of the Urban Crisis: Race and Inequality in Postwar Detroit* (Princeton, NJ: Princeton University Press, 1996).

13 Sandra Smith, "'Don't put my name on it': Trust and Job-Finding Assistance among the Black Urban Poor," *American Journal of Sociology* 111:1 (2005), 1–57; Sandra Smith, "A Question of Access or Mobilization? Understanding Inefficacious Job Referral Networks among the Black Poor," in *Social Capital: Advances in Research*, ed. Nan Lin and Bonnie Erickson (New York: Oxford University Press, 2008), 157–81.

14 Loïc Wacquant, *Punishing the Poor: The Neoliberal Government of Social Insecurity* (Durham, NC: Duke University Press, 2009).

15 Reed, *Stirrings in the Jug*, 30.

16 See, for example, William Julius Wilson, *The Declining Significance of Race: Blacks and Changing American Institutions (Chicago: University of Chicago Press, 1978)*; Mary Pattillo, *Black Picket Fences: Privilege and Peril among the Black Middle Class* (Chicago: University of Chicago Press, 1999); Karyn Lacy, *Blue-Chip Black Race, Class, and Status in the New Black Middle Class* (Berkeley and Los Angeles: University of California Press, 2007).

17 See, for example, Rufus Browning, Dale Marshall, and David Tabb, *Protest Is Not Enough: The Struggle of Blacks and Hispanics for Equality in Urban Politics* (Berkeley: University of California Press, 1984).

18 Reed, *Stirrings in the Jug*.
19 John Mollenkopf, "Neighborhood Political Development and the Politics of Urban Growth: Boston and San Francisco, 1958–1978," *International Journal of Urban and Regional Research* 5:1 (1981), 15–39.
20 John Logan and Harvey Molotch, *Urban Fortunes: The Political Economy of Place* (Berkeley: University of California Press, 1987).
21 Leonard Moore, "The School Desegregation Crisis of Cleveland, Ohio, 1963–4," *Journal of Urban History* 28:2 (2002), 135–57.
22 Reed, *Stirrings in the Jug*; Thompson, *Double Trouble*.
23 Reed, *Stirrings in the Jug*.
24 Committees on Governance, or COGs, are the organizations that distribute federal funds regionally. They are very important, very opaque, and poorly understood institutions. Stokes was prepared to make a big deal of the representation issue, but pressing matters like the Glenville riot prompted him to take a deal that nearly quadrupled Cleveland representation, but that still amounted to underrepresentation for the city.
25 Burten suffered an untimely death at age 40. He represented the last gasp of black reformist politicians in the city. He did battle with council president George Forbes and the local housing authority. The conflict was visible enough nationally that Ralph Nader sided with him publicly. Burten responded by saying that his fight with Forbes was absolutely none of Nader's business. The implication was that it was not the place of whites to interfere in the internecine struggles of Blacks. Though, more important, the incident demonstrated how tone-deaf a white progressive could be to the dynamics of African American politics.
26 Harry Boyte, *The Backyard Revolution: Understanding the New Citizen Movement* (Philadelphia, PA: Temple University Press, 1980).
27 Todd Swanstrom, *The Crisis of Growth Politics: Cleveland, Kucinich, and the Challenge of Urban Populism* (Philadelphia, PA: Temple University Press, 1985).
28 Cunningham interviews with Diane Yambor, Tom Gannon, John Calkins, Kathy Jaksic, and Mike O'Brien, Cunningham Collection, Western Reserve Historical Society, Cleveland, Ohio.
29 Mollenkopf, "Neighborhood Political Development and the Politics of Urban Growth"; Pierre Clavel, *The Progressive City: Planning and Participation, 1969–1984* (New Brunswick, NJ: Rutgers University Press, 1986).
30 Leonard Moore. *Carl B. Stokes and the Rise of Black Political Power* (Urbana: University of Illinois Press, 2002).
31 Doug Guthrie and Michael McQuarrie, "Providing for the Public Good: Corporate-Community Relations in the Era of the Receding Welfare State," *City & Community* 7:2 (2008), 113–39; Michael McQuarrie, "Community Organizations in the Foreclosure Crisis: The Failure of Neoliberal Civil Society," *Politics and Society* 41:1 (2013), 73–101; Jordan Yin, "The Community Development Industry System: A Case Study of Politics and Institutions in Cleveland, 1967–1997," *Journal of Urban Affairs* 20:2 (1998), 137–57.

32 Susan Clarke and Gary Gaile, *The Work of Cities* (Minneapolis: University of Minnesota Press, 1998); David Harvey, "From Managerialism to Entrepreneurialism: The Transformation of Urban Governance in Late Capitalism," *Geografiska Annaler* 71:1 (1989), 3–17.

33 Not surprisingly, given that it was committed to using its funds to pursue the politics of growth and used the withdrawal of funds to help destroy community organizing, the Cleveland Foundation was cited by the Committee on Responsive Philanthropy for pursuing a self-serving agenda rather than the public good.

34 Kim Moody, *Workers in a Lean World: Unions in the International Economy* (London: Verso, 1997).

35 Bruce Adams, "Cleveland: The Partnership City," in *Boundary Crossers Case Studies*, ed. Bruce Adams and John Parr (College Park: University of Maryland Academy of Leadership, 1998); Clarke and Gaile, *The Work of Cities*; Guthrie and McQuarrie, "Providing for the Public Good"; Michael McQuarrie, "Nonprofits and the Reconstruction of Urban Governance: Housing Production and Community Development in Cleveland, 1975–2005," in *Politics and Partnerships: Associations and Nonprofit Organizations in American Governance*, ed. Elisabeth Clemens and Doug Guthrie (Chicago: University of Chicago Press, 2010), 237–68.

36 Stephanie Mudge, "What Is Neo-Liberalism?" *Socio-Economic Review* 6:4 (2008), 703–31.

37 Harvey, "From Managerialism to Entrepreneurialism"; Josh Pacewicz, *Partisans and Partners: The Politics of the Post-Keynesian Society* (Chicago: University of Chicago Press, 2016).

38 Doug Guthrie and Michael McQuarrie, "Privatization and Low-Income Housing in the United States Since 1986," *Research in Political Sociology* 14 (September 2005), 15–51; Guthrie and McQuarrie, "Providing for the Public Good"; McQuarrie, "Nonprofits and the Reconstruction of Urban Governance."

39 The logic of this directly affects this form of housing. For example, sponsors are strongly incentivized to "cream" the most affluent people who can meet the bar of "low-income."

40 Josh Pacewicz, "Tax Increment Financing, Economic Development Professionals and the Financialization of Urban Politics," *Socio-Economic Review* 11:3 (July 2013), 413–40.

41 Kevin Fox Gotham, *Race, Real Estate, and Uneven Development: The Kansas City Experience, 1900–2000* (Albany: SUNY Press, 2002); Jesus Hernandez, "Redlining Revisited: Mortgage Lending Patterns in Sacramento, 1930–2004," *International Journal of Urban and Regional Research* 33:2 (2009), 291–313; Douglas Massey and Nancy Denton, *American Apartheid: Segregation and the Making of an Underclass* (Cambridge, MA: Harvard University Press, 1994).

42 The foreclosure crisis made it clear that this was a disastrous policy paradigm for the city. I discuss this at length in McQuarrie, "Community Organizations in the Foreclosure Crisis."

43 John Arena, *Driven from New Orleans: How Nonprofits Betray Public Housing and Promote Privatization* (Minneapolis: University of Minnesota Press, 2012); Reed, *Stirrings in the Jug.*

44 Mary Pattillo, *Black on the Block: The Politics of Race and Class in the City* (Chicago: University of Chicago Press, 2007).

45 Nicole Marwell, "Privatizing the Welfare State: Nonprofit Community-Based Organizations as Political Actors," *American Sociological Review* 69:2 (2004), 265–91.

46 Thompson, *Double Trouble.*

47 Gotham, *Race, Real Estate, and Uneven Development.*

ACKNOWLEDGMENTS

It is fitting that a book offering critical histories of urban neoliberalism grew from a collective intellectual project. The chapters in this volume had their origins in a series of lively workshops on race, ethnicity, political economy, criminal justice, and urban public policy. Our collaboration here is the first step in an ongoing transnational project considering the history of urban neoliberalism and its entanglements with political economy, race and ethnicity, governance, and grassroots activism in Europe and the United States. We received generous support from the French Commissariat général à l'égalité des territoires (CGET); Institut Français; Metro-Univers-Cité; New York University; Sorbonne Université; Université Paris Ouest-Nanterre-La Défense; Université Paris 8—Vincennes-Saint-Denis; and University of Pennsylvania. Thomas Sugrue also received support from a Carnegie Fellowship granted by the Carnegie Corporation of New York.

We deeply appreciate our colleagues who commented on these chapters and shared their work and ideas with us as the project evolved, especially the anonymous referees for New York University Press. We would like to express special thanks to our collaborators and critical readers: Salah Amokrane, Sébastien Chauvin, Nathan Connolly, Elsa Devienne, Michael Foley, Laurence Gervais, Phil Harper, Jeffrey Helgeson, Romain Huret, David Huyssen, Cedric Johnson, Andrew Kahrl, Thomas Kirszbaum, Sherry Linkon, Tracy Neumann, Caroline Rolland-Diamond, John Russo, Julien Talpin, Luisa Valle, and Caitlin Zaloom.

—Andrew J. Diamond and Thomas J. Sugrue

Thomas Adams is Senior Lecturer in History and American Studies and Academic Director of the US Studies Centre at the University of Sydney. He is the co-editor of *Remaking New Orleans: Beyond Exceptionalism and Authenticity* (2019) and *Working in the Big Easy: The History and Politics of Labor in New Orleans* (2014). His writing has also appeared in *The Huffington Post*, *Jacobin*, and *ABC Australia*.

Andrew J. Diamond is Professor of US History at the Sorbonne University in Paris, where he directs the research center Histoire et Dynamique des Espaces Anglophones (HDEA). He is the author or editor of several books, including *Mean Streets: Chicago Youths and the Everyday Struggle for Empowerment in the Multiracial City, 1908-1969* (2009) and *Chicago on the Make: Power and Inequality in a Modern City* (2017), which won the Jon Gjerde Prize from the Midwestern History Association.

Megan French-Marcelin is the Fair Hiring Project Coordinator at JustLeadershipUSA. She is a twentieth-century historian of urban policy and planning and received her PhD in US History from Columbia University.

Michael McQuarrie is Director of the Center for Work and Democracy and Associate Professor in the School of Social Transformation at Arizona State University. He is the co-editor of *Remaking Urban Citizenship: Organizations, Institutions, and the Right to the City* (2012) and *Democratizing Inequalities: The Promise and Pitfalls of the New Public Participation* (2015).

Donna Murch is Associate Professor of History at Rutgers University. She is the author of *Living for the City: Migration, Education, and the Rise of the Black Panther Party in Oakland, California* (2010), which won the 2011 Phillis Wheatley Prize from the Northeast Black Studies Association.

Mary Pattillo is the Harold Washington Professor of Sociology and African American Studies and Faculty Affiliate at the Institute for Policy Research at Northwestern University. She is the author of *Black Picket Fences: Privilege and Peril among the Black Middle Class* (1999) and *Black on the Block: The Politics of Race and Class in the City* (2007), and coeditor of *Imprisoning America: The Social Effects of Mass Incarceration* (2004).

Kim Phillips-Fein is Professor of History at the Gallatin School of Individualized Study at New York University. She is the author of *Invisible Hands: The Making of the Conservative Movement from the New Deal to Reagan* (2009) and *Fear City: New York's Fiscal Crisis and the Rise of Austerity Politics* (2017), which was a finalist for the 2018 Pulitzer Prize in History.

Thomas J. Sugrue is Professor of Social and Cultural Analysis and History at New York University, where he directs the Metropolitan Studies Program. He is the author of *The Origins of the Urban Crisis: Race Inequality in Postwar Detroit* (1996), *Sweet Land of Liberty: The Forgotten Struggle for Civil Rights in the North* (2008), *Not Even Past: Barack Obama and the Burden of Race* (2010), and, with Glenda Gilmore, *These United States: America in the Making, 1890–Present* (2015).

Sylvie Tissot is Professor of Political Science at the University of Paris–8. She is the author of *Good Neighbors: Gentrifying Diversity in Boston's South End* (2015). Her new book is a comparative study of gay-friendly attitudes in New York and Paris based on fieldwork in Park Slope in Brooklyn and Le Marais in Paris.

INDEX

Abu-Lughod, Janet, 54
Abzug, Bella, 79
affirmative action, 113
African Americans. *See* black political
power; black power; civil rights activism; electoral politics: black voters; racial
inequality
Aid to Families with Dependent Children
(AFDC), 141
Albany, NY, 80, 84
Alexander, Robert E., 55–57, 59–60
American Civil Liberties Union (ACLU),
140, 144
anti-communism, 4, 57, 59
anti-welfare policies, 2–3, 8. *See also* austerity
budgets; welfare state: cuts to
artists, 155–56, 165–66
Association for a Better New York, 82
Atlanta, GA, 7, 20, 183
austerity budgets, 1, 3, 6, 78–94, 98, 117, 199;
resistance to, 79–81, 86–94, 115

Babcock, Henry A., 55–57, 59–60
banks, 89, 193
Barbaro, Frank, 92
Barney, Clarence, 106, 119n6
bars, 167–68
Barthelemy, Sidney, 117
Bass, Karen, 142
Beame, Abraham, 79, 85, 90–91
Berger, Stephen, 89
Beverly Hills, CA, 52
black freedom struggle. *See* black power;
civil rights activism
Black Lives Matter movement, 174, 177
Black Metropolis, 177
Black Panthers, 83, 132, 185; and Coalition
Against Police Abuse (CAPA), 144–45

black politics, 99–108, 113, 121n20, 131, 139–
41, 184. *See also* electoral politics: black
power; black voters
black power, 1, 83–84, 103, 132, 143–45, 157.
See also Black Lives Matter movement;
Black Panthers; civil rights activism
Black United Front, 92
Boal, Sam, 60
Bobo, James, 125n68
Bonaventure Debates, 49–50, 63, 71n4
Bonaventure Hotel (Los Angeles, CA). *See*
Westin Bonaventure Hotel (Los Angeles,
CA)
Bond, Julian, 119n6
Boston Courant (MA), 166
Boston, MA, 7, 154–70; Prudential Tower,
158; SoWa district, 165–67; South End Historical Society, 156, 158–70; Washington
Gateway, 167–70, 171n20
Bourdieu, Pierre, 169
Bowly, Devereux, 19, 22, 27
Bowron, Fletcher, 54–55, 57
Boyte, Harry, 186
Brief History of Neoliberalism, A. See David
Harvey
Bradley, Tom, 137–39, 141
Bronx Community College (New York, NY),
88
Brown, Wendy, 5, 11n9, 15–16
Burbank, CA, 67
Burten, Lonnie, 184, 204n25
Bush, George H. W., 134–35, 141–42

California. courts, 61–64, 135; Department
of Corrections (CDC), 132, 135; Highway
Patrol (CHP), 130; Proposition 18, 58,
62–64; Proposition 21, 136; Southern
California, 49, 53, 55, 68–69, 128, 130, 140;

www.ingramcontent.com/pod-product-compliance
Lightning Source LLC
Chambersburg PA
CBHW020253030426
42336CB00010B/735